Public Sector Accounting

Public Sector Accounting

Michael Rogers

Stanley Thornes (Publishers) Ltd

First published in 1995 by
Stanley Thornes Publishers Ltd
Ellenborough House
Wellington Street
Cheltenham
Glos. GL50 1YD
UK

A catalogue record for this book is available from The British Library.

ISBN 0 7487 1908 3

Typeset by
Northern Phototypesetting Co Ltd, Bolton
Printed and bound in Great Britain by
T.J. Press (Padstow) Ltd, Padstow, Cornwall

Contents

Acknowledgements

I am grateful to all those colleagues and friends who helped me to compile this book and also to Francis Dodds and Sandy Marshall of Stanley Thornes for their support and forebearance.

Michael Rogers
July 1995

Abbreviations used in the text

AAT	Association of Accounting Technicians
ACG	Annual Capital Guideline
ACOP	Accounting Code of Practice
AMRA	Asset Management Revenue Account
ASB	Accounting Standards Board
ASC	Accounting Standards Committee
BCA	Basic Credit Approval
C and AG	Comptroller and Auditor General
CBF	Cross Boundary Flows
CC	County Council
CCAB	Consultative Committee of Accountancy Bodies
CCT	Compulsory Competitive Tendering
CEC	Central Establishment Charges
CFO	Chief Financial Officer
CHC	Community Health Council
CIPFA	Chartered Institute of Public Finance and Accounting
CMA	Costs of Management and Administration
DHA	District Health Authority
DLO	Direct Labour Organisation
DMU	Directly Managed Unit
DoE	Department of the Environment
DRG	Diagnostic Related Groups
DSO	Direct Service Organisation
ECR	Extra Contractual Referrals
EFL	External Financing Limit
FHSA	Family Health Service Authority
FRC	Financial Reporting Council
FRS	Financial Reporting Standards
GLC	Greater London Council
GPFH	General Practitioner Fund Holder
HCHS	Hospital and Community Health Service
HRA	Housing Revenue Account
IBD	Interest bearing Debt
ICAEW	Institute of Chartered Accountants in England and Wales
LASAAC	Local Authority, Scotland Accounts Advisory Committee
LRT	London Regional Transport
MBO	Management Buy-Out
MCC	Metropolitan County Council
MRP	Minimum Revenue Provision
NAO	National Audit Office

NHS	National Health Service
NHSE	National Health Service Executive
NNDR	National Non-Domestic Rate
NSGC	National Steering Group on Costing
PCL	Provision for Credit Liabilities
PDC	Public Dividend Capital
PES	Public Expenditure Survey
PFI	Private Finance Initiative
PTA	Passenger Transport Authority
PTE	Passenger Transport Executive
RHA	Regional Health Authority
RSG	Revenue Support Grant
ROCE	Return On Capital Employed
RTIA	Receipts Taken Into Account
SFI	Standing Financial Instruction
SIFTR	Service Increment for Teaching and Research
SLA	Service Level Agreement
SOLACE	Society of Local Authorities' Chief Executives
SORP	Statements of Recommended Practice
SRA	Summary Revenue Account
SSA	Standing Spending Assessment
SSAP	Statements of Standard Accounting Practice
SSSC	Statements of Support Service Costs
UBR	Uniform Business Rate
UITF	Urgent Issues Task Force

Preface

This book was first planned in the autumn of 1993. It was then clear that there was a need for a practical and up-to-date student text on public sector accounting for those taking public administration courses. Much of the existing material caters for academics and practitioners rather than those new to the subject.

Recent national developments have meant that this has been a good time to produce this book. A new NVQ-based AAT assessment structure was introduced in 1993. The broad structure and financing of local government and the NHS appears settled, at least for the immediate future. CIPFA has published an updated version of its Accounting Code of Practice, which contains clear and long awaited recommendations on the thorny subject of capital accounting in local government. Government Regulations have determined likely directions of both an internal market in local government and Compulsory Competitive Tendering. On the health side, the National Health Service Executive has issued *Finance for Health Service Managers* and an accounting manual as well as new national guidance on the form of accounts. Having said all that, there will no doubt be sufficient developments to require a regular updating of this work. Little stays still for long in what remains of the public sector.

1 The public sector – scope and financing

This chapter considers the scope of the public sector and the types of organisations within the United Kingdom public sector. It looks at relationships between central government and those organisations and then at recent important developments in public administration. The accounting needs and objectives of the public sector are considered, before finally looking at public expenditure and how the government keeps the nation's books.

What is the public sector?

Introduction

The simplest definition of the public sector is: *All organisations which are not privately owned and operated.*

In essence, the public sector consists of organisations where control lies in the hands of the public, as opposed to private owners, and whose objectives involve the provision of services where profit is not a primary objective.

The public sector primarily exists:

- to provide services which are beyond the private means of people using those services
- to provide a benefit to everyone within socially acceptable norms
- to achieve certain minimum standards of service, e.g., roads, education and training schemes)
- to substitute central or local planning in place of consumer choice
- to ensure a consistent approach to certain practices or procedures
- to aid control and economic regulation in key areas.

These objectives within the public sector will be significantly influenced by the central government. The relationship between central control and of local democracy is an important political consideration, and while the concept of what the public sector provides is fairly universal, the means of control over the different organisations providing these services can differ.

Types of organisation within the United Kingdom

Public sector organisations can be classified into five major groups in the UK:

- departments of central government
- nationalised industries, public corporations
- local authorities
- health authorities
- bodies set up for a specific purpose:
  - universities
  - the Royal Mint
  - HM Stationery Office.

Unlike the private sector of the economy, where there is a clear objective and motivation in making profits or a return on capital, the public sector has a multitude of demands and objectives. Primarily, however, the public sector is concerned with providing services to the general public which would not otherwise be available or provided adequately within the financial resources of all individual members of the public. The nationalised industries and public corporations are required to meet certain criteria set by the government in the form of a return on capital.

The obligation to provide public services by the different types of organisation almost invariably derives from statutes or legislation passed by Parliament. This legislation may be either general, applicable to the whole country, or 'local', relating to just one area. From an accounting point of view, a knowledge of certain aspects of this legislation is important because not only will the relevant statutes set out the financing powers for raising money to pay for the provision of services, but also associated regulations may provide accounting and audit requirements.

Each type of public sector organisation has its own accounting objectives and it is these that will influence the form and content of its accounts and accounting arrangements. Some, however, are common to all and the first of these is stewardship. The use of public money, particularly if it is acquired through taxation, demands that the accounts show that monies have been properly and lawfully used. This requires the publication of sufficient information which can be easily understood by the public.

Another essential feature is to provide systematic records for estimating financial requirements and the measurement of the use of these financial resources to establish relative efficiency and effectiveness. Value for money is of the utmost importance and is especially so when taxation or charging levels are high or increasing rapidly. Accounting procedures must be directed towards ensuring that the maximum benefit is obtained from the limited resources.

A further feature is to provide the structure for financial control. Without profit and the motivation and disciplines that go with it, financial control must be exercised through a sound budgeting and accounting system. A control system will normally be supported by written internal regulations or instructions concerning expenditure and income procedures and their associated accounting arrangements.

Commercial and non-commercial factors

Financial classification
The types of organisation within the public sector fall broadly into three groups, with regard to financing:

- those met wholly from charges recovered for the services rendered
- those met largely from taxation
- those partly met from charges but with taxation meeting any deficit.

Financing met wholly from charges
Those in this category include most of the public corporations such as the Post Office.

The Acts incorporating these bodies require them to cover their revenue expenditure by sufficient user charges made for their services. In addition, central government also sets financial targets in the form of a specified rate of return on capital employed. These industries therefore are placed in very much the same position as private commercial organisations, albeit some enjoying monopoly powers. The fact that these organisations are treated as similar to the private sector has encouraged them to adopt private sector accounting practices wherever possible.

Most of the bodies from this category have recently been sold to the private sector, e.g., British Gas, British Telecom, the electricity industry and, in December 1994, British Coal.

Financing met largely from taxation
This category relates to those services provided by central and local government, financed either wholly or mainly from taxation. There is no profit motive and the chief objective is the provision of a service. The basic accounting requirements are to record and account for expenditure and ensure it is adequately financed.

There is thus a very considerable difference between the accounting requirements of the private sector and this part of the public sector.

Central government expenditure is recorded on the receipts and payments (cash) basis for both revenue and capital items. Taxation is used as the main source of financing, but any difference is met by borrowing. No distinction is made between capital and revenue and the accruals basis is not needed to ensure the correct calculation of profit or loss, or to provide 'true and fair' balance sheets as in the private sector.

Financing met only partly from charges
This third category covers those organisations or activities which are a mixture of the two previous types. These organisations meet the bulk of their requirements from user charges, but have to resort to subsidies from taxation in order to avoid excessive charges. The best example is British Rail (where privatisation has commenced).

The circumstances of each organisation dictate its general accounting features, but commercial practices are accepted where possible. With public corporations such as British Rail, subsidies will be restricted by government targets.

Capital structure
In all of these circumstances, the capital structures are not the same as in commerce. In the public corporations and local government, capital is mainly financed by borrowing. Apart from a few exceptions, there are no shareholders or proprietors as such. Debt is repaid during the life of assets and when new assets are required, further loans will be sought unless reserve funds have been accrued. The main source of borrowing is through central government, which now borrows not only to meet its own needs but also to lend to the public corporations and local authorities.

Accounting information

All public sector organisations have an obligation to publish financial accounting information. The non-trading elements of central and local government tend to use tabular formats to analyse expenditure over services and activities. Local government also produces revenue and capital accounts, with balance sheets normally on a historical cost basis. Public corporations and trading undertakings of the other sectors tend to produce accounts in full commercial format, wherever possible. Presentation is in narrative form, to highlight the trading nature of these activities.

Organisations in the public sector

Introduction

The United Kingdom has adopted a society in which many services and activities are provided by the State. Such services and activities are administered by central government via central departments and a variety of public sector organisations operating at national, regional and local levels. The activities undertaken by the many branches of the public sector in the United Kingdom amount to about 20 per cent of gross domestic product. Clearly, therefore the manner in which those activities are managed has an important impact on the operation of the economy as a whole.

The public sector is made up of diversely differing organisations. This diversity stems mainly from the differing objectives of public sector organisations. There are those organisations such as the nationalised industries which operate on commercial lines and sell their products in the market place. At the other end of the spectrum of public sector organisations are bodies like local authorities and health authorities which exist, in the main, to provide services which are not sold on the open market. These differing objectives lead to a diversity of financial accounting practices, control procedures and management structures in public sector organisations. The four major public sector organisations that are currently operating in the United Kingdom

- central government departments
- nationalised industries
- ad hoc bodies and public corporations
- NHS and local authorities

are now briefly described.

Central government departments

Central government departments are staffed by civil servants but headed by either ministers or Secretaries of State who are politicians. The departments are mainly based in London but often have regional or local offices throughout the country. The departments' prime function is to implement Acts of Parliament; like all public sector organisations, government departments can only undertake things for which they have Parliamentary power. The size of the task often requires that implementation is achieved through other organisations such as local authorities or health authorities. Thus central departments can both influence and direct the decisions and actions of many other public sector organisations via letters and circulars.

The Secretary of State who heads the department is directly accountable to Parliament for the actions of their department. The Secretary of State is assisted by junior ministers. The civil servants running the departments are headed by the person occupying the post of Permanent Secretary.

Examples of central departments and their functions are outlined below.

Department and departmental head	Functions and responsibilities
The Department of Education, headed by the Secretary of State for Education.	Planning and monitoring the educational requirements and standards of the country at all levels – nursery, primary, secondary, further and higher. This work entails a close involvement with local education authorities.
The Department of Social Security, headed by the Secretary of State for Social Security.	The implementation of social by welfare policies such as the provision of pensions and welfare benefits. This is usually achieved via the local offices of the Department of Social Security.
The Department of Health, headed by the Health Secretary.	The Department's main function is controlling and directing the National Health Service provided by regional and district health authorities. Such services include hospital care, family practitioner services and community health.
Department of Transport, headed by the Minister of Transport.	Implementation of transport policy in respect of roads, buses, railways, ports, canals etc. This obviously involves working closely with local authorities, British Rail and other public sector bodies.
The Treasury, headed by the Chancellor of the Exchequer but note the Prime Minister is the First Lord of the Treasury.	Planning and implementation of national economic policies via the control of the public sector borrowing requirement, the money supply, taxation, balance of payments, etc. The Treasury has a major influence on other public sector organisations as provider of advice to Parliament on the total level of public expenditure in any one financial year.
The Department of the Environment, headed by Secretary of State for the Environment.	Concerned with overall planning for such services as the housing, urban renewal, planning, water resources and supply. This overall responsibility brings the Department into close contact with local authorities, new towns and water authorities.

Next step agencies

A report in 1988 recommended that executive functions of government should be delivered by executive units or agencies. The first agency was the Vehicle Inspectorate, established in 1988, quickly followed by Companies House. As at 1 January 1993 there were 76 agencies as well as 30 executive units in Customs and Excise and 43 executive offices in the Inland Revenue which employed 300,790 people. This ranged from 30 people employed at Wilton Park Conference Centre to 63,100 employed at Wilton Park Conference Centre to 63,100 employed by the Social Security Benefits Agency.

More recent agencies relate to District Audit (see Chapter 11), Highways, The Prison Service and the Resettlement Agency which runs residential units to help homeless people. In March 1995 there were about 100 agencies in action.

From 1994, the District Audit Service was transferred at 'arm's length' from the Audit Commission to a new agency. Its title is now *District Audit* and its first executive is David Prince, formerly Chief Executive of Leicestershire County Council. The new agency will now compete with private firms for Audit Commission audit and consultancy work.

Each agency operates within well-defined frameworks in which the policy, budget, specific targets and results are set out. This framework consists of a framework document, a corporate plan, business plan and the annual report and accounts.

Framework document

This specifies the agency's framework of responsibilities as delegated by the appropriate minister to the agency's chief executive. It briefly summarises the following items:

- the agency's relationship with its parent department and responsible minister
- the aims, objectives and performance targets detailed for the agency
- its resources and financial and accounting arrangements, including its delegated powers.

Agency framework documents are reviewed at three-yearly intervals to appraise whether it should continue as an agency or whether it should be contracted out, privatised or abolished.

The agency's management framework and objectives will be set out in its corporate and business plans. These do not have to be published if the agency operates in a competitive market, or if operational reasons require the maintenance of responsibility.

The plans should comprise:

- plans for a five-year period
- a business plan for assessing the prospects and planned activity levels. It will consider client requirements, the consequence of competitive tendering and how the agency proposes to deal with these
- outline resources requirements, improvements in their use and raising quality standards, performance pay, market testing, internal charging and developing management systems
- detailed financial projections and key targets.

Annual report

All the agencies have to produce and publish commercial-style annual reports and accounts, which reveal the agency's financial performance and achievement against key targets and the work programme detailed in the business plan. The financial statements should be certified by the Comptroller and Auditor General.

Nationalised industries

The nationalised industries are a group of industries which are publicly owned, separate legal entities created by special laws other than the Companies Acts, which obtain their funds by borrowing from the Treasury or the public. The industries also sell their goods and services to the public to generate revenue. The industries making up this group are liable to change over time depending on central government's policy towards public ownership. An example of an industry currently falling into this definition is British Rail. The nationalised industries are separate legal entities and as such differ from the central government departments mentioned earlier. This distinction is highlighted by the fact that the employees of nationalised industries are not civil servants.

Parliament, in creating a nationalised industry, appoints a minister or secretary of state who is responsible to Parliament for implementing the legislation. The minister is aided in this by civil servants from particular government departments often called sponsoring departments.

The minister appoints the board of the nationalised industry, approves the industry's capital investment proposal, receives the annual accounts from the auditors and has the power to consult with, and direct, the industries on matters which affect the public interest. Parliamentary control of the nationalised industries is exercised via Parliamentary Select Committees of MPs, who consider the policies and the performance of the nationalised industries. The boards of nationalised industries are made up of appointed members with experience either in the particular industry or as senior managers in another, often related, industry. The boards contain part-time as well as full-time members. Often responsibility for a particular function of the industry is delegated to a particular board member, e.g., the personnel function or research and development. The minister is entitled to reports as to the progress of the industry from board members.

The industries operate within strict financial targets set by the appropriate minister. In addition, the industries are required to obtain specified rates of return on new investments. The major source of finance of the industries is borrowings from the National Loans Fund. Such loans are repaid over predetermined periods at an appropriate rate of interest. Overall the industries operate within external financing limits or cash limits prescribed annually by the minister. In general terms the nationalised industries are required to ensure that their combined revenues are sufficient to meet charges taking one year with another.

Ad hoc bodies and public corporations

Some organisations are set up by Parliament to provide a specific function. Such bodies include Development Corporations for New Towns, the Bank of England, Crown Agents, the British Broadcasting Corporation, and Her Majesty's Stationery Office. These bodies are established under various Acts of Parliament usually in response to a particular problem or to administer a specific function. They are bodies made up of members appointed by the appropriate Minister and as such are a separate legal entity. They are financed by a mixture of government grants, revenue from sales of goods and services, and borrowing. Two particular bodies need mentioning at this point:

The Audit Commission for Local Authorities

The Audit Commission for Local Authorities in England and Wales was established by the *Local Government Finance Act 1982*. This is a body independent of both central and local government with its income coming entirely from fees for audit work undertaken for local government and the National Health Service.

Under the terms of the *National Health Service and Community Care Act 1990*, from 1 October 1990 the Audit Commission assumed responsibility for the external audit of the National Health Service in England and Wales.

Members, totalling 16, are appointed jointly by the Secretary of State for the Environment and the Secretary of State for Wales. They come from all walks of life, e.g., industry, trade unions, accountancy bodies, local government, etc.

The Commission is supported by paid officials led by the Controller of Audit. The Commission has two principal objectives:

- to promote the integrity of local government by ensuring that local authorities spend their money and report their financial situation in accordance with the law and adopt suitable safeguards against fraud and corruption
- to promote value for money in local government.

This is achieved by the Commission in two ways:

- by appointing auditors to audit the accounts of all local health authorities in England and Wales (including NHS trusts)
- by undertaking studies which make recommendations for improving economy, efficiency and effectiveness of services, and which encourage authorities to learn from one another and apply good management practice which has proved effective elsewhere.

Further details of the Commission's work are contained in Chapter 11.

The National Audit Office (NAO)

The NAO is established under the *National Audit Act 1983*. It is headed by the Comptroller and Auditor General. This title indicates two distinct responsibilities of this post holder. As Comptroller General it is his/her responsibility to authorise the issue of public funds to central government departments and other public bodies. But it is the other role as Auditor General which takes up the major part of the NAO's time. This involves certifying the accounts of all government departments. It also involves reporting the results of examinations into all aspects of the financial operations of government departments back to Parliament. Thus this department plays a key role in the accountability and stewardship of public monies.

As well as the traditional auditing role, the NAO has statutory powers to carry out examinations of economy, efficiency and effectiveness in relation to the use of resources by various departments. These 'value for money' studies are published and presented to Parliament with any key issues being followed up by the Public Accounts Committee of the House of Commons. This Committee studies the reports, gathers evidence, calls witnesses, produces reports and makes recommendations to which the Government responds. Thus the independence and professional approach of the NAO in examining the operation of government departments is an essential element in monitoring central government's performance.

The NAO audits over 500 public sector accounts and has a staff of almost 1000 split into various service and functional divisions.

The National Health Service and local authorities

A detailed description of the structure and financing methods of these organisations will be given in a later chapter of this book.

Characteristics of public sector organisations

The major characteristic which public sector organisations have in common is that they derive their powers from Parliament and ultimately are all responsible to Parliament. It is usual for a minister to be made responsible to Parliament for the activities of a public sector organisation.

The functions undertaken by public authorities are strictly determined by the legislative authority granted by Acts of Parliament. Parliament, through the appropriate legislation, also determines the particular structure within which the various functions are to operate, although the structure does vary in different parts of the country. Thus the various tiers of administration in public sector bodies, e.g., county and district councils of local government in England, are prescribed by Parliament.

A public sector body which provides a product or service for which there is no statutory basis is said to have broken the doctrine of ultra vires, i.e., beyond the powers. This means the organisation has overstepped its statutory limits and as such the expenditure incurred is illegal. Often it is quite difficult to decide whether expenditure has any statutory basis or not because the decision involves interpretation of Acts of Parliament. For example under the *Local Government Act 1972* a local authority has power to undertake anything which would facilitate the discharge of any of its functions.

In some public sector organisations, notably the nationalised industries, managers operate on broadly commercial lines. In other words the success of the organisation is measured to a large extent by the amount of profit the organisation generates. Obviously the nationalised industries have objectives other than profit maximisation, e.g., improving the standards of service, but at the end of the day profit, or its absence, is available as a measure of efficiency for this type of public sector organisation.

In other public sector organisations, which can be labelled 'not-for-profit organisations' the profit measure is not available as a means of measuring performance. In providing services such as education, health care, housing, etc., the objectives are not centred on generating profits but on improving the social welfare of society. This absence of the profit measure can make financial control more difficult to achieve, because the focus of control tends to concentrate on the quantity and quality of the service provided.

The crux of control is the measurement of the objectives of the organisation in order that performance can be monitored. Thus one could argue that absence of the profit measure makes financial control in parts of the public sector a more subjective task because measurement of objectives is often difficult if not impossible.

Relationships between central government and public sector organisations

The impact of central government

The preceding sessions should have left no doubt as to the considerable influence central government has on the policy direction of local government and the National Health Service, and, indeed, on any 'branch' of the public sector.

Basic principles

At the present time there is conflict between central government and many public sector organisations. When these arguments are explored it is often the case that they arise because there is no clearly defined relationship between the different levels of government. This is particularly true in respect of financial arrangements. As long ago as 1976 the Layfield Committee in its report on Local Government Finance (Cmnd 6453) commented:

It is open to question whether there is a system for local government finance and, if there is, who purports to control that part of the system that lies in the hands of the government. There are few evident signs of either a system or a coherent set of related arrangements so far as Whitehall is concerned. Some instruments are evident. The major instruments are the power to control borrowing, the ability to use grants to influence expenditure or bring about economy in spending, the negotiations about grant distribution and the production of the public expenditure white papers.

A close relationship between these several arrangements was not apparent on initial inspection. Indeed the opposite sometimes appeared to be the case; for instance, there was no clear relationship between the public expenditure White Paper figures and those used in the grant negotiations.

Such comments are equally true today and as applicable to the different parts of the public sector.

Overall central–local relations demand a balance of control and independence, in other words a partnership between central government and the public authority. However, it should not be forgotten that there is a legal basis for the national control over public sector bodies namely that they have no powers other than those conferred on them by statute. Thus public authorities largely carry out the administration of general policy decided by the national legislature. For example, the basic constitutional rules of local government are set out in the *Local Government Act 1972*.

The position in the UK

The central government retains responsibility for matters relating to the national interest such as defence, foreign affairs, internal security (Home Office) currency regulation and control, and national economic development. Central departments also retain overall responsibility for development of the country's infrastructure through the departments of energy and transport, and for the co-ordination of and establishment of minimum standards for essential services – such as health, social security, housing, environment, education and science.

So far as the infrastructure is concerned services are administered by public corporations dealing with such matters as electric power, coal, railways, airways, steel production and postal services. Up to about 40 years ago some services such as gas and electricity were provided by local authorities. The huge capital investment required and the development of national grid systems brought about the transfer of these services to the public boards which themselves administer the services throughout the country on a regional basis.

Other services which were previously under the control of local government are personal health, water supply and sewerage services which have, because of the large capital investment needed to build hospitals, pumping stations, filtration plants, etc., been brought under the control of larger regional authorities, whose administration is then sub-divided on an area or divisional basis.

Then one comes to those services which are administered by the local councils. Even in this area, up to 1974 local councils differed considerably in size, resources and range of services to be provided. Local resources available can still differ substantially but re-organisation did do much to reduce the number of and increase the size of local government units. In effect it was a compromise between moving centres of administration further away from the people and the benefits in terms of economies of scale that can be derived from larger administrative units.

The relationship with local authorities

In a *Review of Central Government Controls over Local Authorities* published in February 1979, the comment was made:

> The Government has announced its determination to reduce substantially the number of bureaucratic controls over local government activities. This should give local authorities more choice and flexibility and allow them to become more efficient in their use of both money and manpower.

> The Government has been guided in this exercise by the following principles. Democratically elected local authorities are wholly responsible bodies who must be free to get on with the tasks entrusted to them by Parliament without constant interference in matters of detail by the Government of the day. On the other hand, there are certain national policies which it is the Government's duty to pursue even though they may be administered locally; for example, where by statute the responsibilities are shared between central and local government or where the Government of the day may have secured a particular mandate at a general election. It would be inappropriate therefore to abandon all control over local government; to do so would be an abdication of the Government's proper role.

It is apparent from the actions of various governments since the Second World War that this has been the underlying policy of their relationship with public sector bodies. This, coupled with a strong political will at central government has resulted in quite far reaching changes being implemented through new legislation.

An example of one of the major pieces of legislation in England and Wales is used to illustrate the underlying political influences which affect the provision of local government services.

Local Government, Planning and Land Act 1980

The major features of this legislation are as follows:

a) *Capital expenditure controls*

For the first time, central government was able to specify to the last pound how much individual local authorities could spend each year on capital account. Hitherto, control on amount had been restricted to loan financed capital expenditure.

b) *Introduction of direct labour organisation accounting requirements*

The *1980 Act* introduced special accounting arrangements for direct labour.

Local authorities who employ direct labour (i.e. labour which is retained to undertake construction and maintenance work, rather than appointed for specific functions) are required to maintain separate accounts to identify fully the costs involved, to earn a return (a profit) in real terms on the capital employed, and demonstrate a measure of competitiveness with outside contractors who might similarly be placed to undertake the work. The accounting requirements are an additional discipline upon local authorities in their management of the activities involved; in itself this is not a bad thing of course. It illustrates, though, the political influence at work in introducing legislation about a topic which previously had been subject to much investigation, amidst assertions of malpractice and innuendo about the true purpose of direct labour forces.

In introducing the legislation, the Secretary of State for the Environment stated that the Act would enable 'the true facts about direct labour organisations to emerge'.

c) *Introduction of block grant*
The novel feature about the block grant is not the nature of the arrangements themselves; nor have philosophies changed. The rate support grant has existed in much the same way for many years.

However, the new mechanism (method of calculating grant entitlement) has enabled the Secretary of State to control an individual authority's grant entitlement; hitherto the control was mainly on the total and the general allocation.

The block grant arrangements in the *1980 Act* emphasise once more the involvement of political influence. In this case it was a political belief that local authorities were spending too much of the nation's resources. The government was being frustrated in its ability to influence individual local authorities because of the general nature of existing legislation. The continuation of this influence was seen in the White Paper *Rates (Proposals for Rate Limitation and Reform of the Rating System)* (Cmnd 9008). The opening chapter states 'the Government has become increasingly concerned about the divergence between actual levels of local government's expenditure and the planned levels set out in the Government's own public expenditure White Paper'.

d) *The power to issue codes of recommended practice*
This part of the *1980 Act* is important, not so much because of any direct and draconian imposition changing a fundamental feature of local government fabric; but because it emphasises once more the extent to which central government can influence without having to dictate.

In the Act the Secretary of State merely 'took powers' to issue recommended codes of practice, and has to date issued the following codes:

- explaining the Local Authority Rate Bill
- local authority annual reports
- publication of manpower information by local authorities
- Accounting Code of Practice
- compulsory competitive tendering.

Types of central government controls over local authorities

Government control and influence through departmental communications
- Professional or operational advice given through the issue of circulars.
- Control over certain local authority officer appointments and dismissals such as Home Office approval to appointment of Chief Constable.
- Excessive detailed supervision of local services such as the approval of budgets, for example, in the magistrates courts service.
- Monitoring of financial results via rate support grant forecasts, grant claims, statistical returns, etc. The need for such information is recognised. However, the number and scope of such returns bears witness to the detailed control and indicates the amount of effort applied by local authorities to meet central government's requirements.
- Numerous statutes give ministers powers to act where local authorities 'default' in the provision of services, i.e., the authority is not discharging a function properly.
- Ministers have extensive powers to approve county structure plans and compulsory purchase orders.

- Central departments have the power to inspect and ensure the operational efficiency of certain services such as visiting schools, police and fire.
- Ministers can act as an arbiter in disputes between local authorities and individuals, e.g., at a planning enquiry.

Government control via the Commissioners for Local Administration (local ombudsmen)

The ombudsmen, established in 1974, can investigate administrative decisions but not policy decisions of a local authority, police authority or regional water authority. Complaints can either be made direct by the inhabitants or via an elected member. The ombudsmen may recommend how a situation should be resolved.

Control via the external audit of local authorities

The Audit Commission is empowered to appoint external auditors to whom general duties are laid down in the *Local Government Finance Act 1982* (Section 15). The duties are briefly as follows:

… an auditor shall by examination of the accounts and otherwise satisfy himself:

a) that the accounts are prepared in accordance with the Accounts and Audit Regulations 1983;

b) that proper practices have been observed;

c) that proper arrangements have been made for securing economy, efficiency and effectiveness.

The key points of the Accounts and Audit Regulations 1983 are as follows:

- accounting control systems, form of accounts, etc.
- internal audit
- records to be kept when paying in money
- accounts to be made up and balanced
- preparation of statement of accounts
- appointment of date for the exercise of public rights
- public inspection of accounts
- alteration of accounts
- notice by advertisement of public rights
- written notice of proposed objection
- signing of statement of accounts, etc.
- notice by advertisement of conclusion of audit, etc.
- publication of statement of accounts
- extraordinary audit.

In addition, members of the public, under Section 17 of the *Local Government Finance Act 1982*, have the right to inspect, question and object to the local authority accounts.

The *Local Government Act 1988* amends and extends the provisions of the *1986 Local Government Act* and in doing so implements some of the recommendations of the Widdecombe Report and thus extends the powers of the external auditor.

Section 30 of the *Local Government Act 1988* enables the auditor of a local authority to issue a prohibition order on an authority, or one of its individual officers, requiring it or them not to adopt or continue with a specified course of action. The auditor can issue such an order if he/she believes the authority/officer is about to:

a) make a decision (or has taken a decision) which would lead the authority to incur unlawful expenditure; or
b) take a course of action (or has taken a course of action) which would be unlawful or cause the authority to incur a loss or deficiency; or
c) make an unlawful entry in its accounts.

An order remains in force until:

a) it is revoked by the auditor or
b) it is quashed by the High Court following an appeal.

Financial relationships between central and local government
A detailed explanation of the main sources of local authority revenue income is given in Chapter 2. This next section will examine the underlying financial relationships between central and local government.

A local tax (previously rates and community charge, now the council tax) – is levied locally and thus paid directly by the recipients of local services. Grants in aid of local services are paid through the government and financed from the national taxpayer. In some cases, they may be one and the same person but national taxation is drawn from a number of different sources and is levied on different bases from that used for the local rate as outlined earlier. The government grants in aid are mainly in the form of a block grant (the revenue support grant) rather than grants for specific services, and are intended through their distribution to take account of the widely differing local needs and resources that exist throughout the country.

Two things stand out:

a) the large bulk of taxing powers, and thus income, from taxation remains with the central government.
b) where taxing powers are transferred or allowed, as exists with local government, the controls from the centre are very numerous.

A Green Paper issued in 1972 on the future shape of local government stated that:

> The central government, whilst wishing to give greater freedom to local authorities, cannot evade their own responsibility for management of the national economy, nor can they evade their duty to ensure minimum standards for essential services throughout the country. The problem for central government is how to resolve this dilemma within these constraints.

The dilemma has arisen because even today no clear-cut definition of the relationship between central and local government exists. There is no written constitution. The complex web that exists today has evolved from an endless stream of statutes, circulars, White Papers, etc., and has the advantage of being flexible and thus responsive to changing conditions. On the other hand it leads to a lack of understanding on the part of the public as to which level of government is responsible for a particular service, and also between central and local government there is often complete misunderstanding or lack of understanding of each other's roles.

Local government expenditure in the UK tends to grow at a faster rate than the national economy but the local tax base (the rate) is inelastic and thus an increasing demand arises for additional sources from the centre.

Local authorities argue that they should have more local powers and discretion, combined with greater taxation powers and additional sources of revenue from the government. The government itself wishes to extend the degree of local autonomy that exists in so far as that extension can be allowed without reducing the government's overall ability to manage the national economy and ensure minimum service standards. In recent years, as shown earlier, local powers tend to have been reduced in that services such as health, water, sewerage, etc., have been taken away from local councils and transferred to large regional authorities.

Additional finance to local government would in itself involve additional controls which mitigate against more local freedom and discretion. Certainly one can argue for a basic situation where:

a) Services imposed on local authorities by central government as a statutory duty – i.e., the local authorities act merely as agent – should be financed by the central government to the extent that minimum service standards are achieved.
b) Where additional standards above national minimum standards are provided as a result of local decision then the additional expenditure should be financed from local resources and local taxation.
c) Purely local services should be financed as at (b) above.

Co-ordination of the various sections of administration at different levels of government to achieve common goals is an important factor, as it is in any complex organisation.

The relationships between central and local government can be summarised therefore by saying that local powers and discretion should be developed to the extent that they do not impinge upon the central government's own role and responsibilities.

Where duties and financial resources are transferred from central government then controls must be applied to see that those duties are being undertaken effectively and efficiently and that the financial resources are being used for those purposes for which they were allocated. The need exists to match local spending patterns with national economic plans.

Centralisation of services
In recent times there has been a decline in the number of services provided by local authorities. Services such as personal health services which were originally administered locally, are now seen as national services administered on a regional basis. The question students should consider is whether there is any scope for further centralisation of local authority services. There are various advantages that might accrue from such a policy:

- It should be easier to achieve and maintain common standards of service e.g., in services such as housing, education, police and social services. This would involve creating local administrative centres concerned with administering the services locally; the funds would be allocated on a regional basis from the centre.
- Centralisation should remove local taxation in the form of the rating system with all its attendant weaknesses. This would rationalise the taxation system.
- There is a possibility of cost savings arising out of the dismantling of the local government structure e.g., the expenses of the elected member would disappear. Obviously the extent of any cost savings would depend on the total cost of operating a central administration.
- It should be easier for central government to control both total expenditure and patterns of expenditure. This would assist the government in controlling the national economy.
- Because policy comes from the centre it should be easier to avoid clashes on policy e.g.,

with locally elected members. The political battle would move to a national level.

On the other hand further centralisation could bring two major disadvantages:

- Policy-making would become more remote by increasing the bureaucracy at the centre. Such centralisation would reduce the opportunities for participating in decision making, particularly if the locally elected member was dispensed with.
- The ability to raise revenue locally would be removed, leaving little room for authorities to deal with local service needs. Local choice would be severely curtailed.

Central government controls over other public sector organisations

There now follows a brief description of the types of control experienced by other public sector organisations. These controls are very similar to those experienced by local authorities. There is however, a major difference when one is evaluating the extent of these controls as compared to local government. This difference lies in the fact that local government members are elected in part to look after local interests. Thus any detailed central control of local government can be viewed as a threat to local democracy.

Health authorities
Examples of central controls are as follows.

- Legal basis of health authorities is contained in *National Health Service Act 1977*.
- Key roles are played by the Department of Health and Secretary of State in planning and monitoring the NHS on a national scale.
- Members of regional health authorities are appointed and dismissed by Secretary of State.
- The major source of finance for revenue and capital expenditure is central government grants.
- Cash limits are imposed for revenue and capital expenditure.
- Health authorities are required to submit regular financial returns to the Department of Health e.g., on level of bank balances.
- Health authorities are required to produce annual accounts as prescribed by the Department of Health.
- The annual review process where a health minister meets the chairman of each regional health authority. They discuss how well policy is being implemented and also the efficiency and effectiveness in the use of resources. Prior to the meeting the regional chairman has had similar meetings with the chairmen of health districts in the region.
- Health authorities required to publish performance indicators, e.g. unit costs, manpower statistics, clinical activity, etc.

Nationalised industries
Examples of central controls are as follows:

- Legal basis of industries is contained in statute.
- Chairmen and members of corporations are appointed by Secretary of State.
- Central departments and Secretary of State oversee activities.
- The industries are ultimately accountable to Parliament and Select Committees of MPs.
- Capital investment programmes and borrowings are centrally approved.
- External financing limits or cash limits are set and enforced.

- A target rate of return upon capital employed is agreed.
- Consultation takes place on the revision of charges and tariffs to consumers.
- Copies of annual reports and audited accounts are produced and submitted to the Secretary of State.

Conclusion

This section has examined several of the welter of controls exercised by government departments over the actions of public authorities. Many of the controls extant in many cases from legislation passed in eras vastly different from that of today. It is certainly time for a close scrutiny of the controls in conjunction with government if the autonomy of local authorities in particular is to be strengthened and if wasteful and costly duplication of work and administration is to be avoided.

Accounting needs and objectives

In the private sector, accounting techniques have been devised to depict clearly the profits made by organisations and how those profits are disbursed, or appropriated. These techniques and their underlying rules and conventions are increasingly in use in the public sector as more areas become open to competition and the 'rate of return' requirements. Public sector accounting is, however, principally concerned with ensuring value for money, through the publication and dissemination of unit costs and statistics derived from published final accounts. Being ultimately responsible to Parliament and with their powers and taxing/charging methods derived from that source, there are considerable pressures on the public sector to see that finances are wisely employed. Securing economy, efficiency and effectiveness in the provision of services, are key requirements of a public sector body and there is increased emphasis on these aspects by external auditors.

The development of the Accounting Code of Practice, detailed in Chapter 3, has been substantially driven by the need for consistency in the preparation of accounts so that statistics produced from them can form a useful starting base from which further enquiries can be made.

In looking at the published accounting requirements of local government, the needs of external providers of finance are a prime consideration. The central government, local taxpayers and users of services need information to tell them what is going on and how the money which they have contributed has been spent. Financial reports of these organisations have therefore traditionally emphasised the stewardship function and recent developments have been slanted towards wider accountability aspects, including responsibility for performance.

Central government accounting

Central government services are administered through the various government departments which operate their accounting systems on a fund basis. The basic system is that all government income from taxes and other revenues is paid into a central fund and the various departments draw off this fund to finance the services they provide.

The accounting system operated within central government is unique. The two main methods of accounting are:

- *vote accounting* – all revenues and payments go into and out of one central fund, and spending can only take place if authorised, or voted, by Parliament
- *accrual accounting* – the system used by the trading services based on normal commercial practice of accounting for accruals and prepayments.

This section will give an overview of the vote accounting system used by central government and detail the format of estimates, appropriation accounts and trading accounts of the various government services. The section also gives an insight to the bookkeeping system operated between the Treasury and the various government departments.

The Public Expenditure Survey

Public expenditure is all the spending by central government, local authorities and the external financing limits of nationalised industries. There are three main areas of spending which are known as economic categories:

a) current expenditure on goods and services and capital expenditure on physical assets, e.g., defence, education and health;
b) subsidies, social security and other benefits and various grants, e.g., Regional Development Grant;
c) lending and similar transactions, e.g., overseas lending.

The funds available to finance public expenditure are allocated between the various government departments. The size of the allocation to an individual department depends on the political and social priorities of the government. Of particular importance in recent years has been the government's commitment to reduce the level of public expenditure coupled with achieving better value for money from every pound spent providing the various government services.

The Public Expenditure Survey (PES) is the planning system by which the government reviews and plans the level of public expenditure for the next three years in the light of the estimated funds available to finance that expenditure.

The amount of money available for public expenditure is subject to cash limits. Spending by a department in any year is stated in cash terms, that is the prices prevailing in the November of the previous year plus an amount to cover forecast inflation in the next year. The total level of expenditure is controlled within this cash limited amount, and the Treasury is responsible for monitoring spending and reporting to the government on the level of spending by the various departments throughout the financial year.

Vote accounting

The current system of vote accounting operated by central government has its foundation in the *Exchequer and Audit Department Act 1866*, as amended by the *National Loans Act 1968*.

All cash limited expenditure on the provision of services by government departments is financed from taxation and other government income collected and paid into the consolidated fund. If there is a deficit in any year, that is if the income of the consolidated fund is less than the expenditures charged to the fund for supply and standing services, then a payment is made from the national loans fund to the consolidated fund to finance that deficit.

The consolidated fund

The operation of the consolidated fund is governed by the *Exchequer and Audit Department Act 1866*, as amended by the *National Loans Act 1968*, which provides that total tax revenue and other public monies collected by central government shall be paid into one general fund. This fund, the consolidated fund, is operated by Treasury staff at the Bank of England and is exemplified below:

Example _____

Consolidated fund
Account of receipts and payments for the year ended 31 March 19X8

Receipts	£m	Payments	£m
Inland Revenue	64,509	Supply services	104,875
Customs and Excise	44,737		
Vehicle excise duty	2,645	Consolidated fund standing services:	
Total tax revenue	111,891	Payment to the national loans fund in respect of service of the national debt	9,599
		Northern Ireland:	
Interest and dividends	1,096	share of taxes, etc	2,219
Miscellaneous receipts	9,982	Payments to the European Contingencies fund – Union, etc.	3,789
repayments	4,215		
		Other standing services:	
		Civil List	4
		Annuities and pensions	7
		Salaries and allowances	2
		Courts of Justice	38
		Miscellaneous services	48
		Issues to contingencies fund	4,195
			124,776
		Surplus transferred to the national loans fund	2,408
Total receipts	127,184	Total payments	127,184

National loans fund

The operation of the national loans fund is regulated by the *National Loans Act 1968* and is maintained on a receipts and payments basis. The national loans fund records all the movements of government borrowings.

If in any financial year, 1 April to 31 March, there is a deficit on the consolidated fund this is financed by a payment/transfer from the national loans fund. On the contrary, if there is a surplus on the consolidated fund, as in the year ended 31 March 19X8, there is a payment/transfer to the national loans fund. An illustration of the national loans fund is given below:

Example

National loans fund
Account of receipts and payments in the year ended 31 March 19X8

Receipts	£m	Payments	£m
Interest, etc		Service by the national debt	
Interest on loans repayable		Interest	16,233
to the national loans fund	5,657	Management and expenses	173
Profits of the issue			
department of the Bank			16,106
of England	1,144	Issues in respect of loans	14,171
Miscellaneous receipts	6	Exchange equalisation	
Service of the national debt:		account issues of sterling	
balance met from the		capital	18,100
consolidated fund	9,599	National debt: sums repaid	149,540
		16,406	
Consolidated fund:			
Surplus transferred	2,408		
Repayment of loans	10,038		
Exchange equalisation account:			
repayments of sterling capital	7,850		
National debt: sums borrowed	161,515		
Total receipts	198,217	Total payments	198,217

The statutory authority for government departments to spend money on the provision of services is contained in the *Appropriation Act* which approves the estimates submitted by the various government departments. As the passing of this Act does not normally take place until the summer of each year and government departments have to incur expenditure from 1 April in order to provide services, *votes on account* are passed by Parliament to authorise spending in the intervening period.

The following are two funds which are available for meeting government spending that cannot be forecast when estimates are prepared, e.g., the financing of the Falklands War and the gales of October 1987.

a) *The reserve fund*
The reserve fund is credited with a proportion of all planned spending which is not allocated to government departments in the supply estimates cycle. The fund is credited each year with this unallocated amount and in any financial year Treasury ministers can allocate money to a department which incurs expenditure of an unforeseen nature.

b) *The contingencies fund*
The contingencies fund is administered under strict rules agreed by Parliament. If a department requires funds urgently for additional expenditure then an advance is made from this fund. When Parliament approves the additional expenditure, the advance has to be repaid.

The structure of a supply estimate

A supply estimate is approved by Parliament as a vote. One or more estimates are presented, by the Treasury, for each government department. Each estimate will detail the expenditure on services provided and administered by an individual department and for which the department concerned will be accountable to Parliament.

A vote is therefore an area of expenditure which is the responsibility of a single government department and for which that department is accountable to Parliament. Some departments have responsibility for more than one vote, in which case the votes are grouped together into a class. There are currently over 180 votes grouped into 18 classes. Class XII, for example, groups together all the supply estimates or votes which are the responsibility of the Department of Education and Science.

The estimates for each class are presented to Parliament for approval on Budget Day each year.

All estimates are in a standard format and contain the following information:

Introduction

– Whether the vote is subject to cash limits
– A general description of the expenditure
– Details of any important changes, e.g., expenditure previously contained in other classes
– A note on the level of service to be provided.

Part I – The ambit and net provision

– The vote title
– Total net provision on the vote
– The ambit
– The department involved
– Net total of the vote
– Money already voted on account
– Balance outstanding.

The ambit describes the purposes for which the estimates relate. When Parliament approves the estimates as a vote the funds cannot be used for any other purpose without the approval of Parliament. However, the system does provide for a limited transfer of funds from an underspending area to an overspending one (known as virement) within the estimate sub-heads.

Part II – Summary and subhead detail

This section of the estimate details the gross and net provision which is put forward for Parliamentary approval. The estimates are analysed by subhead, grouped into sections each covering a particular aspect of the service and show comparative figures for earlier years.

Appropriations in aid is the term used in the central government accounting system to describe income received by a department. The income is used to finance the expenditure on services by a department and is therefore deducted from the gross expenditure on a vote, reducing the amount that is needed to be issued from the consolidated fund to finance expenditure.

Part III – Extra receipts payable to the consolidated fund

This section details the extra receipts, above the level approved as appropriations in aid by Parliament or of a type not authorised for such appropriation, which are surrendered to the consolidated fund. Receipts under this latter category might relate to the proceeds from the sale of land and property.

Part IV – Analysis of the vote by type of expenditure

Some departments make payments to finance the provision of central services by local authorities and other bodies. These payments are usually in the form of grants. The Home Office pays a grant to local authorities to part finance the running of the police force in their administrative area. The Department of the Environment pays the revenue support grant to local authorities to part finance the expenditure incurred by them in running services such as education and social services in their administrative area.

Where a particular vote includes this type of payment to other public sector organisations, it is detailed as follows:

a) *Public expenditure* – This is split between current and capital expenditure. Expenditure on land, buildings, plant and machinery which have a useful life of more than one year is classified as capital expenditure. Expenditure on the day-to-day running of a department and on the delivery of services, salaries, wages, electricity for example is classified as current expenditure.

b) *Other expenditure* – These are the payments made from central government to other public bodies, e.g., from the Home Office to a police authority.

Example _____

From the following information, you are required to prepare the Part II Summary Supply Estimates for Vote 1, Schools, further education and other educational services, contained in Class XII, Department of Education and Science Supply Estimates, for the year to 31 March 19X6.

	19X3/19X4 Net outturn £'000	19X4/19X5 Total net provision £'000	19X5/19X6 Gross provision £'000
Schools	40,223	42,032	54,253
Higher and further education	105,593	123,096	133,463

Miscellaneous educational services, research and administration 22,887	25,111	28,170

Notes

Estimated appropriations in aid are as follows:

	£'000
Schools	289
Higher and further education	4,297
Miscellaneous educational services, research and administration	182

Method

The completion of this type of question only requires the production of the summary in the standard format as contained in the Treasury guidelines on estimate preparation and presentation.

Solution

19X5/19X6 Class XII, Vote 1
Schools, further education and other educational services

Part II – Summary

19X3/19X4 Net outturn £'000	19X4/19X5 Total net provision £'000		19X5/19X6 Gross provision £'000	Appropriations in aid £'000	Net provision £'000
40,223	42,032	Schools	54,253	289	53,964
105,593	123,096	Higher and further education	133,463	4,297	129,166
22,887	25,111	Miscellaneous educational services, research and administration	28,170	182	27,988
168,703	190,239	Total	215,886	4,768	211,118

The appropriation account

At the end of each financial year, each spending department is required by the *Exchequer and Audit Department Act 1866* and the *National Audit Act* to produce an annual statement of its transactions, an appropriation account, for each vote.

The appropriation account shows how the supply grant voted by Parliament has been spent. The format of the appropriation account is laid down in guidance notes issued by the Treasury and it follows closely the format of the supply estimates already described. This allows a comparison to be made of actual with authorised expenditure.

As appropriation accounts are prepared on a receipts and payments basis, there is no system for accounting for capital expenditure other than in the year of purchase or sale. No balance sheets are produced and therefore no capital accounting system is operated to record such things as the depreciation of fixed assets. This feature is unique to central government and you should compare the central government accounting system with that of public corporations to emphasise this fact.

Appropriation accounts are produced by the finance branches in spending departments and it is the responsibility of the accounting officer, usually the permanent head of a department, to sign the appropriation account confirming its accuracy and confirming responsibility for the propriety and regularity of the department's expenditure.

The *National Audit Act 1983*, lays down that appropriation accounts have to be submitted for audit by the Comptroller and Auditor General (C and AG) as soon as possible after 31 March each year. This Act outlines the duties of the C and AG. As auditor general he has to ensure that supply grants have only been spent as authorised and whether value for money has been obtained. At the end of the audit of each appropriation account the C and AG signs a certificate which gives his opinion that sums expended have been applied for the purposes authorised by Parliament and the account properly presents the expenditure and receipts of that vote. The certificate is printed at the end of each appropriation account.

When all appropriation accounts have been audited they are submitted to the Public Accounts Committee for scrutiny on behalf of the House of Commons. It is assisted in its scrutiny by the C and AG and the Treasury Officer of Accounts and can request departmental accounting officers to appear before it to answer any questions or queries there may be in relation to the contents of an appropriation account, or the system of financial administration within a spending department.

The Public Accounts Committee presents a report on its findings to Parliament where the contents of this report and the appropriation accounts are debated.

The structure of an appropriation account

The booklet containing the appropriation accounts for each vote making up a particular class starts with a report by the C and AG on the class as a whole. The next section is the summary appropriation accounts for the whole class and it contains all the individual appropriation accounts for all the votes in the class. The appropriation account for each individual vote is preceded by a summary of outturn, i.e., actual payments in a financial year and a comparison of estimated expenditure with actual expenditure. The final section details any receipts payable to the consolidated fund.

The name of the department's accounting officer is shown at the foot of the accounts, followed by the Audit Certificate signed by the Comptroller and Auditor General.

It will be useful at this stage to look at a summary appropriation account.

Example ———————————————————————————

Appropriation account 19X5/X6
Central Administration (Department of Education)

	£m
Budgeted gross expenditure (45,276 + 7,631 + 1,397)	54,304

Authorised appropriations in aid	2,145
Supply grant (54,304 – 2,145)	52,159
Actual gross expenditure (45,020 + 7,440 + 1,325)	53,785
Appropriations in aid applied	2,145
Net expenditure (53,785 – 2,145)	51,640
Gross expenditure saving (54,304 – 53,785)	519
Deficiency in appropriations in aid	Nil
Amount surrendered to consolidated fund (52,159 – 51,640)	519

Trading accounts

A number of central government services are managed and administered on a commercial basis under legislation contained in the *Government Trading Funds Act 1973*. Various funds have been established such as the following:

a) *Her Majesty's Stationery Office Trading Fund* – This organisation supplies stationery and office equipment to central government departments and other public sector bodies and also publishes and sells government publications.

There are various HMSO shops throughout England which are run on a commercial basis, selling books and stationery in addition to government publications.

b) *Royal Mint Trading Fund* – The Royal Mint produces all the banknotes and coins for circulation. It also produces and sells gold coins and commemorative coins and medals.

The *Government Trading Funds Act 1973* lays upon the minister responsible for each fund the duty:

a) to manage the funded operations so that the revenue of the fund is not less than sufficient, taking one year with another to meet outgoings which are properly chargeable to revenue;
b) to achieve such further financial objectives as the Treasury may from time to time, by minute laid before the House of Commons, indicate as having been determined by the responsible minister (with Treasury concurrence) to be desirable of achievement.

An example of this further financial objective is that for the three-year period 1990/91 to 1992/93, the Royal Mint is to achieve an annual average return of 12.5 per cent on net assets.

The accounting methods and format of the final accounts of the trading funds compare with those of private sector commercial organisations.

Resource accounting

A concerted move from cash to 'resources' or 'accruals' accounting was spelled out by the Chancellor of Exchequer in his November 1993 budget speech. A Green Paper was subsequently issued in July 1994 and this will eventually bring Whitehall accounting into line with the private sector.

They also entail substantial changes in the annual system of public expenditure review which began in the 1960s in the wake of a report by Lord Plowden. Parliament, ministers and departments will have to start thinking of periods much longer than a single year.

Between now and the end of the decade, the plan is to phase in a new way of assessing how the recipients of public money spend it. In the jargon, it is called resource accounting (based on UK Generally Accepted Accounting Practice and in particular the requirements of the *Companies Act 1985*, adjusted to reflect differences between private and public sectors). It entails measuring what government departments produce not just in relation to the cash they are allocated by the Treasury, but also how effectively they have managed their buildings, plant and capital.

For the first time, in principle, departments might be able to claim that spending some cash now (for example on new technology) is an investment that will reap rewards in the future and justifies flexibility on cash spending. Whether the Treasury would accept this and allow the longer run to be played off against short-run cash considerations remains to be seen.

At the end of each financial year, departments would write up a balance sheet – not dissimilar to those drawn up for private companies – showing movement in the value of assets and liabilities as well as cash expended. Changes in a 'value' for the product of a department would indicate the skill in managing its resource base, as well as its success in keeping cash targets.

It will be, according to Mr Clarke 'a much more accurate way of looking at how departments link inputs and outputs'. He could be right, but a lot depends on who is doing the looking – will this (as Whitehall fears) be just another lever for Treasury penny-pinchers to pull, or will the Government for the first time start to recognise that there is a difference between public money paid out in current spending and money invested for future returns? 'It will require a substantial change in the way departments are run,' says the Chancellor, 'in the accounting and information systems they use and in their working methods and culture.'

The technical leader of the team managing the reform is Andrew Likierman, the head of the Government's Accountancy Service and chief accounting adviser at the Treasury. He takes the line that accruals accounting was starting to happen anyway – in the National Health Service, among executive agencies and in local authorities – and there is an inevitability about its arrival in Whitehall.

The intention will be to produce the three main financial statements on an historical cost basis, but with fixed assets included at current value. The new accounting systems are due to be in place by April 1997, with the first full set of accounts – those for 1998/99 – available for internal consumption. 1999/2000 will see the first set of publicly available statements. Central government moves a little more slowly than when overseeing change in local government.

The Private Finance Initiative

The PFI was launched by Norman Lamont as Chancellor of the Exchequer in November 1992. The intention was to encourage private sector finance to secure infrastructure investment and save public expenditure. The Private Finance Panel is a limited company with a finite life. It had three main targets: to complete an individual project such as a hospital, to create a model or template for similar types of development and to identify and remove problems preventing the use of private sector finance. The Chancellor set the Panel a target of £5 billion of private sector finance by the end of 1995, and that is well on target.

Road funding transportation and projects within the national health service are high on the list of areas of greatest potential. Input to date from local government has not been great, but education is clearly a field earmarked for future growth. Urban Development Corporations have been involved in a number of projects, including those in the former London Docklands including parts of the Docklands Light Railway.

2 Local government – structure and functions

This chapter examines the present structure of local government in England and Wales and outlines proposals for the future being prepared by the local Government Commission. The statutory position of the chief financial officer is set out. The division of services and functions between local government is examined and new ways of providing local services are considered. The chapter concludes with an examination of the relationships between central and local government.

Framework of local government

Definition of local government

Local government is that part of the administration of a country that deals mainly with such matters as concern the inhabitants of a particular place or district, including those functions which the central government has considered it desirable to be so administered at a local level.

The bodies entrusted with these matters are known as local authorities and are, in the main, elective. A local authority means any body of persons empowered to spend money derived from the proceeds of a local tax. Parliament decides the structure and scope of local government and the powers of local authorities are determined by statute.

In the United Kingdom, many services and activities are provided by the State. They are administered by central government, acting through departments and a number of public sector organisations – nationalised industries (many of which in recent years have been privatised), local government and health authorities. These bodies have differing objectives which lead to a variety of accounting practices, control procedures and management structures. A characteristic which all public sector organisations have in common is that they derive their powers from Parliament and ultimately all are responsible to Parliament.

Derivation of powers

The functions undertaken by public authorities are strictly determined by the legislative authority granted by Acts of Parliament. Parliament, through the appropriate legislation, also determines the particular structure within which the various functions are to operate, although the structure does vary in different parts of the country. Thus the various tiers of administration in public sector bodies, e.g. county and district councils of local government in England, are prescribed by Parliament.

A public sector body which provides a product or service for which there is no statutory basis is said to have broken the doctrine of *ultra vires*, i.e., beyond the powers. This means the organisation has overstepped its statutory limits and as such the expenditure incurred is illegal. Often it is quite difficult to decide whether expenditure has any statutory basis or not because the decision involves interpretation of Acts of Parliament. For example under the *Local Government Act 1972* a local authority has power to undertake anything which would facilitate the discharge of any of its functions.

The present framework of local government

In 1966, the late Richard Crossman as Minister of Housing and Local Government in a Labour Government, set up a Royal Commission under the chairmanship of Sir John Maud (Lord Redcliffe-Maud) to review functions and areas in England and Wales (excluding London). It was, however, debarred from considering local government finance.

The Maud Commission reported in 1969 proposing that over 1,000 local authorities should be replaced by 61 new local authority areas. Of these areas 58 were to be all-purpose authorities – enlarged county boroughs given the name unitary – while in the other three (centred on Birmingham, Liverpool and Manchester) a two-tier form of metropolitan government, similar to London, was proposed.

The Labour government accepted the report with modifications but it was opposed by the Conservatives, who became committed to maintaining the two-tier system and formed the government after the 1970 general election. Peter Walker took over as Minister of Housing and Local Government (the post was soon upgraded to Secretary of State for the Environment) and he made it clear that the unitary structure was too revolutionary. Evolutionary was to be the style of the new local government system.

His solution was a compromise embodied in the *Local Government Act 1972*. It recognised the special needs of the major centres of population by introducing two-tier metropolitan government in six areas. These were the three proposed by the Maud Commission (West Midlands, Merseyside and Greater Manchester) plus West Yorkshire, South Yorkshire and Tyne and Wear. All six metropolitan county councils (MCCs) were abolished on 31 March 1986.

For the rest of the country a traditional two-tier county/district structure was laid down. Amalgamations at county and district level brought a drastic reduction in the number of authorities – 39 counties and 296 districts in England, eight counties and 37 districts in Wales.

The Conservative Party included in its 1983 general election manifesto a promise to abolish the Greater London Council and the six metropolitan county councils. The manifesto said these authorities were a 'wasteful and unnecessary tier of government'. It promised to abolish them and return most of their functions to the boroughs and districts with those services which needed to be administered over a wider area, such as police and fire, being run by joint boards. There was bitter opposition, but the *Local Government Act 1985* resulted in the GLC and the six metropolitan counties ceasing to exist after 31 March 1986.

The Inner London Education Authority was retained as a directly elected authority, responsible for education in inner London but it was abolished by the *Education Reform Act 1988* on 1 April 1990. Each London borough is now responsible for education.

The changes were presided over by residuary bodies, set up in London and the metropolitan counties in September 1985 by the Secretary of State for the Environment who appointed chairmen and members. They assumed responsibilities for dealing with the assets and liabilities of the former authorities and have themselves now been wound up.

New police authorities were set up for the metropolitan county areas of Greater Manchester, Merseyside, South Yorkshire, West Midlands and West Yorkshire. In addition, the Northumbria Police Authority was extended to take in Tyne and Wear. All the metropolitan districts nominate councillors to serve on the new police authorities but, as in county police authorities, one third of the membership of each authority have to be non-elected magistrates appointed by joint magistrates committees. These magistrates do not have to live in the county area.

Seven new fire and civil defence authorities were set up in the areas administered by the abolished authorities. In London, each of the 32 London boroughs, plus the City of London, nominate one councillor to serve on the London Fire and Civil Defence Authority. In the six metropolitan areas the number of nominations of each district is dependent on its size. Districts, in their nominations to the new bodies, are required to reflect the political balance of their councils as far as is practical.

Six new passenger transport authorities were set up in the metropolitan areas. Their membership is based on the same criteria as the fire and civil defence authorities. London local government has not had any involvement in passenger transport since London Regional Transport, a government appointed body, was set up in 1984 to take over GLC underground and bus powers.

A more commercial environment

The period of local government in this country since the Second World War, has been dominated by the loss of local control over traditional local services. Local health services and hospitals are now within the NHS. Water, gas and electricity have now all been privatised. In more recent years, and particularly since the present Conservative government came to power in 1979, legislation has severely reduced the powers of local government, particularly in the major services of police, education and housing. Few services have been transferred the other way, the most notable being community care under the *NHS and Community Care Act 1990*.

The *Local Government, Planning and Land Act 1980* introduced direct labour organisations into local government. This legislation required significant areas of local government work, particularly those associated with manual workforces, to be placed on a commercial accounting basis and to make a rate of return on capital employed (see Chapter 7).

Compulsory competitive tendering (CCT) is being applied to all local government services (at present only the central support services remain to be tested and they have been held up by reorganisation). Thus, a far more commercial environment in the provision of local services has been created by the government. This is having a considerable impact on the structure and financial administration of local government.

Further structural changes

The *Local Government Act 1972* set up the Boundary Commission for England and Wales, with powers to recommend the abolition of a local government area, the amalgamation of authorities, the abolition of any principal area of local government or the constitution of parishes.

The English Boundary Commission was charged with reviewing all counties, metropolitan districts and London boroughs between 1984 and 1989. Some county boundaries were changed in 1985 and there have been recommendations for places like Humberside but the Commission has not had a major effect.

Local authorities could make proposals for changes to their own boundaries and these had to be passed on by the commission to the Secretary of State with their comments.

District councils have a duty to keep parish boundaries under review. They could propose changes to the Boundary Commission. They had to act on a request for a review from a parish council, or from at least 30 parish electors.

The *Local Government Act 1992* provided for the replacement of the English Boundary Commission by a new Local Government Commission which has considered the structure of English local government, area by area, and made recommendations to the Secretary of State.

A uniform solution throughout the country is not envisaged, rather flexibility to allow for local circumstances with the emphasis on communities. The Commission will be required to reflect the identity and views of local communities as well as the need for effective and convenient local government. Such a reconciliation will be a very difficult task. It is one that has bedevilled all previous views.

The Secretary of State has issued guidelines for the Commission, which initially will confine itself to England outside London and the metropolitan counties, although inevitably when looking at surrounding areas they may make proposals affecting them. In gauging a community's identity the commission should consider:

- people's preferences
- work, shopping and leisure patterns
- topography, geography and the history of the area.

The Commission's work to date has produced recommendations for county areas which have caused vigorous national and local opposition, including High Court judicial reviews. In March 1995 the Commission chairman, Sir John Banham, suddenly resigned after differences with the Environment Secretary about the final shape of the English map. John Gummer was disappointed that so few unitary authorities had been proposed when that was clearly the original intention of the Government. Sir David Cooksey, Chairman of the Audit Commmision, has taken over the task, with completion by June 1996.

Wales did not have a Local Government Commission. Instead, the Secretary of State for Wales announced, in May 1993, that he favoured 27 unitary authorities and a map of his proposals was published.

Provider to enabler

The changing role of local government has accelerated in recent years particularly since 1979. In early 1994, the Financial Secretary to the Treasury told an audience of prominent local government and public sector figures that he would like to see their role diminish to that of a purchaser of services, which would almost wholly be provided by the private sector. The 'enabling' authority is seen as one mainly concerned with policy direction, the allocation of resources, determining standards and priorities and then monitoring the results. The widening of compulsory competitive tendering (CCT) is an important move in this direction, as is 'outsourcing', where local services are provided by a private company under contract, without the need for CCT.

The role of the Chief Financial Officer

The *Local Government Act 1972* abolished specific statutory reference to the need to appoint a 'treasurer' and to the 'making of safe and efficient arrangements for receipts and payments'. What it did do, however, was to impose wider but more general responsibilities for the financial administration of local authority affairs. *The 1972 Act* stated:

- 'a local authority shall appoint such officers as they think necessary for the proper discharge ... of their functions' (Section 112);
- 'every local authority shall make arrangements for the proper administration of their financial affairs and shall ensure that one of their officers has responsibility for the administration of those affairs' (Section 151).

The *Local Government Act 1988* strengthens the position of the *1972 Act* by:

- requiring all Section 151 officers to be properly qualified
- specifying those issues on which Section 151 officers must report to the council.

The title 'Chief Financial Officer' is widely used, but other titles also exist (e.g. 'Treasurer', 'Director of Finance'). The duties of such a post vary widely. In some small district councils the Chief Financial Officer may, even today, be little more than a bookkeeper, receiver and paymaster for the authority. In practice it is for the members of an authority to determine the role of the Chief Financial Officer and to specify the terms and conditions of his appointment, and thus in other authorities he will have a very senior and high profile role.

At the time of the 1972 reorganisation of local government CIPFA made the following statement about the place of finance in the internal management structure of a local authority. The statement is equally applicable to other public sector organisations:

that the accounting, financial administration and control system of a local authority should be the responsibility of a chief financial officer who is independent of the main spending arrangements of management;

that the chief financial officer should be a member of the management team, and be required to contribute to the management of local authority financial advice and information;

that the chief financial officer should continue to be under public obligation to maintain the integrity of the financial administration and control system;

that, to maintain the objectivity and integrity of financial administration and control, the chief financial officer should continue to be responsible for ensuring that the financial implications of the local authority's activities are taken into account throughout the authority and at all levels, and that therefore the chief financial officer should have the right of direct communication to all levels of the local authority management;

that Standing Orders of a local authority should provide that no decision to expend resources should be taken without advice from the local authority's chief financial officer.

As well as fulfilling the statutory duties set out above, the Chief Financial Officer (CFO) will be responsible for the accounting, budgeting and budgetary control, internal audit, receipts and payments and other key areas of financial work – insurances, investments, grant claims and financial returns, as well as the management of the finance department.

At the end of 1993, CIPFA issued a Statement on the duties of a CFO, for the first time since just before the 1974 reorganisation. The timing of this new Statement reflects the significant changes in local government over that period and into the future.

The Cadbury Report on corporate governance

Reference is made to this report in paragraph 23 of the CIPFA Statement above. The report was published late in 1992 and was the result of a Committee of Inquiry chaired by Sir Adrian Cadbury. The Committee was established to ask some searching questions about the way in which companies are run and the relationship between shareholders, executives and auditors. The Cadbury Committee recommended a Code of Conduct for the way in which companies are run, setting out specific roles for the chairman and chief executive, and the public responsibility of auditors.

Aspects of the Cadbury Report are certainly relevant to the public sector. The NHS Executive began to introduce parts of it into the NHS from April 1994. CIPFA has issued a discussion paper entitled 'Corporate Governance in the Public Services'. This is a subject that will develop, but it received an unexpected boost in the spring of 1995 with the appointment, by the Prime Minister, of a committee under Lord Nolan to report on standards in public life. This followed several instances of misconduct by Members of Parliament. The Nolan brief is wide-ranging and includes local government; the first report of the committee was delivered in May 1995.

Structure, functions and services

Present structure

The *Local Government Act 1972* contains the statutory provisions which established the local government structure in England and Wales and that operated from 1974.

The *Local Government Act 1985* abolished the six metropolitan county councils and the Greater London Council from 31 March 1986. The services which they administered, were transferred to metropolitan district councils as joint authorities. The present structure and information about the services provided by each type of authority and electoral arrangements are shown in Appendix 2.1 at the end of this chapter.

Functions and services

Appendix 2.2 sets out the principal functions and services provided by each type of local authority in England.

Mandatory and discretionary services

The services provided by local authorities fall into two main categories as follows:

- *Discretionary* – allotments, recreation, airports, cemeteries and crematoria
- *Mandatory* – planning, education, highways and transportation, social services, trading standards.

Local government in Wales

Eight new counties were set up by the *Local Government Act 1972*. The former county boroughs, boroughs, rural and urban districts were combined into 37 new districts.

Functions in Wales and England are allocated similarly. The differences are:

- refuse disposal is a district function in Wales
- Welsh districts, with the consent of the county council, can provide on-street and off-street car parks (English districts can only provide off-street parking)
- Welsh districts may be allowed to administer libraries and some consumer protection functions.

English parishes

All parishes and parish councils survived under the *1972 Local Government Act*, but without the added powers which were proposed for them by the Royal Commission, whose recommendations meant they would have been the only tier of local government under the large, all powerful unitary authorities. The 1972 Act said all parishes with over 150 people must have a council.

Parishes are very much the grass roots of local government and as such can be important pressure groups. It is quite common for parish councillors to serve as district and/or county councillors, which means they have an additional platform for advancing the cause of their parishes.

Parish councils (often retaining traditional titles of town or city council) vary enormously – from the 150 minimum population to over 30,000. There are nearly 200 in metropolitan areas. After the 1974 reorganisation, a number of 'disappearing' authorities, mostly with a population under 20,000, gained special dispensation to continue in parish form (known as town councils).

Welsh community councils

These are the Welsh parish councils. They automatically took over where there was a parish council before the *1972 Act.*

Powers and duties of parish councils

Most services provided by parish councils are concurrent with the district council. Transport services may be undertaken with the permission of the county council. In addition, the district council, if requested, must notify the parish council of all planning applications concerning the parish council. The parish council may then comment on these applications.

Parish councils are responsible for the provision and/or maintenance of the following services:

- allotments
- cemeteries and crematoria
- conveniences
- village halls
- war memorials
- public baths and wash houses
- public footpaths and incidentals to public highways
- recreation grounds and open spaces.

Joint working between local authorities

Local authorities, especially shire county councils and their districts, perform many functions which cannot be exercised independently of each other, e.g. refuse collection of a district and refuse disposal by the county council (in Wales, the districts are responsible for both). Thus, there are many opportunities for co-operation by sharing resources and expertise. Such arrangements may take a number of forms, e.g. a formal principal and agent relationship, or a pooling of resources necessary to establish a purchasing consortia.

Agency agreements

Agency agreements are frequently set up between counties and districts and they are most common for highway matters and refuse disposal. Formal agency agreements are not allowed under existing legislation for education, social services, police and fire.

Section 101 of the *Local Government Act 1972* allows a local authority to arrange for the discharge of most of their functions by another local authority. This 'agency arrangement' is where one authority sets up a formal agreement which allows another authority to act on its behalf. Thus, if road maintenance was delegated by a county council to one of its district councils, the district, as 'agent', would act on behalf of the county as 'principal'. This agreement would be subject to a formal and legally binding contract, which would contain detailed arrangements for, among other things, the scope of work to be covered, financial arrangements, penalty clauses, insurance, arbitration and internal audit.

Other forms of co-operation

Outside of formal agency arrangements, there is plenty of co-operation between authorities in the efficient provision of services. Examples of such arrangements are IT and computer facilities, central purchasing, building, printing and internal audit.

Whatever form the co-operation takes it is necessary to examine its feasibility prior to entering into any agreement. The following criteria, at least, should be satisfied.

• The overall standard of service should at least be as effective as that presently provided.
• Economies should, where possible, accrue to all parties.
• The actions of joint arrangements should be influenced by local members, officers, the electorate and the consumer of the service. The service must be both flexible in its actions and accountable for its performance.
• Co-operation should not generate high levels of capital expenditure on buildings and equipment. Obviously there are exceptions such as joint use facilities or a central store but in the main the aim should be to make better use of existing resources.

When entering into an agreement on co-operation, a formal contract to which all parties are agreeable should be prepared. This clarifies the responsibilities and expectations of all the parties. The following points should be included in any contract:

• The period of time to be covered by the arrangements; is there a time limit or are the arrangements open-ended?
• The exact relationship of the authorities involved, e.g. are they equal partners or is it an agency arrangement with a principal and agent?
• The method or arrangement for determining policies of the joint facility. Particularly, is there to be a committee of members and/or officers to operate the facility? Section 102 of the *Local Government Act 1972* allows local authorities to appoint a joint committee to advise on any matters relating to the discharge of the function.
• Details of the procedures for preparing the annual revenue and capital estimates.
• The procedures for the incurring of expenditure throughout the year, e.g. expenditure may only be incurred with prior approval of the principal.
• The respective responsibilities and methods of accounting for the facility or function.
• Details of the audit arrangements, particularly the right of access by all parties to the records of another authority.
• The procedures for the reimbursement of expenditure; is it to be quarterly, annually, etc.?
• Will one of the authorities be able to reclaim an administrative charge from the other authorities? How will such a charge be calculated?
• The basis of sharing the costs and revenues between co-operative authorities, e.g. will it be on a population basis, a time basis, a floor area basis, etc.?

Co-operation with other bodies
Co-operation arrangements discussed thus far, have been those between different parts of the public sector. However it is possible for public authorities to enter into agreements with outside bodies, who will help to discharge one of the authorities' functions. This is an area where there has been a considerable growth as public authorities have found their own resources insufficient to carry out their duties. The 'outsourcing' of certain central services (see below) is a good example of this development.

Many voluntary non-profit-making organisations can assist public authorities in the discharge of their functions. A current example is that of registered charities assisting health authorities to integrate the mentally handicapped into the community. Other examples in health care are in home nursing, care of young children, etc. Local authorities are able to call on the assistance of housing associations, non-maintained schools, youth organisations, and charities caring for the elderly.

Such bodies can share the burden of providing the service. The public sector organisation can make a grant to the voluntary body where there is statutory authority to do so.

Outsourcing and management buy-outs

Outsourcing is a comparatively recent development of considerable administrative importance to local government. This involves the placing of bulky, routine work with a specialist private sector company, with the local authority remaining responsible for policy decisions. To date, most outsourcing has related to local taxation billing and/or its subsequent recovery; debt collection and aspects of information technology. Capita plc is a major public sector outsourcing company.

Another growing form of 'privatisation' is the sale to a team of local government officers of the functions of a particular department, under a management buy-out (MBO). The new company then contracts with the local authority to provide financial services, but is also free to trade in the wider market. Recent significant MBOs have been in the finance departments of Berkshire CC and the London Borough of Croydon. However MBOs are particularly relevant in the area of direct labour organisations where the new company will be able to trade free from the constraints of local government.

The local government ombudsmen

The Commissioners for Local Administration (local ombudsmen) were established in 1974. There are three in England, and one each for Wales, Scotland and Northern Ireland.

Anyone wishing to complain about maladministration by one of the authorities mentioned above may make a direct approach to the ombudsman. When an ombudsman receives a complaint there are usually informal talks with the authority before making a decision on whether or not to investigate. Once a decision to investigate has been taken, an authority has 14 days to provide formal comments. An investigating officer will talk to the complainant and then study all relevant records (papers must be made available) and interview councillors and officers. All investigations are private.

The ombudsmen can investigate administrative decisions, but not policy decisions, made by a local authority (not a parish or town council), but they cannot investigate subjects that affect the majority of the inhabitants, contractual matters, personnel, a number of educational matters involving schools, and anything in which a person has the remedy of an appeal to the courts or to a minister.

There are three findings open to an ombudsman when making the report: no maladministration; maladministration but no injustice; or maladministration causing injustice. The report may recommend how the matter should be put right.

One copy of the ombudsman's report goes to the complainant, one to the authority complained about, and one to any other person named in the report. The authority must make the report available for public inspection – it has to advertise this in the local press. Copies of the report are also made available to the press (unless the ombudsman rules the matter should be kept private, which is rare), but people involved in the complaint are not named in the press copies.

If the report criticises an authority, it has to consider the report within three months and tell the ombudsman the action it has taken or how it proposes to put the matter right. A decision not to take any action on the report can only be taken by the full council. If the authority fails to make what the ombudsman considers to be a satisfactory response, or decides to take no action then he may make a further report and require the authority to publish a statement in any two newspapers circulating in the area. If he believes that there has been maladministration involving a member of a council, or that the member's conduct has breached the National Code of Conduct then the ombudsman must identify the individual member concerned and give his name unless he is of the opinion that it would be an injustice to do so.

There his powers end and he cannot force an authority to take action. However, in the vast majority of cases and, particularly in view of the publicity, agreement between the ombudsman and the local authority is reached.

The Commission for Local Administration is paid for by local authorities.

Relationships with central government

Introduction

The main central government departments with which local authorities are involved are set out in Chapter 1.

Local authorities have no powers except those granted by statute and any function not authorised by the general law must be sought by the promotion of a special private bill which will, in due course, become a local Act. There are powers contained in Section 137 of the *Local Government Act 1972* to spend limited sums on expenditure which in the opinion of the authority will be in the interests of the authority or its inhabitants. This expenditure is limited annually to £5 per adult in London and metropolitan areas and £2.50 per adult in shire counties and districts.

Forms of control

Control over the administration of local government is exercised by central government in many ways, but principally through the Secretary of State for the Environment and other government departments which have regular responsibility for local government through various Acts. Parliament has given wide powers to ministers to make rules, regulations and orders to control the day-to-day operations of local authorities. Parliament also authorises local authorities to make local by-laws, particularly those for the 'good government of their areas'.

Reasons for controls

Unlike individuals who can do anything that they are not expressly forbidden to do, local authorities can only do things that they are authorised to do by way of an Act of Parliament, or which can be reasonably inferred from the terms of one. To facilitate business the courts have held that local authorities can do things reasonably incidental to their main powers; and the *Local Government Act 1972* empowered them to do things 'calculated to facilitate, or be conducive or incidental to, the discharge of any of their functions'. However, although at first sight this might seem to give a wide discretion it does not mean local authorities can do what they like. The words of the Act are likely to be interpreted quite narrowly by the courts who have said that 'incidental to' does not mean just being convenient to do.

The need for some measure of central control cannot, in general, be refuted. Many local services have national characteristics and it would be wrong if at least minimum national standards were not available throughout the country, e.g. fire protection, traffic control and building controls.

Another reason for control is that the government provides the bulk of the money that local authorities spend and although it is possible to argue that this should not necessarily mean strict central control, in practice the old adage that 'he who pays the piper calls the tune' has great force.

Judicial control is only one of many controls: the others are *legislative control* by Parliament, and *administrative* and *financial control* by central government.

Control over local government has increased greatly in the last decade. Legislation has been introduced giving the government power to prohibit excessive poll tax and council tax increases and to control local authority budgets. Other controls limit the use of capital receipts, prohibit political advertising and seek to control the way that a local authority conducts its business.

Legislative control

Almost every piece of legislation passed by Parliament affects local authorities in some way, either adding to or taking away from their powers. Private Bills sponsored by local authorities are, of course, subject to rejection or amendment by Parliament.

There are three types of Act – mandatory, adoptive or permissive:

- a *mandatory Act* compels a local authority to take certain action, like selling council houses under the *Housing Act 1980*
- an *adoptive Act* is one which gives a local authority power to carry out a function but which needs a resolution by the authority to adopt the Act before it applies
- a *permissive Act* is one which gives a local authority discretion over taking on new powers, generally minor ones.

A local authority can exercise a subordinate legislative function by making by-laws (subject to controls). A by-law is a local regulation governing such matters as the use of a municipal park or library. Model by-laws are suggested by the Department of the Environment but each authority can frame its own, subject to the approval of the department. If they wish to extend their powers they must get a local Bill through Parliament.

The exception is the freedom to spend an amount per head of population (£2.50 in counties and districts; £5 in metropolitan districts and London boroughs) on anything for the benefit of their area provided that the benefit received is commensurate with the expenditure. The *Local Government Act 1986* restricted the use of this discretionary money on publicity. It forbids expenditure on any material which sets out to affect public support for a political party, or anyone identified with a political party.

Administrative control

This is exercised by central government departments, who are generally concerned with seeing that minimum standards of service are maintained throughout the country. Ministers and departments do not have overall detailed control of the work of local authorities, but a number of Acts make provision for supervisory powers.

For instance, the *Education Act 1944* requires the Secretary of State for Education and Science 'to secure the effective execution by local authorities, under his control and direction, of national policy for providing a varied and comprehensive educational service in every area'. This is achieved through school inspectors.

The *Local Authority Social Services Act 1970* laid down that 'local authorities shall, in the exercise of their social services functions, including the exercise of any discretion conferred by any relevant enactment, act under the general guidance of the Secretary of State'.

Central departments also have the power in some services, notably the police and fire, to inspect and ensure operational efficiency.

Other legislation requires local authorities to submit schemes for the development of services, like those they were required to bring forward for the introduction of a comprehensive system of education.

Ministers can act in a quasi-judicial manner, acting as arbiters in disputes between local authorities and individuals. This occurs most commonly in planning, where individuals may appeal to the ministers against a decision of the planning authority. An inquiry will be held followed by a ruling on the dispute.

Other powers enable a minister to act if an authority is not discharging a function properly. Alternatively, he may, in such circumstances, appoint commissioners to act in place of the authority.

Financial control

Financial controls on local authorities by central government were increased under the *Local Government Finance Act 1982*, which removed the power to levy supplementary rates or precepts. It forbade an authority to increase its rate or precept during the year but allowed a substitute rate or precept at a lower figure.

Further controls came with the *Rates Act 1984*, which gave the Secretary of State for the Environment power to limit the rates levied by specified authorities (or for all authorities after Parliamentary approval). This power was extended to the poll tax and the council tax and the budgets of all local authorities. In addition, the government controls money from the uniform business rate and borrowing as well as the use of capital receipts.

Judicial control

The courts can be used to compel a local authority to carry out its statutory duties. In this case an application is made to the high court for an order of *mandamus*, which orders the carrying out of a public duty. Mandamus cannot, however, be used to compel a local authority to carry out a permissive or discretionary duty.

Two other judicial remedies against local authorities are *prohibition* and *certiorari*, which can be used against them when they act, or propose to act, without jurisdiction, or are in breach of natural justice.

Declarations and *injunctions* are further legal remedies against local authorities. An action for either enables the legality of an act or decision of a local authority to be tested in the courts.

A declaratory judgment is a finding by the court on a question of law or rights; an injunction is used to stop an authority doing something, or requiring it to do something.

An individual who wishes to take out an injunction against a local authority must ask the attorney-general to take the action. The action will be at the individual's expense. Individuals may also take action against local authorities for negligence. Authorities may be held to be responsible for any action, or lack of action, by them or their employees.

The role of central government

Bearing in mind the impact the public sector as a whole has on the operation of the economy, central government is always concerned about what is happening in the various public sector organisations. However not all the organisations operate in the same way, nor are their respective constitutions drawn up in the same manner. In fact, the degree of influence the government has, varies considerably. In the public sector, for example, the health services operated by Health Authorities are much more closely controlled by central government than are local authorities.

Anyone working in, or who has been closely connected with public sector organisations in recent years will have been unable to avoid noticing the significant changes which occurred in attitudes about the provision of public sector services.

As an example, the *Local Government, Planning and Land Act 1980* increased central government's control over the capital expenditure of local government, the operation of direct labour organisations and manpower levels. On the other hand, central government is narrowing its control on the public sector by selling off many public sector bodies to the private sector, e.g. British Aerospace, British Telecom, etc. The Rates Act 1984 introduced the concept of 'capping' local authority expenditure.

The sources of income
The different public sector organisations finance their operations in various ways and usually by a combination of several methods such as a direct payment by clients for the work done or the goods received; a mandatory levy or tax; subsidy or grant from central government. The sources of income of the different public sector organisations will influence not only the level of services provided but also the methods of financial control employed. It is a feature of the funding of public sector services that if service levels are not to be curtailed as a result of cutbacks in expenditure, then income other than taxation must be raised. There are two major limitations on public sector organisations maximising their sources of income:

- central government, via taxes, provides a majority of the finance for revenue and capital expenditure in the public sector.
- many of the services provided by public sector organisations are provided for socially desirable purposes, e.g. housing, health care or education and as such politicians are often reluctant to increase charges in line with rising costs.

Providers of services rather than goods
A majority of public sector expenditure is spent on the provision of intangible services rather than tangible goods. Unlike organisations which can control the quality and level of

the product they produce, public sector organisations tend to provide services. The quality of such services is difficult to measure because what is a good service depends so much on the preference of the individual receiving and providing the service. Managers in the public sector are often able to measure the quantity of service provided but cannot readily measure the quality of service. This characteristic can make the control of certain public sector organisations that much more difficult.

Central government departments

Types of government control and influence through departments

- Professional or operational advice given through the issue of circulars.
- Control over certain local authority officer appointments and dismissals such as Home Office approval to the appointment of the Chief Constable.
- Excessive detailed supervision of local services such as the approval of budgets, for example, in the magistrates courts service.
- Monitoring of financial results via revenue grant forecasts, grant claims, statistical returns, etc.
- Numerous statutes give ministers powers to act where local authorities 'default' in the provision of services, i.e. the authority is not discharging a function properly.
- Ministers have extensive powers to approve county structure plans and compulsory purchase orders.
- Central departments have the power to inspect and ensure the operational efficiency of certain services such as visiting schools, police and fire.
- Ministers can act as an arbiter in disputes between local authorities and individuals, e.g. at a planning enquiry.

Government control via the Commissioners for Local Administration (local ombudsmen)

The ombudsmen, established in 1974, can investigate administrative decisions but not policy decisions of a local authority, police authority or regional water authority. Details are contained earlier in this chapter.

Control via the external audit of local authorities

The Audit Commission is empowered to appoint external auditors whose general duties are laid down in the *Local Government Finance Act 1982*. Details are contained in Chapter 11.

Inspectorates

A number of government departments have Inspectorates, with statutory facilities to examine, in detail, the efficiency with which local authorities deliver the major mandatory services which have been entrusted to them. This applies particularly to the schools, police and fire services.

Development of Codes of Practice for local government

The *Local Government, Planning and Land Act 1980* contained an important provision confirming the extent to which central government can directly influence local administration without having to rely upon legislation, or edicts issued thereunder.

In this Act, the Environment Secretary took powers to issue recommended 'Codes of Practice'. These are documents, worked in conjunction with the local authority associations and which local authorities are exhorted to follow upon pain of further legislation if they do not. From local government's viewpoint such procedures are an important way of getting specialist input to a regulatory document, resulting in a finished product which should command a greater measure of support than further detailed, formal prescription.

The main codes that have been issued to date are set out on page 12. Codes will be dealt with in other chapters, as appropriate.

Relationship of local government financing to national finances

Local authority expenditure is a response to the demands of the local community expressed in political terms at both national and local elections for the provision of certain public goods which are not provided by the market. The level of response to, or interpretation of, those demands is affected by many factors, including the political control of the central government and of the local authority, economic and financial pressures (including inflation), physical and demographic factors, and public expectation. Even so a difficulty for local authorities is to find effective methods of assessing the actual demand for services prior to deciding upon the degree and form of response to that demand.

Having established its policy the local authority can then only develop that policy in the light of what has gone before. In other words, irrespective of any other constraints which may exist a local authority cannot change the course of its activities except gradually. A major factor which prevents radical changes is prior capital expenditure. For example, a local authority which has built an old persons' home or a school has an asset which it has to finance and for which an alternative use cannot easily be found. This commits its future use of resources and thus reduces the opportunities for changes in expenditure patterns in the future.

A decision to provide capital assets usually takes between three and five years to come to fruition (depending upon the type of scheme) and once the scheme is completed the only savings the local authority can make are in the running costs (heating, lighting, staffing, etc.) because it cannot avoid paying the capital charges, that is, the interest on money borrowed and the repayment of the loan.

Apart from the problem created by capital expenditure influencing future revenue spending, other factors in practice limit local authority discretion over the amount of money which it can spend despite the fact that it may be argued that in theory it has considerable discretion over its spending. These factors include the following:

- national pay agreements
- the requirement, by statute to provide many services and meet government requirements/standards
- maintenance of service standards
- local demographic factors
- national economic requirements.

The total amount of public expenditure planned for the next financial year, is announced by the Chancellor of the Exchequer in the National Budget each November. Since 1993, that budget announces taxation as well as spending plans. The totality of planned public spending (£253 billion in 1994/95) is allocated to Departments of State and then to individual sectors and programmes and is cash-linked.

Decisions about the level of resources available to public authorities emanate from the government annual budgeting exercise, and are linked to the policy decisions made by the cabinet during the summer months which lead to the Chancellor of the Exchequer's budget in November.

Within these cabinet discussions, the level of spending for each major government spending department was formulated, based upon Treasury forecasts of trends in demand, likely levels of inflation and interest rates, and was specifically geared to central government's own policy of cash limiting the total volume of public sector spending.

Following the Chancellor's autumn announcement local authorities are informed of the agreed totals of revenue support grant for local authorities, and also the expected levels of local authority expenditure generally. Details about individual local authority spending are announced later and this fits into an individual local authority's own budgeting cycle.

At this time too the Department of Health notifies regional health authorities of their likely cash allocations and starts the budget cycle for individual regional and district health authorities.

Following the November budget announcements, the government publishes its White Paper on public expenditure, summarising and setting out in more detail the implications and purposes of the government's economic strategy. It acts as a backcloth to the budget which formalises the funding, i.e. decisions about taxes, necessary to meet the announced levels of public expenditure.

The Budget White Paper in effect reflects the political objectives of central government for the public sector as a whole.

The amounts of money to be made available to local government through the Revenue Support Grant or through capital expenditure allocations are, effectively, fixed at this point and those sums are employed in negotiations with local government before council capital and revenue spending plans are finalised for the new financial year. Further information and details of the ways in which the central government 'caps' the expenditure of individual local authorities are set out in Chapter 4.

Appendix 2.1

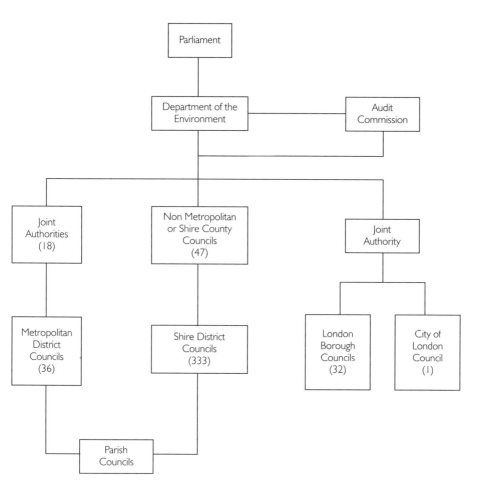

Structure of local government in England and Wales as at November 1994

Local government elections

County councils: every 4th year, when the whole council is elected.

Other authorities: elections are held either every 3rd year, when the whole council is elected, or every year, when one third of the council is elected. No elections are held in county council election years.

Appendix 2.2

Functions and services of local authorities

(a) London boroughs/City of London	Joint boards/statutory bodies etc.

Planning
New unified development plans
Planning applications
Caravan sites (including gypsies)
Historic buildings and monuments

Transport	**Transport**
Roads	London Transport run since 1984
Footpaths	by London Regional
Traffic management and parking	Transport a government-appointed body

Emergency services	**Emergency services**
Police (City of London only)	Police – Metropolitan Police
Emergency planning	under control of Home
	Secretary
	Fire service and civil defence –
	London Fire and Civil Defence
	Authority

Education

Economic development

Environmental services	**Environmental services**
Refuse collection	Refuse disposal:
Building regulations	1 London Waste Regulation
General environmental services	Authority
Street cleaning	2 Four statutory waste
	disposal authorities
	3 Three voluntary joint
	boards

Housing

Personal social services

Trading standards	**Trading standards**

Recreation and Arts	**Arts**
Libraries	

Allotments

Registration
Births, deaths and marriages
Electoral register

Superannuation

Cemeteries and crematoria

Council Tax
(collection)

(b) Metropolitan districts	**Joint boards/statutory bodies etc.**

Planning
New unified development plans
Planning applications
Caravan sites (including gypsies)
Historic buildings and monuments

Transport
Roads
Footpaths
Traffic management and parking

Transport
Public transport – passenger
transport authorities in each of
the six metropolitan areas

Emergency services
Emergency planning

Emergency services
Police – under Local Police
Authority
Fire and civil defence – fire and
civil defence authorities in each
of the metropolitan areas

Education

Economic development

Environmental services
Refuse collection
Building regulations
General environmental services
Street cleaning

Environmental services
Refuse disposal – voluntary
joint arrangements in South
Yorkshire, Tyne & Wear,
West Midlands and
West Yorkshire; statutory
authorities in Greater Manchester
(except Wigan) and Merseyside

Housing

Personal social services

Trading standards

Trading standards

Recreation and Arts
Libraries

Arts

Airports

Airports
If there is no voluntary
agreement between districts,
control lies with the Passenger
Transport Authority

Allotments

Registration
Births, deaths and marriages
Electoral register

Superannuation

Cemeteries and crematoria

Council Tax
(collection)

(c) Counties

Planning
Structure planning
National parks
Caravan sites (including gypsy sites)*
Historic buildings*

Transport
Highways and on-street parking*
Traffic management
Footpaths and bridleways*
Transport planning

Emergency services
Fire
Police**
Emergency planning*

Environmental services
Refuse disposal

Recreation and Arts
Parks and open spaces*
Swimming pools*
Support for the arts*
Museums*
Encouraging tourism*

Smallholdings

Registration
Births, deaths and marriages

Consumer Protection
Trading standards etc.

Education

Economic development*

Libraries

Youth Employment Services

Superannuation

Personal Social Services

Non Metropolitan Districts

Planning
Local plans
Planning applications
Caravan sites (including
    management of gypsy sites)*
Historic buildings*

Transport
Unclassified roads
Offstreet car parking*
Footpaths*

Emergency services
Emergency planning*

Emergency services
Refuse collection
Building regulations
General environmental services
    (including pollution control,
    food hygiene, control of
    diseases and conditions of
    shops and offices)
Street cleaning

Recreation and Arts
Parks and open spaces*
Swimming pools*
Support for the arts*
Museums*
Encouraging tourism*

Allotments

Electoral registration

Cemeteries and Crematoria

Council Tax and Business Rate
(collection)

Housing

Economic development*

* Concurrent services
** Police and Magistrates Courts Act 1994
As from April 1995, police authorities have been reconstituted and made more accountable to the Home Secretary. Budgets are now prepared independently of local government and both budgets and membership of police authorities are subject to the Home Secretary's approval. Chairmen of authorities are now appointed by the Home Secretary to bring greater business skills into local government.

3 The local authority accounting environment

This chapter reports on the statutory environment within which local authority accounting is placed. It also considers the national accounting standards position and the relationship between the two, encapsulated in the *1993 Accounting Code of Practice* (ACOP).

Capital and revenue

As in the commercial world, there are two aspects of finance: the source of funds and their utilisation; in other words, income and expenditure. In practice, however, a further distinction must be made; namely, between capital and revenue transactions.

Very broadly, expenditure of a *capital* nature may be described as that which is incurred on some object of lasting value even though that value may diminish in the course of time, whereas *revenue* expenditure is usually of a constantly recurring nature and produces no permanent asset. The cost of erecting a school by a local authority is an example of capital expenditure producing an asset with a 'life', whilst the expenditure on the general maintenance of the school – teachers' salaries, cleaning, heating and lighting, etc. – is of a revenue nature.

This distinction between capital and revenue expenditure is of great significance. It affects the way in which such expenditure may be financed, and this is important because of the incidence of the expenditure upon the user, taxpayer, or ratepayer. A local authority can spread the cost of its capital expenditure over a prescribed period of years not usually exceeding the assumed life of the asset. It meets the cost of revenue expenditure in the year in which it is incurred. A local authority is able to spread the cost of its capital expenditure over the life of the asset because it has the power to borrow money to finance capital expenditure.

By borrowing, a local authority is able to meet heavy expenditure in one year without undue financial stress and, by repayment of the amount borrowed over a period related to the life of the asset, some of the burden (or alternatively the incidence) is transferred to the ratepayers and taxpayers of the future, who may be expected to derive benefit from the expenditure. But a local authority cannot borrow to finance revenue expenditure except temporarily, pending the receipt of revenue. On the other hand, a local authority does not have to borrow to finance capital expenditure and it may decide to charge such expenditure against its rate and grant revenues. The extent to which a local authority can charge capital expenditure to revenue depends upon the financial resources of the authority concerned.

Many authorities, for example, do not borrow money for the purpose of buying comparatively inexpensive and short-lived assets such as motor vehicles and concrete mixers; even the smallest authority would hesitate to borrow the money for a typewriter! Borrowing costs money and interest charges can be avoided by financing expenditure from revenue. But given high inflation levels there are advantages in paying off one's liabilities in depreciated pounds, particularly when the cost in terms of interest is less, and perhaps substantially less, than the rate of inflation. These factors along with many others influence the decision of a local authority as to whether it should meet the cost from revenue.

Fund accounting

In the commercial world, financial reporting is usually discussed in terms of the organisation, e.g. the company, as a whole – a separate entity, with a separate legal identity. Companies Act law requires the directors to prepare accounts giving an account of their stewardship and this is particularly important for a major public quoted company with millions of shareholders.

This concept of stewardship and public accountability is also a feature of financial reporting for the public sector. However, while the rules of double-entry bookkeeping remain the same for any organisation, the conventions for processing and presentation of financial data may vary considerably within the public sector. Many public sector organisations are commercially orientated and follow reporting practices which are compatible with profit-orientated undertakings, e.g. the British Coal Corporation prepares financial statements which comply with Companies Act requirements. Other public sector bodies are not commercially orientated in that they supply essential services (e.g. the Police Authority) and the reporting procedures therefore follow the principles and conventions appropriate to the public sector. These principles have conventions which use terminology and layouts not compatible with the Companies Act but which are drawn up in accordance with statutory requirements and established practice.

Local authority accounting is based on certain unique conventions and this involves accounting terms which may not be readily understandable to those in the private sector. A key aspect of local authority accounting is the concept of fund accounting and this is now explained.

The fund theory of accounting developed from commercial concerns about accounting for and defining an individual organisation, unit or entity. Company law requires that a company be viewed as a whole for reporting purposes and thus a local authority, responsible for a wide range of individual services and financial functions, should also consolidate those disparate transactions.

A fund could be, therefore, the internal audit section, an administrative building or the housing service. The accounting system will be designed so as to define specific funds or cost centres where financial reports demand. Thus, a separate revenue account and balance sheet for each activity or service provided by the local authority could be prepared.

Obviously, each individual revenue account and balance sheet must be aggregated or consolidated, to give a total picture of the whole of the local authority's operations. This operation, therefore, mirrors the action of a large commercial company whose final accounts and balance sheet bring together the results of individual trading subsidiaries.

In local government, the system for recording and processing cash is similar to that in commercial undertakings, although there may be minor variations on points of detail. For example, each different activity or service requires that the cash book should be analysed accordingly so that receipts and payments in relation to each fund can be suitably identified and the total cash position reconciled with bank accounts.

The needs of legislation, stewardship, accountability and control suggest that accounts should be based on services within authorities, and within services, on divisions of service. This is known as an objective classification, where the budget and financial accounts are maintained according to the purpose of the expenditure. Thus accounts for a police authority would show divisions of the service, e.g.:

- criminal investigations
- traffic control
- motorway patrol
- beat policing
- community policing, etc.

Similarly, accounts for the education service would show the separate 'objective' divisions of the service, e.g.:

Age groups	
Nursery	3-5
Primary	5 0
Middle school	8-14
Tertiary colleges	14-16
Higher education	16+

This need for accounting to be service-based leads to one fundamental division of accounts, namely between those which are *general fund services* and those which are *trading services*.

Example _____

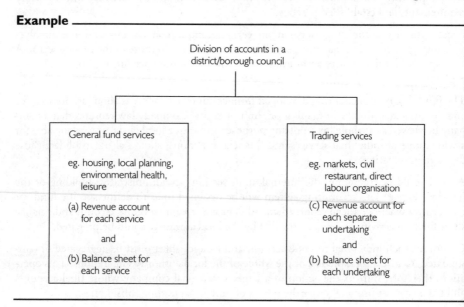

Division of accounts in a
district/borough council

General fund services

eg. housing, local planning,
environmental health,
leisure

(a) Revenue account
for each service

and

(b) Balance sheet for
each service

Trading services

eg. markets, civil
restaurant, direct
labour organisation

(c) Revenue account for
each separate
undertaking

and

(b) Balance sheet for
each undertaking

General fund (in a county council, the county fund)

(a) and (b) both relate to general fund services, i.e. those services which are financed (paid for) directly from income from the community charge/council tax and business rate.

(a) is equivalent to a profit and loss account in a commercial organisation, though the composition of items is different. Revenue accounts contain items of revenue expenditure relating to current expenditure of the financial year where the benefit from that expenditure relates to the same financial period.

(b) is a list of balances at the year end on that service.

Trading services

(c) and (d) both relate to services where the authority has the power to determine charging policy and where the aim of the service is to at least raise sufficient income to meet its expenditure.

(c) again is a list of expenditure and income for a financial year and (d) shows the year end balances of capital items and the sources of their finance.

This type of analysis and reporting is a response to the diversity of functions within an authority.

To meet these requirements of a service-based accounting system, the idea of fund accounting has been developed whereby it is possible to segregate expenditure or services so that separate accounts are kept for each service. This separation enables records to be kept so that expenditure on a service can be identified, and the means of financing it can be shown and compared with the original budget.

The accountant or cost centre dealing with a service has the flexibility to decide on the size of a reporting unit, and to arrange a coding structure to analyse different functions, or different expenditures. When the annual accounts have been prepared on a service basis there can be, as in the private sector, a consolidation of fund balance sheets to provide a single summary for the whole authority. Any items which are not under the control of the authority must be excluded from the consolidation, e.g. trust funds administered by an education authority.

A detailed discussion of revenue accounts is contained in Chapter 4 and of balance sheets in Chapter 6.

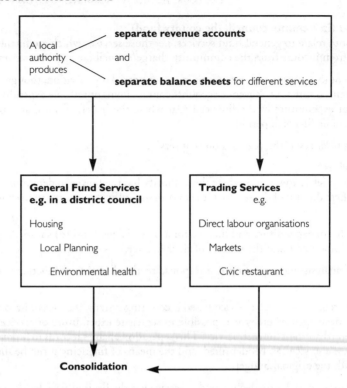

To produce an annual summary of the effect of all transactions on the whole authority, e.g.:

	Gross expenditure £	Income £	Net expenditure
General fund services (detailed) Trading services (detailed)			
TOTALS			

and a

Consolidated balance sheet for the whole authority

Local authority financial reporting

Local authorities publish four main types of financial reports.

- an annual revenue budget and capital programme (budget)
- an information leaflet or mini-report to be sent to all council taxpayers with the council tax demand note
- a statement of accounts (traditionally referred to as an abstract of accounts)
- an annual report.

The form and content of these reports is largely standardised, and must comply with four types of external requirements:

- statutory requirements, including Acts of Parliament and Accounts and Audit regulations
- government directions in the form of codes of practice and notes of guidance
- professional standards, including statements of standard accounting practice (SSAPs), statements of recommended practice (SORPs) and financial reporting standards (FRSs) and the CIPFA's *Code of Practice on Local Authority Accounting* (the latest edition in 1993)
- generally accepted accounting principles, consistently applied.

Local authorities are legally required to publish a statement of accounts (an 'abstract of accounts'), and may publish an annual report.

The *Accounts and Audit Regulations 1983* (issued under the *Local Government Finance Act 1982*) define what statements should appear in the statement of accounts, but not their precise form. The *Local Government and Housing Act 1989* defines the proper accounting practices to be observed.

The CIPFA *Code of Practice on Local Authority Accounting for Great Britain (1993)* specifies the form and content of the individual financial statements which comprise the statement of accounts, and these are considered generally in Chapter 3 and specifically in Chapters 4, 5, 6 and 7.

The *Accounts and Audit Regulations 1983* make the following provisions for local government:

- As soon as possible after the conclusion of an audit, a body to which these regulations apply shall give notice by advertisement that the audit has been concluded and that the statement of accounts is available for inspection by local government electors.
- The abstract shall contain such detail of the audited balance sheets and audited revenue and capital accounts, together with any necessary explanations, as the local authority considers necessary. The availability of the abstract for public inspection shall be advertised and copies should be available for purchase by the general public.

Statutory requirements

Provisions concerning local authority accounts in England and Wales are contained in the following enactments:

- Local Government Act 1972

- Local Government Finance Act 1982
- Accounts and Audit Regulations 1983
- Local Government and Housing Act 1989.

The *Local Government Act 1972* refers to the keeping of a general rate (now a 'general fund' following the replacement of domestic rates by the council tax) by district and borough councils and county funds by county councils, and specifies that accounts are to be kept by receipts carried to and payments made out of the appropriate fund (Section 148). Section 151 provides that every local authority shall make arrangements for the proper administration of its financial affairs and that one of its officers will have responsibility for this.

The *Local Government Finance Act 1982* requires that accounts be made up to 31 March in every year, or such special date as the Secretary of State may determine, and shall be audited by auditors appointed by the Audit Commission.

Under the 1982 Act the Secretary of State has the power to make regulations controlling in detail the form, content and presentation of local authority accounts (Section 23). The *Accounts and Audit Regulations 1983* were issued under this power.

In 1985 the Department of the Environment published proposals for the form of local authority accounts, but these were withdrawn and replaced in 1987 by CIPFA's own Code of Practice on Local Authority Accounting which was updated in 1991 and 1993, by CIPFA. The 1993 Code is reproduced in Appendix 3.3.

The *Local Government and Housing Act 1989* introduces a new system of central government control over local authority capital expenditure and finance.

Accounts and Audit Regulations 1983

These regulations place upon the 'responsible financial officer' (subject to instructions from the employer) the responsibility for determining the accounting system, form of accounts and supporting records. Further, that officer has a duty to ensure that the accounting systems determined by him are observed and that the accounts and supporting records are kept up to date.

The regulations contain several sections that are particularly relevant and these are now detailed.

- Internal audit is required. The responsible officer shall maintain an adequate and effective internal audit of the accounts of the body and shall have a right of access at all times to such documents of the body which relate to the accounts of the body as appear to him to be necessary for the purpose of the audit and shall be entitled to require from any officer of the body such information and explanation as is required for that purpose.
- The responsible financial officer shall ensure that all accounts are made up and balanced as soon as practicable after the end of the period to which these accounts relate, and in any event not later than the expiry of six months beginning immediately after the end of that period.
- Section 7 of the regulations concerns the preparation of the statement of accounts. The statement of accounts shall include the following:
  a) Summarised statements of the income and expenditure of each fund or undertaking in relation to which the body is required by or by virtue of any statutory provision to keep a separate account.

b) A summarised statement of capital expenditure, differentiated in respect of different services and showing the sources of finance of the year's total capital expenditure.

c) A consolidated balance sheet.

d) Balance sheets for consolidated funds.

e) A statement of source and application of funds (but see below).

In respect of all but (b) above, any corresponding amounts for the preceding period shall be shown. With regard to (a) the publication of summarised statements is now at the authority's discretion.

- The requirements relating to the statement of accounts apply to the following bodies:
  a) The council of a county, a district or a London borough.
  b) Any committee of such a council which is required to keep separate accounts.
  c) Any joint committee of two or more such councils.
  d) Any combined policy authority.
  e) Any fire authority constituted by a combination scheme.

- A statement of accounts shall include particulars of the main principles adopted in its compilation and those particulars shall draw attention to any changes of practice which in the opinion of the body have a significant effect on the results shown by the statement. The regulations list the main principles as follows:
  a) The basis on which debtors and creditors outstanding at the end of the relevant year are included.
  b) The nature of substantial reserves, provisions, contingent liabilities and deferred charges included.
  c) The basis of provision for the redemption of debt.
  d) The basis on which capital works or expenses are recorded and assets are shown in the balance sheet.
  e) The basis of valuation of real property and investments.
  f) The basis of depreciation provisions.
  g) The extent to which central support costs are allocated over services.

Local authorities commonly combine the publication of the above main principles with the statement of accounting policies required under the CIPFA *Accounting Code of Practice*. Details of the accounting concepts and principles to be followed in the Code of Practice are given in Appendix 3.2.

The statement of accounts is the summary financial statement on which the external auditor gives his opinion.

Annual reports

The Code of Practice *Local Authority Annual Reports* was issued by the Department of the Environment in 1981. The purpose was to encourage every local authority to publish an annual report with at least the minimum contents specified in the Code.

Briefly, the Code recommends the following contents for the annual report.

- Details of revenue expenditure, plus prior year figures, including the following analysis.
  - An analysis, service by service, of gross expenditure and income, comparing out-turn with budget and explaining major variances.
  - Comments on any changing pattern of expenditure between services within the authority and any corporate strategy underlying this.

- A summary of capital expenditure service by service and an overall statement of sources of finance.
- A summary subjective analysis of gross revenue expenditure by category and income by source for the financial year.
- General statistics for major functions, including scale of service provision, size of client group, usage, costs, etc., together with prior year figures.
- A set of key service indicators selected by the authority which where possible measure performance, including productivity where appropriate. The information should be at least for the year of account. The figures for the authority should also be compared with actual and average figures of other authorities based at least on the figures for the year of account. But authorities may wish to make such comparisons on a more recent estimated basis as well.
- A manpower statement summarised by staff category and by service.
- Details of how interested parties may follow up queries, and a timetable showing key dates in the financial and management planning process.

The aim of the Code of Practice is to encourage the production of local authority annual reports that will achieve the following objectives.

- To give electors, council taxpayers, ratepayers and other interested parties information about local government activities.
- To make it easier for such persons to make comparisons of, and judgements on, the performance of their authorities.
- To enable elected councillors to form judgements about the performance of their authorities.

Statements of accounts

Background

Regulations pending revision and developments in accounting and audit practices in local authority accounting were introduced by the *Accounts and Audit Regulations 1983*. It was clear that these regulations were produced on an interim basis pending more permanent arrangements.

In 1987 CIPFA published the *Code of Practice on Local Authority Accounting* which was franked by the ASC as a SORP and had effect for the financial years commencing on or after 1 April 1987. The Code was produced in the context of the reporting requirements already established for local government in the *Code of Practice on Annual Reports*.

The 1987 Code applied to local authorities in England and Wales and was superseded in 1991 and the *1991 Code of Practice* was updated by CIPFA in September 1993. There has been some updating to the detail in the 1991 Code and a major addition in respect of the accounting treatment of capital expenditure. The 1993 ACOP is examined later in this chapter and is set out in Appendix 3.3.

In June 1995 CIPFA answered that the 1993 ACOP had recently been updated and the 1995 version would apply to accounting periods beginning on or after 1 April 1995. Details of the main changes required by this latest Code are set out in Appendix 3.4.

National Accounting Standards

Brief history of the standard setting process

The accountancy profession issued the first statement of standard accounting practice (SSAP) in 1970, in response to pressure to impose standardised procedures, avoid possible inconsistencies and generally improve the quality and usefulness of financial statements.

Until then, there were relatively few financial reporting requirements for companies and very little help in the *1948 Companies Act*. The accounting profession relied upon a series of recommendations issued by the ICAEW, but a variety of accounting methods still applied in practice.

The standard setting process

The standard setting process is performed in the UK by the Financial Reporting Council (FRC), and specifically the FRC's two subsidiary organisations, the Accounting Standards Board (ASB) and the Review Panel. In addition, there is an offshoot of the ASB known as the Urgent Issues Task Force.

The FRC is responsible for securing finance to operate the standard setting process, and for ensuring that the system is carried out efficiently and economically. In particular, the FRC provides the forum for discussion and support for accounting standards.

Membership of the Council comprises not only members of the accountancy profession but also others who are concerned in some way with the use, audit or preparation of accounting information. This includes accountants from industry, commerce, academia and the public sector. This is a significant departure from its predecessor, the Accounting Standards Committee (ASC) which was controlled and financed by the accountancy profession itself. The FRC took over from the ASC on 1 August 1990.

The Accounting Standards Board

The ASB, whilst only half the size of the FRC, is at the 'sharp end' of the standard-setting process, as it issues standards on its own authority. The FRC has no say over the detail of any individual standard, but the ASB needs to secure the widest possible support for the standards it issues if it is to be successful. The intention is quality rather than quantity, but in the early years of the ASB we can perhaps expect to see a thoroughgoing review of inherited existing standards.

Aims of the Accounting Standards Board

The aims of the ASB are to establish and improve standards of financial accounting and reporting, for the benefit of users, preparers and auditors of financial information. It intends to achieve its aims by:

- Developing principles to guide it in establishing standards and to provide a framework within which others can exercise judgement in resolving accounting issues.

- Issuing new accounting standards, or amending existing ones, in response to evolving business practices, new economic developments and deficiencies being identified in current practice.
- Addressing urgent issues promptly.

The development of a Financial Reporting Standard (FRS)

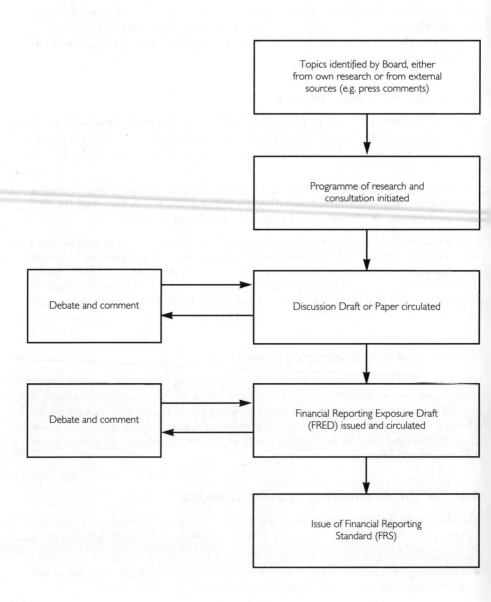

Compliance with standards

The ASB issued a Foreword to Accounting Standards in June 1993, in which it set out the authority, scope and application of accounting standards.

Authority

- FRSs and SSAPs are 'accounting standards' for the purpose of the *Companies Act 1985*. The Act requires the accounts of 'large' companies to state whether they have been prepared in accordance with applicable accounting standards and to give particulars of any material departure from those standards and the reasons for it.
- Members of the professional bodies which comprise the Consultative Committee of Accountancy Bodies (CCAB) are expected to observe accounting standards whether as preparers or auditors of financial information.
- Where CCAB members act as directors or other officers, other than auditors, the onus will be on them to ensure that the existence and purpose of accounting standards are fully understood by fellow directors and other officers.
- Members should also use their best endeavours to ensure that accounting standards are observed and that significant departures found to be necessary are adequately explained in the financial statements.
- Where members act as auditors or reporting accountants, they should be in a position to justify significant departures to the extent that their concurrence with the departures is stated or implied. They are not, however, required to refer in their report to departures with which they concur, provided that adequate disclosure has been made in the notes to the financial statements.

In addition to the statutory powers of the Review Panel, the professional accountancy bodies have the sanction of bringing disciplinary action against any of their members who have failed to observe accounting standards or to ensure adequate disclosure of significant departures from standards. Such actions are invariably well publicised and may result in the member being admonished, fined or, in extreme cases, excluded from membership.

Scope and application

Accounting standards are applicable to financial statements of a reporting entity that are intended to give a true and fair view of its state of affairs at the balance sheet date and of its profit and loss (or income and expenditure) for the financial period ended on that date. Accounting standards need not be applied to immaterial items. They should be applied to UK and Republic of Ireland group financial statements including any overseas entities which are part of those statements, but are not intended to apply where financial statements are prepared overseas for local purposes.

Standards and the Companies Acts

The Foreword explains the circumstances underlying compliance with accounting standards, of which the following is a summary:

- Compliance with standards will normally be necessary for financial statements to give a true and fair view.
- In applying accounting standards it is important to be guided by the spirit and reasoning behind them.

- The requirement to give a true and fair view may in special circumstances require a departure to be made from accounting standards, but the Board envisages that this will only be necessary in exceptional circumstances.
- Particulars of any material departure from an accounting standard, the reasons for it and its financial effects should be disclosed in the financial statements.
- The Review Panel and the Department of Trade and Industry have procedures for receiving and investigating complaints regarding the annual accounts of companies in respect of apparent departures from the accounting requirements of the Companies Act, including the requirement to show a true and fair view. The Review Panel can apply to the court to require the directors to prepare revised accounts.

In November 1994 it was announced that the Accounting Standards Board had set up a public sector and non-profit making committee to improve its ability to scrutinise non-private sector SORPs.

CIPFA welcomed the replacement of the public sector liaison committee but repeated its call for a separate accounting standards body to deal exclusively with this field. Martin Evans, head of the Institute's technical and research division, is a member of the new committee. He said, 'We are pleased that the former committee's role has been extended to the not-for-profit sector, as it was unable to put any significant input into the SORPs for housing associations and universities.'

The committee is expected to discuss the government's green paper on resource accounting and the revision of the SORP on local authority accounting at its early meetings. Half of the ten full committee members are also CIPFA members, as is the observer.

Accounting standards and local authorities

The FRSs and SSAPs issued as at Spring 1995 are listed in Appendix 3.1.

A summary of those FRS's and SSAPs which are considered appropriate to local authorities, together with relevant comments, is given below.

SSAP	Subject	Comments
2	Disclosure of accounting policies	Appropriate to local authorities including the four concepts of 'going concern', accruals, consistency and prudence. A statement of accounting policies must be attached to published accounts.
4	Accounting for government grants (revised July 1990)	Grants towards capital expenditure to be credited to revenue over life of asset by treating the amount of grant as a deferred credit with a portion transferred to revenue annually.
5	Accounting for Value Added Tax	VAT is normally wholly recoverable by local authorities. VAT should be excluded from income or expenditure.
6	Extraordinary items and prior-year adjustment (now replaced by FRS3)	Extraordinary items (now virtually outlawed by FRS3) should be shown separately and included after striking net cost of services. Prior year

		adjustments will also require adjustment to current year's figures.
9	Stocks and long-term contracts	Average price and FIFO probably leave an acceptable basis for stock shown in balance sheets. LIFO will normally result in the need to adjust stock values for balance sheet purposes.
10	Statement of source and application of funds (now replaced by FRS1)	A minimum of netting off should take place, but temporary loans/repayments should be netted. A funds statement for the local authority as a whole should always be produced. A separate statement for capital receipts should also be prepared.
13	Accounting for research and development	Generally should be written off in the period it is incurred. Development expenditure can only be carried forward if related to a product which is commercially viable. If associated with a capital project, it should be included therein.
17	Accounting for post balance sheet events	Material events to be accounted for between date of balance sheet and date of 'responsible financial officer' signing the balance sheet.
18	Accounting for contingencies	Applies to contingencies which have not been resolved at the date the balance sheet is signed by the 'responsible financial officer'.

Of the seven most recent SSAPs (19–25) issued, four are not relevant to local government or the health service (numbers 19, 20, 22, 23). Of the remainder:

- SSAP 21: dealing with accounting for leases and hire purchase contracts certainly apply and the implications are reflected in the *1993 Accounting Code of Practice.*
- SSAP 24: the 1993 ACOP has been revised to incorporate the disclosure requirements of pensions costs and liabilities issued by CIPFA in a statement on SSAP 24 in May 1992.
- SSAP 25: the 1993 ACOP takes on board the requirements of this standard which requires the disclosure of performance in the main 'classes of business', as well as consolidated results.

The application of SSAP24 *Accounting for pension costs* was the subject of consultation at the time of the publication of the SORP, but in 1992 CIPFA issued a separate guide (*The Application of SSAP24 to Local Authorities in Great Britain*). SSAP10 has now been superseded by FRS1 *Cash flow statements* and a cash flow statement will replace the consolidated statement for the 1993/94 accounts. FRS2 *Accounting for subsidiary undertakings* has superseded SSAP14 and FRS3 *Reporting financial performance* has superseded SSAP6.

Individual authorities which do not comply with the SORP must refer to variations in the accounts and the auditor may draw attention to the variation in his report. Most authorities refer to the adoption of SSAPs and any variations in the statement of accounting policies section of their statement of (abstract) accounts.

Standard setting in local government

For many years up to the development of the Accounting Standards Committee, any guidance was issued by CIPFA or by its predecessor body, the Institute of Municipal Treasurers and Accountants. The Standard Form of Published Accounts of Local Authorities, or something similar, had first appeared at the beginning of this century and was revised at regular intervals.

This publication, as its name implies, was substantially an analysis of income and expenditure to be applied to the main general and county fund accounts. There were also recommendations for special accounts, summary revenue accounts and balance sheets. In more recent years, the Institute has published recommendations for individual services based on the Standard Form, which was retitled the Standard Analysis of Income and Expenditure.

The main point about these publications was that they were not mandatory and because they were merely recommendations, their application to local authority accounts was left to the individual local authority. Most did follow the basic analysis and accounting principles underlying them but there was no compulsion to do so and different styles appeared in published abstracts of accounts, a title that has given way to 'statements of accounts'.

When SSAPs first appeared in 1970, their applicability to the public sector other than aspects of central government was not clear. The expectation of the Accounting Standards Committee was that SSAPs would be applied to published accounts except where it was obviously not appropriate for them to do so. SSAPs were primarily prepared for the private sector, where an audit certificate as to the true and fair view of a company's accounts was one that embraced extant Statements unless clear disclosure stated otherwise.

The development by the ASC of Statements of Recommended Practice (SORPs) – statements usually produced by one of the six main accountancy bodies and endorsed or 'franked' by the ASC – was significant in that specific sector interests were being addressed. Since CIPFA's first SORP on standard setting in local government appeared in 1987, this machinery has been used for the development of the Accounting Codes of Practice. ACOPs have been prepared and issued by CIPFA in accordance with the ASBs code of practice for the development of SORPs.

The ACOP publications have been of considerable assistance in clarifying the status of SSAPs and SORPs in local government. Local authorities are now required to follow the Code. In addition the Code of Local Government Audit Practice (page 270), which requires the external auditor to certify that the statement of accounts 'presents fairly' the financial position of a local authority, includes compliance with best or proper practice. Detailed guidelines relating to accounting concepts and principles in local government are published in CIPFA's 1991 ACOP. These guidelines develop and expand the principles of SSAP2.

Although in the past ten years CIPFA has made great strides in tightening up the standard setting process in local government, its ACOP and related documents are still minimum publication requirements and do not stipulate the precise form of statements of accounts, as is the case in the health service. There is still considerable scope for flexibility and innovation in the published accounts of local authorities.

CIPFA Accounting Code of Practice 1993

Background

CIPFA's 1993 Code (ACOP) is based on approved accounting standards and the Urgent Issues Task Force's (UITF) Abstracts, except where these conflict with specific statutory requirements. It has been prepared on the basis of accounting standards and UITF abstracts extant at 30 September 1992. However, FRS2 *Accounting for Subsidiary Undertakings* has not been incorporated at this stage, pending the issue of regulations under Part V of the *Local Government and Housing Act 1989.*

The *Code of Practice* supersedes the second *Code of Practice on Local Authority Accounting,* published by the Institute in 1991. It also supersedes the Statement of Recommended Practice (SORP) on 'The application of accounting standards (SSAPs) to local authorities in Great Britain' (franked by the Accounting Standards Committee and published by CIPFA in 1990).

In England and Wales, the *Code of Practice* constitutes a 'proper accounting practice' under the terms of the *Local Government and Housing Act 1989.* In Scotland, the status and authority of the *Code of Practice* derives from Scottish Office Circular 5/1985 which indicates that local authorities should follow recommendations made by LASAAC (Local Authority, Scotland, Accounts Advisory Committee) regarding the form of accounts and accounting practice.

A Statement by the ASB at the beginning of the 1993 ACOP comments:

> 'The Accounting Standards Board (ASB) has approved the CIPFA/LASAAC Joint Committee (the Joint Committee), a standing committee of CIPFA and LASAAC, for the purpose of issuing recognised Statements of Recommended Accounting Practice (SORPs). This arrangement requires the Joint Committee to follow the ASBs code of practice for the production and issue of SORPs.
>
> The ASBs code of practice provides a framework to be followed by the Joint Committee for the development of SORPs, but does not entail a detailed examination of the proposed SORP by the ASB. However, a review of limited scope is performed.
>
> The SORP is based on accounting standards in issue at 30 September 1992, except where such standards conflict with specific statutory requirements and except for FRS2 *Accounting for Subsidiary Undertakings,* issued in July 1992, which has not been incorporated pending the issue of further Regulations. The ASB notes that the Joint Committee is committed to revising the SORP as appropriate to take account of all newly issued standards and is beginning work on the application to local authorities of FRS3 *Reporting Financial Performance* issued in October 1992.
>
> Other than the matters noted above, on the basis of its review the ASB has concluded that the SORP has been developed in accordance with the ASBs code of practice and does not appear to contain any fundamental points of principle that are unacceptable in the context of current accounting practice or to conflict with any existing or currently contemplated accounting standards.'

The 1993 *Code of Practice* is set out in Appendix 3.3.

Appendix 3.1

Financial Reporting Standards (FRSs) and Statements of Standard Accounting Practice (SSAPs), as at Spring 1995

FRS	Title
1	Cash flow statements
2	Accounting for subsidiary undertakings
3	Reporting financial performance
4	Accounting for capital instruments
5	Reporting the substance of transactions
6	Acquisitions and mergers
7	Fair values in acquisition accounting

SSAP	Title
1	Accounting for associated companies
2	Disclosure of accounting policies
3	Earnings per share
4	Accounting treatment of government grants
5	Accounting for value added tax
6	(superseded by FRS 3)
7	(withdrawn)
8	Treatment of taxation under the inputation system in the accounts of companies
9	Stocks and long term contracts
10	(superseded by FRS 1)
11	(withdrawn)
12	Accounting for depreciation
13	Accounting for research and development
14	(superseded by FRS 2)
15	Accounting for deferred tax
16	(withdrawn)
17	Accounting for post balance sheet events
18	Accounting for contingencies
19	Accounting for investment properties
20	Foreign currency translation
21	Accounting for leases and hire purchase contracts
22	Accounting for goodwill
23	Accounting for acquisitions and mergers
24	Accounting for pension costs
25	Segmental reporting

Appendix 3.2

Accounting concepts and principles as set out in CIPFA's ACOP 1991

Accounting concepts

1 The Statements of Accounts shall be prepared in accordance with the basic accounting concepts described below and the GB SORP, and other relevant accounting recommendations of CIPFA and LASAAC.

2 Presents fairly
A Statement of Accounts shall present fairly the financial position and transactions of the authority. 'Fair presentation' will normally be achieved by compliance in all material respects with proper local authority accounting practices and in particular with this *Code of Practice* as regards form and content, and the broad accounting concepts outlined below. Where the requirements of the Code are not met, then full disclosure and, where relevant, quantification of the departure in the Statements of Accounts is required.

3 Matching
Revenue income and expenditure shall be matched to the services provided in the same accounting period. This requires compliance with the concept of accruals for operating income and expenditure and interest. The matching principle does not preclude the establishment of provisions to equalise the charges for irregular but recurring types of expenditure.

4 Consistency
Consistent policies shall be applied both within the accounts for a year and between years. Generally, a change in accounting policy should not be made unless it can be justified on the grounds that the new policy is preferable to the one it replaces because it will give a fairer presentation of the results and of the financial position.

5 Prudence
The accounts shall be prepared in accordance with the prudence concept. Income shall only be included to the extent that it can be realised with reasonable certainty and proper allowance shall be made for all known liabilities and losses.

6 Substance over form
The accounting statements shall be prepared so as to reflect the reality or substance of the transactions and activities underlying them, rather than only their formal character.

7 Materiality
Strict compliance with this Code, both as to disclosure and accounting principles, is not necessary where the amounts involved are not material to the fair presentation of the financial position of the authority and to an understanding of the Statement of Accounts by a reader.

Accounting principles
1   The following accounting principles are consistent with the Accounting Concepts and shall be followed in respect of the specific areas of income, expenditure and balances listed below.

2   Employee costs
The full cost of employees, including holiday pay, shall be charged to the accounts of the period within which the employees worked. Accrual should be made for wages earned but unpaid at the year end. Where retrospective adjustments or special payments are required, for example through pay awards or redundancy payments, the accounts shall be charged (or credited) with the additional amount as soon as it can reasonably be estimated.

3   Pension costs
The cost of providing pensions for employees shall be charged in accordance with statutory requirements.

4   Premises related expenses
Premises related expenses, including property rents payable under operating leases, shall be accrued and accounted for in the period to which they relate.

5   Transport related expenses
Transport related expenses shall be accrued and fully allocated and charged to services in the period to which they relate.

6   Supplies and services
The cost of supplies and services shall be accrued and accounted for in the period during which they were consumed or received. Accrual shall be made for all material sums unpaid at the year end for goods or services received or works completed. Stocks and work-in-progress should be included in the balance sheet at cost less an appropriate provision for obsolescence or loss in value (see the GB SORP – SSAP9).

7   Costs of support services
Costs of support services shall be fully charged to services.

8   Interest
Interest on external borrowings shall be accrued and charged in the accounts of the period to which it relates. Interest charges should be made on a fair basis, and at rates which are equivalent to actual rates in force. In Scotland, see LASAAC's guidance notes on interest on balances.

9   Grants
Revenue based grants shall be accrued and credited to the accounts of the same period in which the expenditure to which they relate is charged; where claims are not settled the best estimate of grant income shall be used. Capital grants should be matched with the cost of the relevant assets.

10   Customer and client receipts
Customer and client receipts in the form of sales, fees, charges and rents shall be accrued and accounted for in the period to which they relate. Provision shall be made for doubtful debts and known uncollectable debts should be written off.

11   Interest income
Interest income shall be accrued and accounted for in the period to which it relates.

12   Investments
Investments in companies established for the promotion of local authority activities and in marketable securities shall be carried at cost less provision, where appropriate, for loss in value. Investments held by superannuation funds shall be carried at market value. Dividends shall be credited to revenue when declared or paid (see also GB SORP – SSAPs 1 and 14).

13   Provisions
Proper provisions are required for any liabilities or losses which are likely to be incurred, or certain to be incurred, but uncertain as to the amounts or the dates on which they will arise. Provisions may also be made for irregular but recurring types of expenditure. In Scotland a Renewal and Repair Fund typically is used for this purpose. All provisions shall be charged to the appropriate service if possible and utilised only for the purpose for which they were established, except where a regular review to determine the appropriateness of the level of the charge and the balance of the provision properly requires a change. Any change in the

use of a provision shall be disclosed.

14   Reserves
Amounts set aside for purposes falling outside the definition of provisions made above shall be considered as reserves, and transfers to and from them shall be distinguished from service expenditure disclosed in the Statement of Accounts. For each reserve established, the purpose, usage and the basis of transactions should be clearly identified.

15   Basis of capital financing
Revenue accounts shall be charged with amounts which cover the minimum revenue provision required by statute (in England and Wales by the *Local Governemnt and Housing Act 1989*; in Scotland by Scottish Office Circular 29/1975). Charges to services may be made on the basis of outstanding debt or on any other appropriate economic basis.

16   Fixed assets
Expenditure on the acquisition of a tangible asset, or expenditure which adds to, and not merely maintains, the value of an existing asset, shall be capitalised and be classified as a fixed asset, provided that the fixed asset yields benefits to the authority and the service it provides for a period of more than one year.

Appendix 3.3

CIPFA Accounting Code of Practice 1993

Introduction
Objective of the Code of Practice
1   This Code of Practice specifies the principles and practices of accounting required to prepare a Statement of Accounts which 'presents fairly' the financial position and transactions of a local authority.

2   The Code of Practice sets out the proper accounting practices required for Statements of Accounts prepared in accordance with the statutory framework established for England and Wales by Regulation 7 of the *Accounts and Audit Regulations 1983* (as amended) and by Sections 41 and 42 of the *Local Government and Housing Act 1989* and, for the audit of those accounts, by Section 15 of the *Local Government Finance Act 1982*. In Scotland, the statutory framework is established by the *Local Authority Accounts (Scotland) Regulations 1985* and, for the audit of those accounts, by Section 99 of the *Local Government (Scotland) Act 1973*.

3   In the unusual event that other statutory provisions require departures from the Code of Practice, then those statutory provisions should be followed. Regard will still need to be given, however, to the need for the Statement of Accounts to 'present fairly' the financial position and transactions of the authority, which may mean the inclusion of additional information in accordance with the provisions of this Code of Practice.

Applicability of the Code of Practice
4   This Code of Practice has effect for financial years commencing on or after 1 April 1993. However, certain provisions have effect only for financial years commencing on or

after 1 April 1994. These provisions are highlighted in the text in italics. Authorities which will cease to exist as a result of the reorganisation of local government in the period up to 1 April 1996 are exempt from the requirements contained within paragraphs 28-39 in Section 3 of the Code of Practice.

5   The Code of Practice applies formally in England and Wales to local authorities, joint committees, joint boards of principal authorities, police and fire authorities. In Scotland, the Code of Practice applies to local authorities, joint committees, joint boards, and water development and river purification boards.

6   The Code of Practice does not apply formally to parish, town and community councils, but the provisions of the Code of Practice may be relevant to them and may be taken into account when Statements of Accounts are prepared.

The context of the Code of Practice's recommendations
7   The Code of Practice is supported by a number of detailed accounting recommendations which have evolved as best accounting practice over many years.

8   The provisions of the Code of Practice are updated where professional or statutory developments make it appropriate and this represents the second such revision to reflect new accounting standards and legislative changes. The Code of Practice has also been revised to incorporate the new system of accounting for fixed assets by local authorities; the requirements of the CIPFA/LASAAC SORP on 'The application of accounting standards (SSAPs) to local authorities in Great Britain' as amended; and the requirements of the CIPFA Statement on 'The application of SSAP24 *Accounting for pension costs* to local authorities'.

9   The Code of Practice sets out the accounting concepts and accounting principles which underpin the Statement of Accounts. The following points are intended to put some of those requirements in context:

● The Code of Practice requires accounting policies to be applied consistently. The over-riding requirement remains that the Statement of Accounts 'presents fairly' the financial position and transactions of the authority. Where there are changes in accounting policies or where the requirements of the Code of Practice are not met, then full disclosure and, where relevant, quantification in the Statement of Accounts is required.

● The Code of Practice represents the minimum requirement for disclosure and presentation (subject to materiality) and is not intended to prejudice the provision of further information by authorities.

● The Code of Practice includes new requirements in respect of accounting for fixed assets. This means that the matching (or accruals) concept is applied to all revenue and capital income and expenditure. The costs of service in the revenue account will include, therefore, capital charges for all fixed assets used in the provision of services.

● The Code of Practice is based on the statutory definition of expenditure which may be capitalised as fixed assets. The classification of deferred charges, representing other expenditure which may properly be capitalised, but which does not result in tangible fixed assets, is retained.

● The new system of accounting for fixed assets means that the balance sheet will normally be prepared on a historical cost basis, modified by the revaluation of certain categories of assets. The Code of Practice includes recommendations on how the financial information relating to fixed assets should be presented.

- The Code of Practice has been revised to reflect accounting standards introduced since 1990. The major change is the replacement of the Statement of Revenue and Capital Movements with a Cash Flow Statement in accordance with FRS1, issued in September 1991. The Code of Practice also reflects the revision of SSAP4 *Accounting for government grants* (July 1990) and the requirements of SSAP25 *Segmental reporting* (June 1990).
- The Code of Practice has also been revised to incorporate the disclosure requirements in respect of pension costs set out in the CIPFA Statement on 'The application of SSAP24 *Accounting for pension costs* to local authorities', issued in May 1992.
- The introduction of the council tax in April 1993 has brought changes in the accounting for the collection fund, which the Code of Practice requires to be consolidated in the authority's consolidated balance sheet.
- The distinction between reserves and provisions as set out in the Code of Practice remains fundamental to ascertaining the cost of services. Provisions are included within the cost of services, whereas reserve movements are treated as separate appropriations.

Accounting standards

10   The 'Foreword to Accounting Standards' issued by the ASB in June 1993 states:

'Where public sector bodies prepare annual reports and accounts on commercial lines, the Government's requirements may or may not refer specifically either to accounting standards or to the need for the financial statements concerned to give a true and fair view. However, it can be expected that the Government's requirements in such cases will normally accord with the principles underlying the Board's pronouncements, except where in the particular circumstances of the public sector bodies concerned the Government considers these principles to be inappropriate or considers other to be more appropriate.'

11   The Code of Practice is based on approved accounting standards, except where these conflict with specific statutory accounting requirements, so that an authority's accounts 'present fairly' the financial position and transactions of the authority.

Purpose of the Statement of Accounts

12   The Code of Practice has been prepared on the basis that the purpose of a local authority's published Statement of Accounts is to give electors, those subject to locally levied taxes and charges, members of the authority, employees and other interested parties clear information about the authority's finances. It should answer such questions as:

- What did the authority's services cost in the year of account
- Where did the money come from?
- What were the authority's assets and liabilities at the year end?

13   It is important for compliance with the Code of Practice that two particular aspects are understood clearly. First, all Statements of Accounts should reflect a common pattern of presentation, although this does not necessarily require them to be in an identical format. One of the main aims of the Code of Practice is to narrow the areas of difference and variety in accounting treatment and thereby to enhance the usefulness of published Statements of Accounts. In particular, it is important that the costs of individual services are defined by local authorities in accordance with the CIPFA Standard Classification of Income and Expenditure.

14   Secondly, interpretation and explanation of the accounts is considered to be extremely important. The Code of Practice requires that there should be an Explanatory Foreword to

the Statement of Accounts. The Explanatory Foreword should explain the more significant features in the accounts. It should be based on the information contained in the Statement of Accounts and local authorities should ensure that it does not contain material inaccuracies or misleading statements in relation to the Statement of Accounts.

15   Wherever possible the Statement of Accounts and the supporting notes should be written in plain English and technical terms or jargon should be used only sparingly. Where the use of technical terms cannot be avoided, they should always be explained clearly in a glossary.

16   Where an authority also publishes a summarised or simplified version of its Statement of Accounts, it should contain a clear reference to the existence of the full Statement of Accounts and to its availability.

Publication
17   The Statement of Accounts should be prepared promptly by authorities in a form which fulfils the purpose outlined above. In Scotland, the accounts must be prepared by 31 August. In England and Wales, authorities are required to prepare their accounts by 30 September and to publish them by 31 December.

18   The publication of a Statement of Accounts is a statutory requirement. However, Statements of Accounts form part of reporting in its wider sense, and must therefore be considered in relation to annual reports. It is recommended that the Statement of Accounts should be included within the annual report. However, where this is not appropriate, the annual report should contain a fair summary of the Statement of Accounts, with a cross-reference to where and how the full Statement of Accounts may be obtained.

19   The Code of Practice states which accounts should be published as part of the Statement of Accounts, and the information to be included in each account. The layout of accounts and terminology used are at the discretion of authorities within the general framework and requirements of the Code of Practice.

20   The accounting statements, statement of accounting policies and notes to the accounts should form the relevant Statement of Accounts for the purpose of the auditor's certificate and opinion. The statements should be grouped together where possible, and published with an audit certificate and opinion in England and Wales and with an audit certificate in Scotland. If the published Statement of Accounts has not been audited, this should be stated clearly on the front of the document.

Accounting concepts
1   The Statement of Accounts should be prepared in accordance with the basic accounting concepts described below, the accounting policies as set out in Section 3 and other relevant accounting recommendations of CIPFA and LASAAC.

2   As stated in the Introduction, the requirement to 'present fairly' will normally be achieved by compliance in all material respects with proper local authority accounting practices and in particular with the requirements of the Code of Practice regarding the form and content of the accounting statements, and the broad accounting concepts outlined below. Where the requirements of the Code of Practice are not met, then full disclosure and, where relevant, quantification of the departure in the Statement of Accounts is required.

Materiality
3   Strict compliance with the Code of Practice, both as to disclosure and accounting prin-

ciples, is not necessary where the amounts involved are not material to the fair presentation of the financial position and transactions of the authority and to an understanding of the Statement of Accounts by a reader.

Going concern

4   A local authority's Statement of Accounts should be prepared on a going concern basis, that is the accounts should be prepared on the assumption that the authority will continue in operational existence for the foreseeable future. This means in particular that the income and expenditure accounts and balance sheet assume no intention to curtail significantly the scale of operation.

Matching

5   Income and expenditure should be matched to the services provided in the same accounting period. This requires compliance with the concept of accruals for revenue and capital income and expenditure.

Consistency

6   Consistent policies should be applied both within the accounts for a year and between years. A change in accounting policy should not be made unless it can be justified on the grounds that the new policy is preferable to the one it replaces because it will give a fairer presentation of the transactions and of the financial position.

Prudence

7   The accounts should be prepared in accordance with the prudence concept. Income should only be included to the extent that it can be realised with reasonable certainty, and proper allowance should be made for all known and foreseeable losses and liabilities.

Substance over form

8   The accounting statements should be prepared so as to reflect the reality or substance of the transactions and activities underlying them, rather than only their formal legal character. In determining the substance of a transaction, it is necessary to identify all of the transaction's aspects and implications.

Accounting policies

1   The following accounting policies are consistent with the accounting concepts and, where appropriate, the relevant accounting standard and should be followed in respect of the specific areas of income, expenditure and balances identified below.

2   As stated in the Introduction, the Code of Practice is based on approved accounting standards, except where these conflict with specific statutory accounting requirements, so that an authority's accounts 'present fairly' the financial position and transactions of the authority.

Accruals of income and expenditure

3   *Customer and client receipts* in the form of sales, fees, charges and rents should be accrued and accounted for in the period to which they relate.

4   *Employee costs:* the full cost of employees, including holiday pay, should be charged to the accounts of the period within which the employees worked. Accrual should be made for wages earned but unpaid at the year end. Where retrospective adjustments or special payments are required, for example through pay awards or redundancy payments, the accounts should be charged (or credited) with the additional amount as soon as it can reasonably be estimated.

5   *Interest* payable on external borrowings and interest income should be accrued and accounted for in the accounts of the period to which it relates.

6   The cost of *supplies and services* should be accrued and accounted for in the period during which they were consumed or received. Accrual should be made for all material sums unpaid at the year end for goods or services received or works completed.

Contingencies

7   Contingencies existing at the balance sheet date should be taken into consideration when preparing the financial statements. The treatment of a contingency existing at the balance sheet date is determined by its expected outcome. Contingent losses will be accrued in the accounting statements where it is probable that a future event will confirm a loss which can be estimated with reasonable accuracy at the date on which the Statement of Accounts is signed and dated. Contingent gains should not be accrued in the accounting statements.

8   Where a material contingency is not provided for in the accounts it should be disclosed by way of notes in order to ensure that the accounting statements do not present a misleading position. Such disclosures should indicate the nature of the contingency, the uncertainties which are expected to affect the ultimate outcome and either a prudent estimate of the financial effect or a statement that it is not practicable to make such an estimate.

Deferred charges

9   Deferred charges should be amortised to revenue over an appropriate period in a consistent and prudent manner.

Exceptional items, extraordinary items and prior year adjustments

10   Exceptional items should be included in the cost of the service to which they relate and, where material, explained within the notes to the accounts.

11   Extraordinary items should be disclosed and described on the face of the consolidated revenue account after dealing with all items within the ordinary activities of the authority and should be explained fully in a note to the accounting statements.

12   Prior year adjustments should be accounted for in the year in which they are identified and disclosed within the notes to the accounts or, where considered necessary for fair reporting, on the face of the appropriate revenue account. However there should not be any adjustment of preceding year comparative figures or of the opening balances of funds. This reflects the requirements to match all expenditure in the reporting period with income from general government grants and local taxpayers. An explanation should be given by way of notes to the accounts of the estimated effect on the prior year figures.

Fixed assets
Recognition

13   *All expenditure on the acquisition, creation or enhancement of fixed assets should be capitalised on an accruals basis.* Expenditure on the acquisition of a tangible asset, or expenditure which adds to, and not merely maintains, the value of an existing asset, should be capitalised and be classified as a fixed asset, provided that the fixed asset yields benefits to the authority and the services it provides for a period of more than one year.

14   Expenditure that should be capitalised will include expenditure on the:

- acquisitions, reclamation, enhancement or laying out of land;
- acquisition, construction, preparation, enhancement or replacement of roads, buildings

and other structures;

- acquisition, installation or replacement of movable or immovable plant, machinery, apparatus, vehicles and vessels.

15   In this context, enhancement means the carrying out of works which are intended:

- to lengthen substantially the useful life of the asset; or
- increase substantially the open market value of the asset; or
- increase substantially the extent to which the asset can or will be used for the purposes of or in conjunction with the functions of the local authority concerned.

16   Under this definition, improvement works and structural repairs should be capitalised, whereas ordinary jobbing maintenance to buildings, including painting and decorating will not be included.

17   *Assets acquired under finance leases should be capitalised and included together with a liability to pay future rentals.*

18   *Where a fixed asset is acquired for other than a cash consideration or where payment is deferred, the asset should be recognised and included in the balance sheet at fair value.*

Measurement

19   *Infrastructure assets and community assets should be included in the balance sheet at historical cost, net of depreciation, where appropriate.*

20   *Operational land and properties and other operational assets should be included in the balance sheet at the lower of net current replacement cost or net realisable value in existing use.*

21   *Non-operational land and properties and other non-operational assets, including investment properties (other than those held by superannuation funds) and assets that are surplus to requirements, should be included in the balance sheet at the lower of net current replacement cost or net realisable value. In the case of investment properties this will normally be open market value.*

Revaluations

22   *When an asset is included in the balance sheet at current value, it should formally be revalued at intervals of not more than five years and the revised amount should be included in the balance sheet.*

23   *The value at which each category of assets is included in the balance sheet should be reviewed at the end of each reporting period and where there is reason to believe that its value has changed materially in the period, and that the change is likely to be other than temporary, the valuation should be adjusted accordingly.*

24   *Where a fixed asset is included in the balance sheet at current value, the difference between that value and the amount at which that asset was included in the balance sheet immediately prior to the latest (re-)valuation should be credited or debited to a fixed asset restatement reserve.*

Disposals

25   *Income from the disposal of fixed assets should be credited to the usable capital receipts reserve, and accounted for on an accruals basis. Where applicable, the proportion reserved (in England and Wales) for the repayment of external loans should be credited to a capital financing reserve.*

26   *Where a fixed asset is disposed of for other than a cash consideration, or payment is deferred, an equivalent asset should be recognised and included in the balance sheet at its fair value.*

27   *Upon disposal, the net book value of the asset disposed of should be written off against the fixed asset restatement reserve.*

Depreciation

28   *Depreciation should be provided for on all fixed assets with a finite useful life, which can be determined at the time of acquisition or revaluation.*

29   *Provision for depreciation should be made by allocating the cost (or revalued amount) less estimated residual value of the assets as fairly as possible to the periods expected to benefit from their use. The depreciation methods used should be the ones which are the most appropriate to the type of asset and their use in the provision of services.*

30   *The useful lives of assets should be estimated on a realistic basis. They should be reviewed regularly and, where necessary, revised.*

31   *Depreciation should not normally be provided for freehold land (whether operational or non-operational) or for non-operational investment properties. However, freehold land should be depreciated where it is subject to depletion by, for example, the extraction of minerals. Investment properties held on a lease should be depreciated over the period when the unexpired term is 20 years or less.*

32   *Depreciation should be based on the amount at which the asset is included in the balance sheet, whether net current replacement cost or historical cost.*

33   *Depreciation need not be provided for where the local authority can demonstrate that it is making regular repairs and maintenance to extend the asset's useful life in its existing use, such that any depreciation would not be material.*

Charges to revenue

34   *General or County Fund services revenue accounts, as defined in CIPFA's Standard Classification of Income and Expenditure, central support services and statutory trading accounts, including DSOs, should be charged with a capital charge for all fixed assets used in the provision of the service.*

35   *As a minimum, such charges should cover the annual provision for depreciation, where appropriate, plus a capital financing charge determined by applying a specified notional rate of interest to the net amount at which the asset is included in the balance sheet. Capital charges to the HRA should at least cover the statutory capital financing charges.*

36   *All expenditure on repairs and maintenance relating to fixed assets should be charged to the appropriate service revenue account.*

37   *Interest payable (including interest payable under finance leases) and provisions for depreciation should be charged to an asset management revenue account.*

38   *Capital charges for the use of fixed assets included in revenue accounts should be credited to the asset management revenue account.*

39   *The amounts set aside from revenue for the repayment of external loans and to finance capital expenditure should be disclosed separately on the face of the consolidated revenue account, below net operating expenditure.*

Foreign currency translation

40   Income and expenditure arising from a transaction denominated in a foreign currency should be translated into pounds sterling at the exchange rate in operation on the date on which the transaction occurred; if the rates do not fluctuate significantly, an average rate for a period may be used as an approximation. Where the transaction is to be settled at a contracted rate, that rate should be used.

41   At each balance sheet date, monetary assets and liabilities denominated in a foreign currency should be translated by using the closing rate or, where appropriate, the rates of exchange fixed under the terms of the relevant transactions.

Government grants

42   Whatever their basis of payment, revenue grants should be matched with the expenditure to which they relate. Grants made to finance the general activities of a local authority or to compensate for a loss of income should be credited to the revenue account of the period in respect of which they are paid.

43   Where the acquisition of a fixed asset is financed either wholly or in part by a government grant or other contribution, the amount of the grant or contribution should be credited to the government grants-deferred account and written off to the asset management revenue account over the useful life of the asset to match the depreciation of the asset to which it relates.

44   Government grants or other contributions should be accounted for on an accruals basis and recognised in the accounting statements when the conditions for their receipt have been complied with and there is reasonable assurance that the grant or contribution will be received.

Investments

45   Investments in listed and unlisted companies established for the promotion of local authority activities and in marketable securities should be carried at cost less provision, where appropriate, for loss in value. Investments held by superannuation funds should be carried at market value. Long-term investments should be identified separately on the face of the balance sheet. Dividends should be credited to revenue when received or receivable. Where the local authority's investment in a company is unlikely to be recovered, the loss should be charged against a relevant reserve or written off to the appropriate revenue account.

Leases

Finance leases

46   Rental payments under finance leases should be apportioned between the finance charge and the reduction of the outstanding obligation, with the finance charge being allocated and charged to revenue over the term of the lease.

Operating leases

47   Rentals payable under operating leases should be charged to revenue on a straight line basis over their term of the lease, even if the payments are not made on such a basis, unless another systematic and rational basis is more appropriate.

Overheads

48   Charges or apportionments covering all support service costs should be made to all their users, including services to the public, divisions of services, trading undertakings, DSOs, capital accounts, services provided for other bodies and other support services.

49   The cost of service management (comprising all management except corporate management) should in the same way be apportioned to the accounts representing the activities managed.

50   The bases of apportionment adopted should be used consistently for all the heads to which apportionments should be made.

51   The costs of corporate management and of regulating any service to the public should be allocated to separate objective heads kept for the purpose and should not thereafter be apportioned to any other head.

52   If any overheads are not charged or apportioned, the reason for not doing so, together with the nature of the overhead and the amount, should be disclosed in a note to the accounts.

Pension costs

53   The cost of providing pensions for employees should be charged to the accounts in accordance with the statutory requirements governing the particular pension schemes to which the authority contributes.

54   Where the statutory charge does not equate to the accrued cost of meeting future pension liabilities on a systematic and rational basis over the period during which the local authority derives benefit from its employees' services (for example, where the scheme is partially funded or unfunded, i.e. payments are made on a 'pay as you go' basis), a statement should be included in the Statement of Accounting Policies to the effect that the revenue account does not include proper provision for the pension costs of employees and that the liabilities included in the balance sheet are understated in respect of pension costs. An estimate of the provision that it would have been necessary to make to meet future pension liabilities should be disclosed in the notes to the accounts.

55   Any variations from the regular cost of pensions (for example, through changes in regulations and the existence of fund surpluses or deficits) should be accounted for appropriately and should be fully disclosed in the accounts, together with the length of the period which has been used to spread the variation (e.g. the average remaining services lives).

Post balance sheet events

56   Where a material post balance sheet event occurs which:

- provides additional evidence relating to conditions existing at the balance sheet date; or
- indicates that application of the going concern concept to a material part of the authority is not appropriate;

changes should be made in the amounts to be included in the Statement of Accounts.

57   The occurrence of a material post balance sheet event which concerns conditions which did not exist at the balance sheet date should be disclosed. The disclosure should state the nature of the event and, where possible, an estimate of the financial effect of the event.

Provisions

58 Proper provisions are required for any liabilities or losses which are likely to be incurred, or certain to be incurred, but uncertain as to the amounts or the dates on which they will arise. Provisions should be charged to the appropriate revenue account. When expenditure is incurred to which the provision relates it should be charged direct to the provision. Provisions should be utilised only for the purpose for which they were established, except where a regular review to determine the appropriateness of the level of the charge and the balance of the provision properly requires a change. Any change in the use of a provision should be disclosed.

Provisions for bad and doubtful debts

59 Provision should be made for doubtful debts, and known uncollectable debts should be written off.

Research and development

60 Expenditure on research and development can normally be regarded as part of the continuing operations of the authority and should be written off as it is incurred.

Reserves

61 Amounts set aside for purposes falling outside the definition of provisions should be considered as reserves, and transfers to and from them should be distinguished from service expenditure disclosed in the Statement of Accounts. Expenditure should not be charged direct to any reserve. For each reserve established, the purpose, usage and the basis of transactions should be clearly identified.

62 Capital reserves are not available for revenue purposes and certain of them can only be used for specific statutory purposes. The fixed asset restatement reserve, usable capital receipts, and capital financing reserves are examples of such reserves.

Stocks and long-term contracts

63 Stocks should be included in the balance sheet at the total of the lower of cost and net realisable value of the separate items of stock or of groups of similar items.

64 For trading activities, the amount recognised in the appropriate revenue account for contract work in progress, for which interim valuations are made, should be the progress payments received and receivable, less related costs and any foreseeable losses, to the extent that the amount exceeds the corresponding amount recognised in previous periods.

65 The amount at which contract work in progress, for which interim valuations are made, is included in the balance sheet should be cost plus any attributable profit less any foreseeable losses and, where relevant, progress payments received and receivable.

Value added tax

66 VAT should be included in income and expenditure accounts, whether of a capital or revenue nature, only to the extent that it is irrecoverable.

The Statement of Accounts

Form and content

1 In its Statement of Accounts, an authority should disclose the information, the accounting statements and the notes as required by this Section. The preparation of the accounting statements should be in accordance with the accounting concepts and policies

set out in Sections 2 and 3. An authority may add such additional information or statements as are necessary to ensure fair presentation of its financial position and transactions.

2   The Statement of Accounts comprises:

- An explanatory foreword
- A statement of accounting policies
- The accounting statements
- Notes to the accounts

3   An authority's accounting statements should comprise those of the following statements that are relevant to its functions:

- Consolidated Revenue Account
- Housing Revenue Account
- Summary Direct Service Organisation (DSO) Revenue and Appropriation Account
- Collection fund (England and Wales)
- Council tax and Non-Domestic Rate Income Accounts (Scotland)
- Consolidated balance sheet (excluding superannuation funds and other trust funds)
- Cash flow statement

4   For England and Wales, the notes to the consolidated balance sheet and the cash flow statement set out in the Code of Practice meet the requirements of the Accounts and Audit Regulations for a summarised statement of capital expenditure and a statement of source and application of funds respectively.

5   The superannuation fund accounts, other trust fund accounts and, in Scotland, the common good accounts are shown separately because they are not part of the consolidated accounts of the local authority.

6   Each authority administering a superannuation fund should also prepare for the fund a separate:

- Statement of Revenue Income and Expenditure; and
- Net Assets Statement.

7   Each authority in Scotland responsible for water and sewerage should also prepare separate summary revenue accounts for these services.

8   All statements should include comparative figures for the previous year.

9   The notes to the accounts should add to and interpret the content of individual statements. They should also provide more explanation or analysis where matters of financial significance cannot adequately be treated in the statements themselves.

Appendix 3.4

Accounting Code of Practice 1995

The recently approved Code of Practice on local authority accounting in Great Britain (1995) (the 1995 Code) applies to accounting periods beginning on or after 1 April 1995.

The 1995 Code was updated to take account of FRS 2, SAS 600 and the SSSC. Revisions to the 1995 Code are now under way. One of the standards to be incorporated into it is FRS 4, Capital instruments. One of the requirements of the standard is that a premium or discount arising on the repurchase of debt is taken to revenue in the year of repurchase. Last year's questionnaire on this matter indicated that straightforward application of this requirement to local authorities would result in a significant change in accounting treatment by them. The CIPFA/LASAAC joint committee is considering the precise implications of FRS 4 for the Code and will produce a discussion paper in the summer opening up debate and seeking views on this and other issues which require revisions to the Code. An exposure draft to amendments to the Code, to be agreed with the Accounting Standards Board, is scheduled for consultation with local authorities and other interested parties at the end of 1995. Until these requirements are incorporated into a new code, local authorities are not required to change their existing accounting policies.

New Code of Practice on local authority accounting in Great Britain

In March, a new Code of Practice on local authority accounting in Great Britain (the Code) was approved by both CIPFA and LASAAC. The changes to the Code reflect principally the requirements of FRS3, 'Reporting financial performance', the statement of support services costs and SAS 600 'Auditors' reports on financial years commencing on or after 1 April 1995.

4 Revenue and trading accounts

This chapter examines the three main types of revenue income available to local authorities and then looks at the main income and expenditure analyses. Tabular and narrative revenue accounts are introduced and the ways in which individual revenue accounts are summarised are dealt with. A selection of standard revenue journal entries precedes an appendix showing CIPFA's standard classification of income and expenditure.

Main types of revenue in local government

Local authorities have four main sources of revenue income, to finance annual revenue expenditure of approximately £44 billion (see Appendix 4.2):

- council tax
- uniform business rate (UBR)
- rents, fees and charges for services.
- government grants.

Council tax

Up to April 1990 rates, a tax based on the value of property owned or occupied, were the backbone of local taxation. Between this date and April 1993 the community charge, or 'poll tax', was introduced, payable by all adults over 18 years, with some relief for those on low incomes. Otherwise all adults in the same local authority paid the same amount.

The rating element differs from the old rating system in two main regards – it is based on capital not rental values, with a reference date of 1 April 1991, and instead of properties being individually valued, they will be placed into one of eight valuation bands:

Band	England values £	Wales values £
A	up to 40,000	up to 30,000
B	40,001 – 52,000	30,001 – 39,000
C	52,001 – 68,000	39,001 – 51,000
D	68,001 – 88,000	51,001 – 66,000
E	88,001 – 120,000	66,001 – 90,000
F	120,001 – 160,000	90,001 – 120,000
G	160,001 – 320,000	120,001 – 240,000
H	over £320,000	over £240,000

There are different bands for England and Wales. The Commissioners of Inland Revenue will allocate properties to valuation bands under the direction of the Secretary of State. The bands are as follows:

The calculation of the rate of council tax is again a simple one, similar to that for the poll tax:

$$\frac{\text{Amount the authority intends to spend-non-council tax revenue}}{\text{Council tax base}}$$

Non-council tax revenue has a similar definition to non poll tax income. The council tax base is determined by regulations made by the Secretary of State, and is similar to calculating a product of a pound rate.

The amount charged for an individual property will be calculated by reference on the basic charge and the proportions for the different valuation bands shown in the table above. Those in the top band H will pay three times as much as those in the bottom band A. Those in Band A will pay two thirds of the amount paid by middle band D. These bands can be altered by an order made by the Secretary of State. Further calculation details are shown under Collection Fund in Chapter 7.

The poll tax element is provided by allowing a 25 per cent discount from the amount payable to single persons households, or where residents fall to be disregarded, e.g. severely mentally impaired, students including student nurses and prisoners. There is a Council Tax Benefits Scheme to help those unable to pay and in all cases there will be one bill per property, not separate ones for each person as in the poll tax. Certain groups such as students are exempt.

Capping

The *Rates Act 1984* introduced the concept of the government 'capping' the expenditure of local authorities if they spent more than government spending assessments. This placed a limit on what they regarded as excessive spending by some authorities. The power to 'cap' rests with the Secretary of State for the Environment (and the Secretary of State for Wales) subject to parliamentary approval. The *Local Government Finance Act* made similar 'capping' provisions for the poll tax and the *Local Government Finance Act 1992* extends it to the council tax. The new provisions provide for the Secretary of State to designate authorities where in his opinion the budget requirement is excessive, or there is an excessive increase between the budget for one year and the next. He will then notify the authority concerned of the total for their budget and they have a right of appeal to him or alternatively may accept his figure. Consequential reductions in the amount of the council tax then have to be made. The present capping rules are summarised in Appendix 4.2.

Uniform business rate (non domestic rates)

Uniform business rates, introduced in 1990, remain in force. They are a property tax paid by occupiers of commercial and industrial property but they are no longer a local tax. They are set by central government and collected by charging authorities for the council tax who hand over the proceeds to central government. The government then redistributes the money to local authorities in proportion to their adult population.

Some non-domestic properties such as churches or agricultural land or buildings are exempt and charitable buildings can receive a reduction.

Properties are valued and given a rateable value by the Inland Revenue based on what the property could have been let for in 1988. The Secretary of State may prescribe other dates. There is a right of appeal to the Valuation and Community Charge Tribunal. The government then sets, each year, the non-domestic rate multiplier (the rate in the pound), separately for England and Wales and this is levied on the rateable value. For example a shopkeeper with a rateable value of £4,000 and a multiplier of 50p will pay 4,000 X 50 = £2,000. There are separate rate multipliers for England and Wales.

National non-domestic rate (or uniform business rate) for 1994/95 was 42.3p. The amount estimated to be raised from central, local and crown lists was £11.2 billion. Total rateable value held on local authority lists at 31 December 1993 was £30.3 billion. The amount to be redistributed to authorities from the pool in 1994/95 was £10.7 billion. The rate for 1995/96 is 43.2p.

There is a statutory requirement to revalue business properties every five years, so that a new valuation list, based on 1993 rental values, became operative from 1 April 1995.

Rents, fees and charges for services

Local government charges for many of its services – housing and industrial rents, leisure facilities, parks and gardens, trade refuse, car parking and planning applications. This area is increasing in importance as national support declines and there is now considerable commercial pressure to make many services self financing. A number of government measures in recent years have encouraged this development, principally by removing central controls over fees and charges, encouraging a move to economic pricing and allowing local authorities to increase certain charges, particularly in the planning field, by well above the rate of inflation. Making local services at least self-funding is now a key financial objective of many local authorities.

Government grants

Central government gives grants to local authorities amounting in total to over 80 per cent of local government expenditure. They come in two main forms:

- Specific grants – to help pay for specific revenue or capital schemes.
- General grants – to pay for general running costs.

Grants are given for the following reasons:

- To achieve a specific purpose – e.g. a specific grant was given to reduce the poll tax.
- To help poor areas.
- To reduce the cost of a service which is either spread unevenly across the country or which is of benefit to the nation as well as the local authority (e.g. coastal defence, police).
- To help fund a service when the government has laid down specific requirements (e.g. fire services).

The major grant introduced in 1990 is called the revenue support grant (RSG) and is a general grant. Its distribution is based on a complex formula, including a number of factors such as road mileage, number of properties and school children, and total population. Payment differs between England and Wales. In England it is paid to all district councils who have to pass most of it on to the county councils; in Wales the districts and counties get their money separately.

To calculate the grant for each area, the government works out how much it thinks it will cost to provide a national level of service per adult – the assessed spending need. If all authorities were to spend at this level, then, in theory the council tax would be the same all over the country, and the government works out what this level would be. This is referred to as the standard charge. The grant each authority receives is then calculated on the difference between its assessed need to spend to the government's level and the amount that it will receive from the national uniform business rate plus its assumed income from a standard level of community charge.

Example

Bramley District Council (population 100,000)	
Needs assessment:	£m
For district	5
Proportion of Bramshire	95
Total needs assessment	100
Income:	
National non-domestic rate	20
'Standard' charge of £300 per head X population of 100,000	30
Total assumed income	50

The shortfall between the needs assessment and calculated income is therefore £50m, which will be the level of revenue support grant and Bramley will have to pass on a substantial percentage to its county council.

The assessment of the spending needs for local authorities, in total and individually, are far below the amount that those authorities claim is the minimum to maintain standards of service in their areas. This is a point of major confrontation between the government and local authorities largely because the government bases its figures on what it believes local government should have spent and local authorities on what they have actually spent. At individual authority level the formula for assessing needs, although complex, does not fully reflect the needs of each area. This has always been a major problem of any general government grant but, now that it is used as the basis for 'capping' excess expenditure, that problem is highlighted.

Revenue accounts – analyses of income and expenditure

Chapter 3 explains the main accounting principles underlying the revenue finances of a local authority, and in particular the fund and reporting requirements, as well as the main divisions of the revenue accounts.

This chapter, which deals with the detailed format of revenue accounts, should be read in conjunction with the fund accounting paragraphs of Chapter 3. There, the framework under which the different types of revenue accounts are drawn up is discussed.

Revenue account formats will therefore be examined in this chapter under two main headings:

- service revenue accounts, e.g. education, planning, social services;
- trading accounts, e.g. markets, catering, transport.

The accounts of direct service organisations are dealt with in Chapter 7.

The standard format of revenue accounts

Regularly, over many years, CIPFA has produced and published recommendations under the heading of 'The Standard Form of Published Accounts of Local Authorities'; the latest base edition is dated 1985. These recommendations have sought to summarise latest accounting developments into best practice. The latest guidance is entitled 'Standard Classification and Summary Service Recommendations (1987)' and it sets out the standard classification of income and expenditure to apply to all published financial statements, relating to the 1987/88 financial year and after.

It is, at this stage, worth a reminder that revenue expenditure is concerned with the day-to-day running costs of local government and its services. Expenditure which creates an asset or is likely to be of benefit over a longer period than the current accounting year is termed 'capital'.

The CIPFA Standard Form recommends that a revenue account should be analysed as follows:

Example _____

- Services – These are the main services, e.g. education, highways, social services.
- Divisions of service – These are objective headings which denote the functional divisions within services. Education, for example, may be broken down into the following sub-divisions: primary and nursery, secondary, further education, etc.
- Sub-divisions of service – These would provide a further objective breakdown of a division of service. Primary and nursery above would then be subdivided into individual schools.
- Standard groupings – The analysis so far is objective into services, divisions of service and sub-divisions of service. The next level of analysis is termed 'stan-

dard groupings'. It is the subjective analysis of service expenditure. Standard groupings are common to all services and are as follows:

Expenditure

- employee expenses
- premises – related expenses
- transport – related expenses
- supplies and services
- agency and contracted services
- transfer payments
- central, departmental and technical support services
- capital financing costs.

Income

- Sub-groups and detail heads – The standard groupings above are then analysed into sub-groups. A detail head for expenditure within each sub-group is used where applicable.

CIPFA's full recommended Standard Classification of Income and Expenditure is shown in Appendix 4.1.

Types of classification

There are three types of classification of revenue expenditure. These are:

- *Subjective classification* – according to the subject or items purchased, for example salaries, books, petrol. This method of classification is simple to use and is appropriate to small organisations but for large organisations it is not helpful for decision-making purposes.
- *Objective classification* – according to the objective to be achieved by the expenditure, for example provision of primary school education, or provision of home help services. This method enables large organisations to come to decisions about changes in expenditure patterns more easily.
- *A combination of both* – in other words an objective classification down to a certain level and a subjective classification below that. This method has the advantage of showing how much has been spent on each objective and also gives further details on precisely what the money was spent on. Local authorities use this type of classification and use three levels of objective classification and three levels of subjective classification as follows:

Objective: Service, e.g. Social Services
             Division of service, e.g. elderly
             Subdivision of service, e.g. residential homes

At this stage in the analysis, all of the expenditure is divided into subdivisions of service, in this case residential homes for the elderly in the social service. The expenditure in each subdivision of service is further classified subjectively as follows:

Subjective: Standard grouping, e.g. premises-related expenses
              Subgroup, e.g. energy costs
              Detail head, e.g. solid fuel.

The 1985 Standard Classification includes a standard objective classification and this can lead to some difficulties because not all of the local authorities have the same internal structure. An example of this at the 'service' level is that some authorities may classify libraries with the service 'education' and others may classify it with the service 'leisure and recreation'. At the 'division of service' level some may deal with elderly mentally ill patients under 'elderly' and others may deal with them under 'mentally ill'.

Thus, having to produce accounts with a standard objective classification structure may result in the authority being involved in extensive reclassification of expenditure after it has been originally collected. This could present some problems, but the alternative would be for authorities to continue to use different objective classifications which makes comparisons between local authorities very difficult.

Coding

A code is defined as, 'A system of symbols designed to be applied to a classified set of items, to give a brief accurate reference facilitating entry, collation and analysis.' *Terminology*.

It will be seen from the above definition that coding is the way that the classification system is applied, i.e. items are classified, then coded. The importance of well designed coding systems cannot be over-emphasised. Coding is important with normal accounting systems, but becomes vital with mechanised and computerised systems. Accordingly an understanding of coding systems is vital to accountants. Coding is necessary:

- to identify uniquely items, materials and parts which cannot be done from descriptions
- to avoid ambiguity which would arise from using descriptions
- to reduce data storage. In the majority of cases a code is much shorter than a description.

Features of good coding systems

- Unique – each item should have one, and only one, code.
- Clear symbolisation – codes should consist of either all numeric or all alphabetic characters. In general, particularly with computer based systems, numeric codes would be preferred. Also, the use of numerous strokes, dashes, colons or brackets should be avoided. The following would be an example of bad notation: 56-503/291:8
- Distinctiveness – codes which represent different items should, so far as practicable, look distinctive. Errors may occur if virtually identical codes describe different items. For example, if a code for raw materials was 9-3816 and a code for a bought in component was 7-3816, confusion may occur even though the codes are unique.
- Brevity – codes should be as brief as possible yet consistent with meeting the requirements of the classification system. In general it has been found that seven digits is the maximum number of digits which can be reliably remembered.
- Uniformity – codes should be of equal length and of the same structure. This makes it easy to see whether any characters are missing. Having fixed length codes also considerably facilitates processing.
- Exhaustive – the coding structure should be exhaustive which means that it should encompass the full range of the classification as it exists and, of equal importance, be able

to cope with new items as they arise. This latter point is a major practical problem when designing coding systems.

- Ambiguity – the notation used for the coding system should avoid ambiguity. If there is a mixed alpha/numeric system, the letters I and O should not be used because of possible confusion with the numerals 1 and 0 (zero). In addition, when an all alphabetic system is used, the letters I, Q, S and G are most similar to other letters and numerals and should be avoided where possible.
- Significant – where possible the coding should be significant. This means that the actual code should signify something about the item being coded. For example, part of the code for vehicle tyres could indicate the actual size of the tyre. Thus a code for a 165 X 3 tyre would include 165.

With computerised accounting systems being common nowadays, the analysis of income and expenditure is frequently obtained by the use of a structured financial coding system, e.g.:

		Code digit						
	1	2	3	4	5	6	7	8
Service	X							
Division of service		X						
Sub-division of service			X	X				
Standard grouping					X			
Sub-grouping						X		
Detail head							X	X
Full code	X	X	X	X	X	X	X	X
		Objective codes			Subjective codes			

Tabular and narrative revenue accounts

As local government has become more commercial, so are more accounts being prepared on a more commercial basis. Trading, or quasi trading, services are those where the authority has the power to levy a charge upon the users of the service and where the overall financial result is likely to be at least a break even situation. These services will tend to have their revenue accounts prepared in a 'narrative' or 'vertical' style, while those which are more in the nature of a public service and where the cost falls upon local taxation, are presented on a 'tabular' basis, sometimes known as 'two sided', or 'horizontal'.

Examples of each of the main types are now shown:

Service accounts

Example ───

Tabular revenue account – Education Service (shown in abridged format)

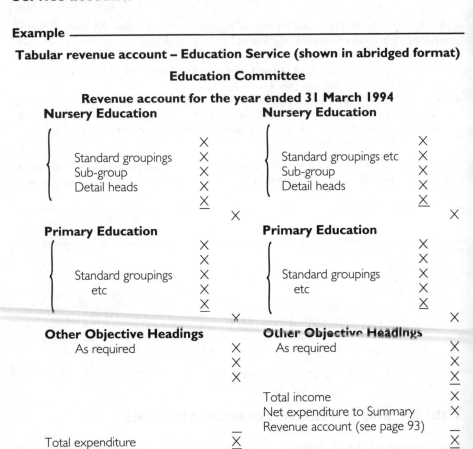

Education Committee

Revenue account for the year ended 31 March 1994

Nursery Education		Nursery Education	
	X		X
Standard groupings	X	Standard groupings etc	X
Sub-group	X	Sub-group	X
Detail heads	X	Detail heads	X
	X		X
		X				X
Primary Education		**Primary Education**	
	X		X
	X		X
Standard groupings	X	Standard groupings	X
etc	X	etc	X
	X		X
		X				X
Other Objective Headings		**Other Objective Headings**	
As required	X	As required	X
	X		X
	X		X
		Total income	X
		Net expenditure to Summary	X
		Revenue account (see page 93)	
Total expenditure	X		X

Trading accounts

Introduction

These are accounts for services and undertakings of a commercial nature which are, or could be, substantially financed by charges made upon the users of the services.

Trading accounts may be kept in two ways, according to local circumstances.

- As part of the general fund, and balanced annually by a transfer to or from the general fund.
- As separate undertakings with separate trading accounts. Surpluses from trading will be retained, i.e. not transferred to general fund, and transferred to a reserve fund. Any loss will be financed by any accumulated surplus in that fund.

Trading services operate to cover their costs and preferably to earn an acceptable surplus. Where the trading service is accounted for as a separate 'fund' the surplus will be used to maintain and expand the service.

Trading services vary between local authorities because of differences in local policies, customs and Local Act powers.

Trading services include the following:

- markets and abattoirs
- car parks and spaces
- cemeteries and crematoria
- catering units
- theatres, piers and entertainments
- harbours, docks and airports.

Revenue accounts of trading services

The revenue accounts of trading services should be drawn up in accordance with the 1985 Standard Classification, but with certain refinements.

- Income should be presented first. Trading income should be separately identified and come before non-trading income in order of presentation.
- A net revenue account and appropriation account should be used in order to achieve the following:
  - The separation of operating income and expenditure from non-operating income and expenditure, and the production of two key figures.

    1) Operating income less operating expenditure equals operating surplus or deficit
    2) Operating surplus or deficit plus non-operating income, less non-operating expenditure equals total surplus or deficit for the year
  - To show how the surplus or deficit for the year, plus the balance brought forward from the previous year, are dealt with (appropriated).

Example _____

Vertical revenue account – Markets undertaking

Revenue account for the year ended 31 March 1994

31.3.93 £		£	£
	Income		
	Customer and client receipts		
	Fees and charges		
	Fees income	X	
	Hire of equipment	X̲	
			X
	Rents		
	Market rents	X	
	Casual lettings	X̲	
			X̲
──	Total income		X̲
──			

Expenditure		
Employee-related expenses		X
Premises-related expenses		
Repairs and maintenance of buildings and grounds	X	
Energy costs	X	
Rates	X	
Cleaning and domestic	X̲	
		X
Transport-related expenses		
Direct transport costs		X
Supplies and services		
Clothing and uniforms	X	
Printing and stationery and general office expense	X	
Subscriptions and grants	X	
Miscellaneous insurances	X	
Miscellaneous expenses	X̲	
		X
Central departmental and technical support services		
Central departmental support		X
Capital financing costs		
Principal	X	
Interest	X̲	
		X
Total expenditure		X̲
Surplus from trading for year		X
Add: Accumulated surplus to date		X̲
Total accumulated surplus		X̲

Example

Net revenue and appropriation accounts

Net revenue account
Operating surplus/deficit

	£

Add: Non-operational income
      (i.e. income arising in the service but not directly
      linked to the level of activity of the service, e.g.
      advertising revenue in a passenger transport
      undertaking, interest on investments)
	———

Less: Debt charges
        Interest
        Principal
      Direct revenue financing
      Transfers to repairs and renewals fund
Total surplus or deficit of the year
	———

Appropriation account

	£
Total surplus (or deficit) for the year	
Add: Balance 1 April brought forward	——
Less: Transfer to reserves contribution to general fund	——
Balance carried forward	——

The final figure from the net revenue account becomes the first figure in the appropriation account. The purpose of this is to combine this year's surplus, with any balance brought forward, and from the combined figure to transfer sums for the general benefit of the undertaking. Normal transfers at this point are to internal reserve funds for the benefit of the undertaking, or a contribution towards the general rate fund to repay what that fund may have paid in the past to support deficits on this trading undertaking. The remaining figure is carried forward to the next period as a surplus or deficit on the undertaking.

There is no strong reason (subject to any statutory requirement) why the accounts of trading services should not be presented in accordance with the 1985 standard form classification.

The close resemblance of trading undertakings to the private sector tends to influence the presentation of accounts. Income is often reported first with distinctions being made in respect of non-trading income and expenditure.

Summary revenue accounts

All local authorities must maintain a county fund (in the case of a county council) or a general fund account (for a district council) in accordance with the *Accounts and Audit Regulations 1983*. The expenditure and income to be carried to the final account includes all expenditure and income of the authority unless otherwise required by statute. Even when separate accounts are required for special services or undertakings, the balances of these special accounts normally fall to be met by the rate fund.

The ultimate balance on the county or general fund account falls to be met by general government grants, e.g. revenue support, block grant, and the remainder by local taxation in the form of precepts or community charge/council tax or business rates.

Inevitably, the amount of net expenditure in any year, and the income from grants and taxation will not match precisely. This leaves a balance which will be carried forward to the following year. Balances can be either as a result of deliberate policy to provide some working capital, or unintended arising through unexpected variations in expenditure or income. In either case an adjustment to balances will be part of the next rate-making exercise and can be used to offset further increases in rates. Deficits carried forward must be recouped in the following period.

The general fund is the major fund of a local authority and the revenue account for this fund is called the General Fund Summary Revenue Account. This account records the sources of income and expenditure on the provision of council services (except those recorded in the accounts of the Housing Revenue Account, the Direct Service Organisation and, where relevant, trust funds).

The sources of income are:

- income from rents fees and charges
- specific grants from the government (for individual services)
- net receipts from the collection fund
- government grants – Revenue Support Grant
- interest from the investment of surplus money.

The income and expenditure on each individual service, e.g. education, is summarised in the General Fund Summary Revenue Account, so that for each service three figures are given – expenditure, income and net expenditure. The income for the individual services includes all the specific income and grants received by that service. The expenditure figure includes all expenditure on the individual service. The income for each service is deducted from the expenditure for each service in the General Fund Summary Revenue Account to give the net expenditure on each service.

Transfers between the general fund and other funds

There may also be transfers between the general fund and other funds which are recorded in the General Fund Summary Revenue Account. Examples of the most common types of transfer are given below.

- Transfer to the Housing Revenue Account. The Housing Revenue Account is now 'ring fenced', which means the general fund cannot be used to fund council housing. In specific circumstances, however, transfers are made to the Housing Revenue Account.
- Transfers from trading accounts. The profits from trading activities increase the funds available for the provision of services. If the trading account makes a loss, there will be a transfer to the trading account from the general fund to cover this.
- Transfers to reserves. If transfers to reserves are necessary, the council tax and business rates must be at a sufficiently high level to allow funds to be available to cover this transfer. There may also be transfers from reserves to the general fund which would reduce the level of council tax and business rates required to fund the services.

The balance on the General Fund Summary Revenue Account

The authority may not plan for a deficit on this account. Thus they must set a council tax which together with business rates covers all their expected expenditure and transfers from the account not financed by government grant or the income from rents, fees and charges. In order to calculate the balance on the general fund which appears on the balance sheet a separate statement is produced which shows the opening balance on the general fund plus the balance on the General Fund Summary Revenue Account for the year to give the closing balance on the general fund account.

The format of the General Fund Summary Revenue Account

A format for this account, which is based on the requirements in CIPFA's *Code of Practice in Local Authority Accounting for Great Britain (1991)*, is given below. Note that the figures in the last column of the account are expenditure figures, so any income is shown as a negative figure in brackets. If the balance for the year is positive, this means that there is an excess of expenditure over income for the year and thus there is a deficit for the year. The figures in the General Fund Balance Statement are reversed from this however so that a positive balance at the year end indicates that there has been a cumulative excess of income over expenditure.

Example _____

General Fund Summary Revenue Account
(1991 Accounting Code of Practice)

Service expenditure

	Gross expenditure	**Income**	**Net expenditure**
Refuse collection	X	X	X
Environmental health	X	X	X
Leisure	X	X	X
Highways	X	X	X
etc	X	X	X
Total service expenditure	X	X	X

Interest and investment income

Surplus or deficit from trading undertakings (not included above) Direct Service organisations, or other operations, including subsidiary and associated companies	X
Contributions to or from reserves	X
Subsidy receivable from/contributions to the Housing Revenue Account	X
Exceptional/extraordinary items	X
Net general fund expenditure	X
Net receipts from the collection fund	X
Government grants – Revenue Support Grant	X
Surplus or deficit for the year	X

General Fund Balance Statement

Balance brought forward	X
Surplus/(deficit) for year	Y
Balance at the end of the year	X

The previous year's figures are also given.

Requirements of the 1993 ACOP

The format of the Summary Revenue Account (SRA) just shown is based on the 1991 ACOP requirements. Those requirements were updated in September 1993 and information now to be included in the Summary Revenue Account is shown below.

In respect of the SRA, the Code comments:

> This statement is fundamental to the understanding of a local authority's activities, in that it reports the net cost for the year of the functions for which the authority is responsible, and demonstrates how that cost has been financed from general government grants and income from local authority's functions, in four distinct sections, each divided by a sub total.

> The first section provides segmental accounting information on the costs of the local authority's different services, net of specific grants and income from fees and charges, to give the net cost of services.

> The second section comprises items of income and expenditure relating to the local authority as a whole. When added to the net cost of services these give the local authority's total net expenditure.

> This third section comprises all appropriations, that is amounts transferred to or from revenue or capital reserves, in the form of amounts set aside from revenue to provide for the repayment of external loans and to finance capital expenditure, in accordance with statutory requirements, or to provide for the future replacement of fixed assets. The sum of these appropriations added to the local authority's net expenditure gives the amount to be met from general government grants and local taxation.

> The fourth section shows the principal sources of financing for the local authority's activities in the period, to give the net deficit or surplus for the year and the amount carried forward in the general reserve.

> The service analysis used in the first section should be in accordance with CIPFA's Standard Classification of Income and Expenditure. Exceptionally, where an authority's management structure differs from the standard classification, the accounts may reflect the local structure, provided that an explanation and adequate supporting information is given. Authorities may, at their discretion, combine minor classes of service expenditure.

> Gross expenditure and income on individual services should include the costs of support services. Other recharges to and from services should be excluded, so that the recharged cost is reflected only in the accounts of the service receiving it.

Example

Information to be included in the General Fund Summary Revenue Account (1993 Accounting Code of Practice)

Gross expenditure (including capital charges, provisions and exceptional items), income and net expenditure on General or County Fund services   X

Gross expenditure, income and net expenditure on the Housing
Revenue Account

Gross expenditure, income and net expenditure on the Water Supply
and Sewerage

Summary Revenue Accounts (in Scotland)	X
Sub-total: Net cost of services	X
Precepts of local precepting authorities	X
The total net surplus or deficit of statutory DSOs	X
Surplus or deficit of trading undertakings (where not included above) or other operations, including dividends from companies	X
Net income or expenditure on the asset management revenue account	X
Interest and investment income	X
Extraordinary items/prior year adjustments	X
Sub total: net operating expenditure	X
The surplus or deficit for the year transferred to or from HRA balances	X
Contributions to or from reserves which are not attributable to the cost of services as above (analysed between reserves)	X
Contributions to or from capital reserves, including provisions for the repayment of external loans and amounts set aside to finance capital expenditure	X
Sub total: amount to be met from government grants and local taxpayers	X
Demands or precepts on the collection fund (England and Wales) or income from the council tax (Scotland)	X
Transfers to/from the collection fund (e.g. in respect of previous year's deficit/surplus)	X
Government grants (not attributable to specific services)	X
Distribution from non-domestic rate pool	X
	X
Total: surplus or deficit for the year	X

Change in general or county fund balance analysed, in England and Wales, between
the amount generally available to the authority and the net amount held by schools
under local management schemes.

Information to be disclosed in notes to the Summary Revenue Account

- The nature and amount of any exceptional items, where appropriate, and of any extraordinary items and prior year adjustments.
- The nature and amount of all material transactions in the asset management revenue account, if not disclosed on the face of the account.
- The amounts of any finance and operating lease rentals paid to lessors in the year, and an estimate of the outstanding undischarged obligations in respect of operating leases.
- The nature, turnover and profits/losses of any significant trading operation.
- Expenditure required to be disclosed in England and Wales by Section 137 of the *Local Government Act 1972* (as amended).
- Expenditure on publicity required to be recorded by Section 5 of the *Local Government Act 1986*.
- The nature and amount of any significant agency income and expenditure.
- Income from bodies under the *Local Authority (Goods and Services) Act 1970* and the related expenditure.
- The following information in respect of the Local Government Superannuation Scheme:
  - The pension costs charged to the accounts, as an absolute figure and as a percentage of the employees' total pensionable pay, together with an explanation of any significant changes in the charge compared to the previous year;
  - any discretionary payments made by the authority in the year, and the expenditure on added years awarded by the authority and any related increases, as an absolute figure and as a percentage of total pensionable pay;
  - the pension costs, as an absolute figure and as a percentage of total pensionable pay, that would have had to have been provided for in the year in order to meet future pension liabilities on a systematic and rational basis over the period during which the local authority derives benefit from its employees' services.
- Where appropriate, the following information in respect of the Police and Fire-fighters pension schemes:
  - the pension costs charged to the accounts, as an absolute figure and as a percentage of the employees' total pensionable pay, together with an explanation of any significant changes in the charge compared to the previous year;
  - the regular cost of benefits, as an absolute figure and as a percentage of total pensionable pay, that would have had to have been provided for in the year in order to reflect the full expected cost of providing pensions;
  - the cost, as an absolute figure and as a percentage of total pensionable pay, or spreading the unfunded accrued liability over an appropriate period; and
  - a brief description of the actuarial assumptions used to calculate the above.
- In respect of the teachers' pension scheme administered by the Department for Education for England and Wales, the rate of contribution set and the amount paid over, together with information regarding any added years' payments awarded by the authority.
- The net amounts charged to revenue in compliance with the statutory requirement to set aside a minimum revenue position for the repayment of external loans (England and Wales).

Standard revenue journal entries

Practical classroom experience has shown the need for a summary of the main journal entries that are required to tackle revenue accounting exercises and particularly final accounts. Most frequently, these take the form of dealing with a list of transactions that require year end adjustments to a summary of receipts and payments or income and expenditure before preparing a set of final accounts.

A journal is merely a record of accounting transactions and provides a ready source of why particular accounting entries have been made and the accounts that have been debited and credited.

		Dr	Cr
1)	Meeting capital expenditure directly from revenue		
	Revenue account – direct revenue financing	X	
	To Cash Account		X
2)	Accruing income		
	Debtors	X	
	To Revenue Account		X
	(appropriate Sub Group/Detail Head)		
3)	Accruing expenditure		
	Revenue Account (appropriate Head)	X	
	To Creditors		X
4)	Writing off of bad debts		
	Revenue Account – Income written off	X	
	To Debtors Account		X
5)	Creation of a Bad Debts Reserve		
	Revenue Account – Provision for bad debts	X	
	To Bad Debts Reserve Account		X
6)	Accounts incorrectly debited or credited		
	(£500 has been charged to supplies and services – catering instead of to transport related expenses – car allowances)		
	Car allowances	X	
	To catering		X
7)	Duplicate payments		
	(A bill for £2,500 in respect of water rates has been paid twice)		
	Debtors – Water Authority	X	
	To premises related expenses – water services		X
8)	Apportionment of Central Support Services costs		
	(The Education Committee has not yet been invoiced for the annual recharge from the Finance Department in respect of financial services provided)		

Education Revenue Account – Central Support Services	X	
To Finance Department Revenue Account		X

Appendix 4.1

CIPFA's Standard Classification of Income and Expenditure

Standard grouping	Sub-group	Detail head

Employees	Employee types
	e.g. operational
	       support
	       administrative
		Salaries and wages
		National insurance
		Superannuation allowances

	Indirect employee expenses	Relocation expenses Training expenses Advertising Severance payments Pension Increase Act payment Transfer values Employee related insurance Interview expenses
Premises-related expenses	Repairs, alterations and maintenance of buildings and grounds	
	Energy costs	Fuel oil Solid fuel Electricity Gas
	Rents	
	Rates	
	Water services	Water charges (metered) Water charges (unmetered) Sewerage and environmental services
	Fixtures and fittings	
	Cleaning and domestic supplies	
	Apportionment of expenses of operational buildings	
	Premises and insurance	
	Contributions to funds	
Transport-related expenses	Direct transport costs	Purchase Repairs and maintenance Running costs Contributions to funds
	Recharge of pooled transport costs	
	Contract hire and operational leases	
	Public transport	Operational Administrative
	Car allowances	Members Operational Administrative
	Transport insurance	Members

Standard grouping	Sub-group	Detail head
Supplies and services	Equipment, furniture and materials	
	Catering	Provisions
		Contract catering
	Clothing, uniforms and laundry	
	Printing, stationery and general office expenses	
	Services	
	Communications and computing	
		General
		Clients
	Expenses	Pupils
		Postages
		Telephone
		Telex
	Grants and subscriptions	Computer
		Subsistence
		Conference
		Members' allowances and financial loss
	Miscellaneous expenses	Miscellaneous insurances
	Contributions to funds and provisions	Interest on balances
		Other
Agency and contracted services	Other committees of council	
	Other local authorities	
	Joint authorities	
	Government departments	
	Voluntary associations	
	Private contractors	
	Pooling contributions	
	Other agency and contracted services	
Transfer payments	School children and students	Mandatory awards
		Discretionary awards
		Other
	Social services clients	
	Housing benefits	Rent allowances
		Rent rebates
		Rate rebates
	Other	Other
Central, departmental and technicalsupport services	Administrative buildings expenses	
	Central departmental support	
	Central support services	
	Departmental administration	
	Democratic representation	
Capital financing costs	Loans fund	Principal repayments
		Interest payments
	Capital fund	Principal repayments
		Interest payments
		Principal repayments

Standard grouping	Sub-group	Detail head
	Debt serviced by other authorities	Interest payments
	Contribution to capital fund	
	Finance leasing charges	Buildings
		Transport and plant
		Equipment
		Other
	Direct revenue financing	
	Debt management expenses	
	Revenue appropriation adjustments	
Income	Government grants	
	Other grants, reimbursements and contributions	Agency reimbursements
		Joint financing contribution
		Contributions from other local authorities
		Contributions for staff board and lodging
		Pooling income
		Receipts from other funds
		Other
	Customer and client receipts	Sales
		Fees and charges
		Rents
	Interest	
	Recharges to other revenue account heads	
	Revenue appropriation adjustments	

Standard subjective classification

The standard subjective classification has three levels – the standard group, the subgroup and the detailed head. The standard groups are given in the section above and details of each standard group are given below.

Employees

This includes the gross remuneration of all staff employed and the employer's contribution for superannuation and national insurance.

Premises related expenses

This includes all the costs of running the buildings and grounds irrespective of what activity takes place in the buildings. Expenditure which is related to the use of the building is included under 'supplies and services'. Thus for instance fixtures and fittings (e.g. light fittings, toilets) are included here but furniture is included in supplies and services.

Transport related expenses

This contains all transport costs including travelling expenses, car allowances and recharges of pooled transport costs.

Supplies and services

This section is for all expenditure necessary to carry out the activity. It thus includes furniture, clothing, catering, printing and stationery. Miscellaneous expenditure which cannot be coded elsewhere is also included here.

Agency and contract services
This category is for payments to other committees of the authority or outside organisations who provide a service which is sufficiently comprehensive to be classified as a subdivision of service. For instance in Social Services – elderly – residential homes, payments to a private nursing home where some of the elderly had been placed would be regarded as payments for an agency's services. On the other hand, payments to an agency for nursing staff would be classified under 'employees', as only one item of service is being received here.

Transfer payments
This is for payments which are made to clients of various kinds and for which no service is received, e.g. student grants.

Central, departmental and technical support services
The central services of the council, e.g. the chief executive's department, treasurer's department are completely recharged over all services. This recharge appears here. Any costs of departmental administration which is allocated over the subdivisions of the services will also be recorded here.

Capital financing costs
In a company the item under this heading would be depreciation. Local authorities do not use depreciation, but instead record the use of the asset in the revenue account according to the method of funding. This is explained in more detail in the chapter on capital transactions. If an asset has been purchased using a loan from the loans fund, then this section will record the principal repayment of the loan paid that year, the interest payments and the debt management expenses payable to the loans fund for organising the borrowing and lending the money. If purchase is made from a loan, then the annual repayment of principal and the payment of interest will be recorded here. If the asset is to be funded directly from revenue then the whole cost of the asset appears in this section under the heading 'direct revenue financing'.

For any asset purchased by lease, the leasing charges will appear in this section.

Finally, if land is transferred from another service then this may result in a cash payment to the service transferring the land. This would appear in this section under 'Revenue appropriation adjustments'.

Income
This includes all specific grants and income on the sale of goods and services. Recharges to other revenue accounts for services given to the other departments are recorded here as income. Also if land has been transferred from this service to another service this may result in a cash payment from the committee receiving the land. Such a payment would be recorded here as income.

In the General Fund Summary Revenue Account (shown earlier in this chapter) the income and expenditure of each service committee is just recorded as a single figure. It is obviously necessary for the local authority to record the income and expenditure of their services and trading activities in much greater detail than this for the purpose of budgeting, budgetary control and planning, and for the calculation of statistics which allow comparison of types of expenditure with other authorities.

Appendix 4.2

Expenditure

Local authority budgeted net revenue expenditure for 1994/95 was (1994/95 cash prices)

Service	£m
Education	18,660
School catering	391
Libraries, museums and art galleries	737
Personal social services	6,497
Police	5,759
Fire	1,206
Other Home Office services	831
Local transport	2,362
Local environment services	5,278
Agricultural services	40
Consumer protection and trading standards	139
Employment	168
Non-housing revenue account housing	378
Housing benefits	4,392
Parish precepts	116
New net current expenditure	44,955
Capital charges	2,534
Capital charged to revenue	705
Other non-current expenditure	3,265
Interest receipts	−611
Gross revenue expenditure	52,849
Specific and special grants outside AEF*	−8,368
Other income	−50
Revenue expenditure	44,432
Specific and special grants inside AEF*	−4,866
Net revenue expenditure	39,566

* AEF = aggregate external finance

In November 1994, the government fixed a TSS for 1995/96 of £43.51 bn a rise of 0.8% on this years TSS of £42.66 bn. TSS planned for 1996/97 is $44.07 bn and £44.57 bn in 1997/98, giving further cuts in real terms.

Capping rules

Capping rules for 1995/96 have been tightened, pushing councils closer to SSAs and limiting the scope for them to make up shoftfalls in government funding through the council tax. Inner London boroughs have fared marginally better because they have received larger increases in SSA provision to help cover repayment of former GLC debt. Separate and slightly more generous capping criteria have been set for police authorities.

For all authorities other than inner London boroughs and police authorities:

- any budget increase of more than 0.5 per cent which gives rise to a budget requirement above an authority's SSA will be excessive

- any budget requirement which is more than 12.5 per cent above SSA will be generally regarded as excessive

For Inner London boroughs:

- any budget increases of more than 2 per cent will be excessive if it exceeds the SSA level
- any budget increase of more than 1.25 per cent will be excessive if the budget is more than 5 per cent over SSA
- any increase of more than 0.5 per cent will be excessive if the budget is more than 10 per cent over SSA.

For police authorities:

- any budget increase of more than 2.5 per cent will be excessive if it exceeds the authority's SSA level plus police grant
- any budger increase of more than 1.5 per cent will be excessive if the budget is more than 5 per cent over SSA plus police grant
- any budget increase of more than 0.5 per cent will be excessive if the budget is more than 10 per cent over SSA plus police grant.

5 Capital finance and accounts

This chapter considers capital finance and accounting in local government, which, for most authorities, is subject to considerable change from the 1994/95 financial year. Published accounts for that year should be produced on the new basis.

The 'present' arrangements for capital accounting and the historical background are described and the impact of recent legislative change upon capital financing is summarised. Much of this will be redundant when the new capital accounting arrangements from CIPFA's (The Chartered Institute of Public Finance and Accounting) 1993 *Accounting Code of Practice* are fully operational.

An outline of the new arrangements is given but it is proposed that further detailed commentary, following the publication of 1994/95 accounts, will be included with practical examples in the separate lecturer's pack.

In many organisations, the distinction between capital and revenue balances is not apparent from published accounts. This is true of both companies and currently the central government, although the new resource accounting proposals outlined in Chapter 1, will make a big difference by the end of the 1990s. In other public sector organisations, of which the health service is a good example, capital and revenue accounts are kept separately, though capital grants can be spent on revenue items and vice versa within certain limits.

In local government, statutory requirements have a significant impact on the way in which local authorities account for capital expenditure. Money borrowed and interest thereon must be charged to the relevant revenue account over an agreed period, so as to extinguish the debt and those costs must then be included in annual local taxation requirements. Thus, the annual provision for repayment of principal is a form of depreciation, although the asset acquired is not written down in the balance sheet.

The following example will show the principles of the way in which local authorities accounted for capital expenditure before the new arrangements, introduced in the 1993 ACOP, which are described later in this chapter.

A county council is to build a new fire sub station for £500,000.00. A specific loan at 6 per cent is raised to finance the spending, which takes place within a year. The loan repayment period chosen by the council is 20 years.

The entries in the accounts would be:

	Dr £	Cr £
Cash account	500,000	
Loans outstanding account		500,000
Raising the loan		
Fixed assets account	500,000	
Cash account		500,000
Payment to the contractor		

and at the end of the first year, the fire service balance sheet would show:

	£
Fixed assets	500,000
Represented by:	
Loans outstanding	500,000

To meet the legal requirements described earlier, the fire service revenue account now needs to start making provision for the loan to be repaid. The annual amount to be debited will be £55,000 – a principal repayment of £25,000 and interest amounting to £30,000. The journal entries would be:

	Dr £	Cr £
Loans outstanding account	25,000	
Interest on loans account	30,000	
Cash account		55,000

Since each of these charges needs to be met from the fire service revenue account, the following entry then needs to be made in respect of the interest which has been paid:

	Dr £	Cr £
Revenue account	30,000	
Interest on loan account		30,000

and, since the repayment of principal which has been made needs to appear in the revenue account, and also needs to show that the total loan outstanding of £500,000 has been reduced by £25,000, the journal entries will be:

	Dr £	Cr £
Revenue account	25,000	
Capital discharged		
(loans repaid) account		25,000

The capital discharged account records the extent to which assets have been financed. The accounts at the end of the first year of loan repayment will therefore be:

Fixed assets account

Balance b/f		Balance c/f	
New Sub Station	500,000		500,000

Loans outstanding account

Principal repayment	25,000	Balance c/f	
Balance c/f	475,000	Loan revised	500,000
	500,000		500,000

Capital discharged account

Balance c/f	25,000	Principal repayment	25,000

Interest on loans account

Interest paid	30,000	Revenue account	30,000

Relevant entries will, of course, appear in the cash book and fire service revenue account, and an extract from the balance sheet at the year end will show:

	£
Fixed assets	500,000
Less capital discharged	25,000
	475,000
Represented by:	
Loans outstanding	475,000

Fixed assets, therefore, continue to be shown at original cost. As the loan outstanding reduces annually, so does the capital discharge figure correspondingly increase.

The way in which fixed assets are financed, therefore, has a significant effect upon the service revenue account and balance sheet. Capital expenditure of £150,000 met fully and directly from revenue, will have a different reporting impact, than if that spending was met from a mixture or wholly from loans, revenue, grants or capital receipts in hand.

These principles are now developed with further examples and some of the terminology specific to local government capital accounting introduced. The historical problems which these principles have caused will then be exposed and the need for new arrangements, set out in CIPFA's 1993 Accounting Code of Practice will be seen.

Capital expenditure and central government controls

Local Government and Housing Act 1989

Part IV of the 1989 Act established a new system of control of capital finance in local government in England and Wales as from April 1990. The new system replaces the prescribed expenditure control contained in the *Local Government Planning and Land Act 1980* and the provisions of the *Local Government Act 1972*. This latter Act contains, in Schedule 13, the powers relating to local authority borrowing and the operation of a consolidated loans fund.

The emphasis of the new system is not on the direct control of capital spending but on limiting the sources of capital funding and especially the amount financed by credit. Thus, external borrowing is limited by annual 'credit approvals' issued by the DOE or the Welsh Office. Credit approvals restrict both an authority's ability to borrow money and its ability to enter into credit arrangements, such as finance leases.

In future, only 50 per cent of capital receipts (25 per cent of housing capital receipts) will be usable by a local authority to finance new capital expenditure; the remainder is to be set aside to redeem existing debt or to meet future debt.

The act repeals a local authority's power to operate special funds such as loans funds. All income and expenditure of the authority must now be specifically charged to a revenue account of the authority rather than to a fund. Therefore, if such funds are to continue they must be retitled to a specific revenue account. Many authorities have maintained them in memorandum form, awaiting the outcome of CIPFA's 1993 ACOP.

A local authority can continue to finance capital expenditure from revenue contributions but the authority must be aware of the impact on its overall revenue budget, on the council tax and on the possibility of charge-capping.

Thus from 1 April 1990 the government has made a major change in the way it controls capital expenditure by switching to a system that controls borrowings rather than expenditure. An authority can spend up to its aggregate credit limit set by the government but cannot exceed it. This limit is calculated by reference to outstanding loans and credit agreements, less provision for their repayment, at 1 April 1990. It is increased by any new credit approvals issued by the Secretary of State and reduced by repayments.

The credit approvals an authority receives in any year can be increased by up to 50 per cent of any capital receipts (money raised from the sale of other assets). This figure is reduced to 25 per cent for money raised from council house sales. The balance of any capital receipts must be used to repay debt.

The local authority has then to finance the schemes itself using one of the methods outlined below:

- borrowing
- using revenue sources (community charge, revenue grants, rents and fees)
- capital receipts (money raised from selling other assets), but see the above comments about the extent to which capital receipts may be used to finance new spending
- capital grants (grants from central government), for example transport supplementary grant

- private sector money, by entering into a joint venture with a private company
- leasing, where assets may be used without being owned.

With the exception of the last two sources, all methods of financing capital expenditure will cost the local authority money and the joint venture is likely to require some money up front:

- if it borrows it will have to pay interest on the loan and repay the loan over a number of years
- if it uses its revenue sources there will be a direct and immediate cost
- if it uses capital receipts it loses the interest it would have gained had it kept the money raised from the sale in the bank. The cost of such financing falls upon the revenue budget and is usually referred to as the revenue implication.

Why do local authorities borrow?

Local authorities borrow to finance capital expenditure for three main reasons:

- it is fairer that all those who will gain benefit from the item should contribute during its lifetime, rather than those who were in the area when it was acquired
- it makes economic sense at time of inflation to pay back with devalued money. However, when interest rates are high, borrowing is expensive
- if it is permissible to finance the expenditure by borrowing, the immediate impact on the revenue account is reduced.

Where do local authorities borrow from?

Local authorities may borrow from the public and private sectors. They can borrow from:

- the Public Works Loan Board (run by the National Investment Office)
- the money market, the financial institutions in the City of London who provide loans for local authorities
- the Stock Exchange, where authorities may float stock, but this is very rare, as is the issuing of local bonds to small investors
- the European Union.

Lotteries

Profits from lotteries may be used to finance small projects specified in the terms of the lottery. They may also finance revenue expenditure. Lotteries were never a major source of money and fewer councils are now running them. Funds may now be available from The National Lottery, provided that local authorities prepare suitable bids for them.

European Union

Local authorities may apply for grants and loans from the EU regional and social funds, the European Coal and Steel Community and the European Investment Bank. In most cases applications have to be made through central government. Grants are mainly payable to areas designated by central government as 'assisted areas' (i.e. areas with particularly high unemployment) though there are other categories which do not necessarily depend upon 'assisted area' status. In addition, grants must be matched pound for pound by central or local government. The total available is small, but some authorities are skilful at obtaining a large share of what there is. All governments, however, reduce local authority capital allocations to take account of EU money.

The European Regional Development Fund, set up in 1975, is the biggest source of EU aid for British local authorities. Its purpose is to correct regional imbalances in the community. The regional fund is divided up into national quotas. Applications are submitted by national governments – in the UK the Department of the Environment and the Welsh, Scottish and Northern Ireland offices select the local authority projects most suitable for submission. The fund can meet up to 30 per cent of the cost of infrastructure projects which contribute to the development of a region. Help is also available from the European Social Fund, which is an employment fund originally established under the Treaty of Rome, to meet the costs of training and retraining in specified categories. Most schemes receiving assistance from this fund are operated by the Training Agency but there has been in increase in the number of local authority projects receiving money.

Calculation of annual spending limits

Each financial year central government notifies each local authority of its annual capital guideline (ACG) covering the key groups of services on which the local authority incurs capital expenditure. The ACG is an attempt to measure the relative need of a local authority to incur capital expenditure. At the same time, central government makes an assessment of the local authority's capital receipts available to finance capital expenditure. This assessment is called *receipts taken into account* (RTIA) and the estimated figure is deducted from the ACG. The net figure is termed the *basic credit approval* (BCA), which covers both external borrowing and credit arrangements to finance capital expenditure. Credit arrangements are forms of credit which do not involve the borrowing of money by a local authority (for example a lease or hire purchase arrangement). The BCA is available for capital expenditure on any local authority service deemed necessary.

These annual arrangements also operate within an aggregate credit limit calculated according to a formula issued by central government. This is a limit requiring local authorities to manage their affairs so that at any time their total outstanding external borrowings and credit arrangements are below the aggregate credit limit.

Most capital expenditure is financed by borrowing. Government controls local authority capital expenditure by means of credit approvals. The credit approval is the total amount which can be advanced to the committees for the purchase of fixed assets. Some of these advances may be from resources within the authority so further borrowing is not necessary.

Authorities are legally required to charge revenue accounts of committees with amounts relating to interest and principal repayments on loans outstanding. The latter is called the minimum revenue provision (MRP) and the *1989 Local Government and Housing Act* specifies that this should be at least 2 per cent of the opening credit ceiling for housing revenue account debt (i.e. on council houses) and 4 per cent for all other debt.

The credit ceiling relates to the amount of advances which have been made to committees, and for which no sums have been set aside to repay. The calculation of the credit ceiling is shown below.

	£
Opening balance	X
Add: credit approvals used in year	X
Less: minimum revenue provision in year	X

Less: reserved part of capital receipts   (X)

Closing credit ceiling   X

The credit approvals used in the year are the total advances made to committees during the year. The Minimum Revenue Provision in the year is the total amount charged to committee revenue accounts and set aside for the repayment of loans. Amounts set aside for the repayment of debt are recorded in the Provision for Credit Liabilities.

The effect capital expenditure has on the revenue account depends upon the method of financing that is chosen: for example, financing by using capital receipts has no effect on revenue, while financing by direct revenue financing has the effect of financing all the capital from revenue immediately. This is proper accounting practice for local authorities, though it is different from the application of the accruals concept as practised in company accounts.

Local authorities do not use depreciation accounting (except within DSO accounts) but arguably charging principal repaid to the revenue account has the same effect, when assets are financed by borrowing. Instead of creating depreciation provisions, local authorities credit individual capital discharged accounts in respect of each type of capital finance, for example capital discharged–loans repaid (alternatively called redeemed), capital discharged–capital receipts applied, etc.

Capital accounting principles and transactions

Before we work through examples of capital accounting, we need to consider balance sheet presentation and terms. The following consolidated balance sheet includes only the capital items.

	£
Net fixed assets (gross amount less capital discharged)	X
Deferred charges	X
Long-term debtors	X
Total long-term assets	X
Financed by:	
Long-term borrowing (loans outstanding)	X
Deferred capital receipts	X
Capital receipts unapplied	X
Provisions	X
Fund balances and reserves	X
Provision for credit liabilities	X
	X

The *Local Government and Housing Act 1989* defined capital expenditure for local government in England. The definition is precise and incorporates the majority of expenditure relating to the following tangible assets:

- the acquisition, reclamation, enhancement or laying out of land, exclusive of roads, buildings and other structures
- the acquisition, construction, preparation, enhancement or replacement of roads, buildings and other structures
- the acquisition, installation or replacement of movable or immovable plant, machinery and apparatus, and vehicles and vessels
- the making of advances or grants or other financial assistance to any person towards expenditure incurred on any of the three previous categories
- the acquisition of share capital or loan capital in any body corporate in so far as it is not expenditure on approved investments
- powers given to the Secretary of State to direct that expenditure which he deems to be capital shall be classed as expenditure for capital purposes (these powers have been exercised subsequent to the act).

CIPFA guidance notes on the 1989 Act indicated that 'Expenditure on the acquisition of a tangible asset, or expenditure which adds to, and not merely maintains, the value of an existing asset, shall be capitalised and be classified as a fixed asset, provided that the fixed asset yields benefits to the authority and the services it provides for a period of more than one year'.

Fixed assets are presented net of *capital discharged.* This is the term used to describe the accumulated payments that have been made out of revenue and other sources, to pay for capital expenditure. Net fixed assets on the balance sheet are thus the total of capital expenditure less the portion that has been paid off.

Deferred charges represent expenditure which has been capitalised in the balance sheet but where there is no tangible asset. A deferred charge arises in two different situations:

- where expenditure is charged to capital and met from borrowing but there is no tangible asset, for example housing improvement grants, the cost of promoting a local act
- where an asset is sold or scrapped and the proceeds are insufficient to clear the outstanding debt, then the residual debt relating to that asset will constitute a deferred charge.

These charges are usually written down on an annual basis by the loan repayments so that their total is equal to the relevant loan debt outstanding.

Let us assume that a capital asset costing £200,000 financed entirely from loan, of which £30,000 remains outstanding, is scrapped. The account in balance sheet form before the asset is scrapped would be:

	£
Fixed asset	200,000
Less: Capital discharged – loans redeemed	170,000
	30,000
Financed by:	
Loans outstanding	30,000

	Dr £	Cr £
When scrapped, the journal entries would be:		—
Capital discharged account – loans redeemed	170,000	
Deferred charge	30,000	
Fixed asset account		200,000

Being the writing out of capital asset scrapped and raising of deferred charge in respect of outstanding loan

The account in balance sheet form would now show that the loan outstanding was not represented by any asset of current value.

	£
Deferred charge	30,000
Financed by:	
Loans outstanding	30,000

Long-term debtors owe amounts to an authority in respect of the sale proceeds of a fixed asset, with the payments being made to the authority over a number of years. This usually relates to council housing.

Long-term borrowing on the consolidated balance sheet is the total amount borrowed from external lenders but not repaid at the balance sheet date. On an individual service balance sheet this would be an internal loan (from the consolidated loans account) and would be classified as advances outstanding. The loans fund accounts record the amounts advanced to committees, and the amounts of external debt.

Deferred capital receipts are the credit side of the item long-term debtors. As payments are received, the deferred capital is written down by a transfer to capital receipts unapplied.

Let us assume that a long-term debtor pays a local authority £9,000. The journal entries would be:

	Dr £	Cr £
Cash account	9,000	
Long-term debtor		9,000

Being receipt of cash from long-term debtor

Deferred capital receipts	9,000	
Capital receipts unapplied		9,000

Being raising of capital receipt

After these journal entries we can see that the local authority has a capital receipt of £9,000 that it holds in cash.

Capital receipts unapplied are the proceeds from the sale of a fixed asset; such capital receipts can be used in one of two ways:

- to repay the debt on assets financed from loan
- to finance new capital expenditure.

With effect from 1 April 1990 the government has prescribed that certain proportions of capital receipts must be used to redeem debt, i.e. 75 per cent of council house sales receipts and 50 per cent of capital receipts from other asset disposals. This is known as the reserved part of the capital receipt and is transferred to the provision for credit liabilities (PCL). The remaining part of the capital receipt is called the usable part, and can be used to finance the purchase of fixed assets.

Financing capital expenditure by the application of capital receipts results in the capital receipts unapplied becoming utilised and being designated 'capital discharged–capital receipts applied'.

Example: capital receipts

A property which originally cost £70,000 and was financed by a loan that is now fully repaid, is sold for £20,000. The useable part of the capital receipt (i.e. £10,000 at 50 per cent) is to be used to finance the purchase of new machinery for the civic library.

Immediately prior to the sale of the property, the account in balance sheet form was as follows:

	£
Fixed asset	70,000
Less: capital discharged – loans repaid	70,000
	–

There is no outstanding finance.

The example above has five individual aspects and requires five separate journal entries. These entries are important to an understanding of the principles and should be carefully followed.

The five aspects (or steps) are:

a) the receipt from the sale and transfer of reserved part to the PCL
b) the writing out of the books (alienation) of the fixed asset sold
c) the acquisition of the new fixed assets
d) the financing of the new fixed assets
e) paying for the new fixed asset.

The journal entries required are as follows:

		Dr £	Cr £
a)	Cash account	20,000	
	Capital receipts unapplied account		20,000
	Capital receipts unapplied account	10,000	
	Provision for credit liabilities		10,000

*Being proceeds of sale of property and transfer of 50 per cent
of capital receipt to PCL*

b) Capital discharged – loans repaid	70,000	
Fixed asset account		70,000

Being alienation of property sold

c) Fixed asset account	20,000	
Creditors		20,000

Being purchase of new machinery

d) Capital receipts unapplied account	20,000	
Capital discharged–capital receipts applied		20,000

*Being financing of paintings by applying
capital receipts*

e) Creditor	20,000	
Cash account		20,000

Being payment of creditor from purchase of paintings

Immediately after all the transactions are recorded the balance sheet would appear as follows:

	£
Fixed asset (machinery)	20,000
Less: Capital discharged–capital receipts applied	20,000
	–

There is no outstanding finance.

Note that after all transactions are completed:

- the original fixed asset and its capital discharged have been completely removed from the ledgers, i.e. alienated
- there is no cash
- the whole of the capital receipt was applied to finance the new expenditure.

The next item to appear on the balance sheet is provisions. These are amounts set aside in the accounts for any liabilities or losses which it is anticipated are likely or certain to be incurred, but cannot be accurately quantified. The future amounts involved and exactly when they will arise are uncertain. This heading would include the balance of Repairs and Renewals account, if one was still operated.

Provision for credit liabilities (PCL) records all the sums set aside for the repayment of debt. These are the minimum revenue provisions (MRP) charged to the revenue accounts committees and the reserved part of the capital receipts. The balance on this account will be reduced when the debt is paid. The resources in this account will also be used to make further advances to committees. This will not result in a reduction on the balance on the account. The practical effect of this is that money set aside for the repayment of loans is used instead for making further advances to committees, so the original loans remain outstanding.

Relationship with revenue expenditure

CIPFA's standard classification of income and expenditure, detailed in Chapter 5, contains an expenditure heading Capital Financing Costs. It is there that the revenue account impact of capital expenditure transactions are analysed and published.

Financing capital expenditure

In addition to financing from capital receipts, capital expenditure may be financed from a number of sources, but principally from:

- loans
- direct revenue financing
- repair and renewals account.

The necessary accounting entries are illustrated below.

Assume a loan is raised for £60,000 and used to purchase a fixed asset. At the end of the year £3,000 of the loan is repaid and the revenue account is charged with the minimum revenue provision of £2,000 to be set aside for the repayment of debt.

The journal entries for the receipt of the loan and the purchase of the asset would be:

	Dr £	Cr £
Cash	60,000	
Loan outstanding		60,000
Being receipt of loan		
Fixed asset	60,000	
Cash		60,000
Being purchase of asset		

There are two sets of journal entries for the recording of the repayment of the loan. The first set relates to the reduction in cash and in the loan outstanding from the repayment of an external loan. These are:

	Dr £	Cr £
Loan outstanding	3,000	
Cash		3,000

The other set relates to the need to reduce the provision for credit liabilities, once part of the provision has been used to repay an external loan. Repaying external debt also creates a provision for capital discharged which only becomes capital discharged when the external debt has been repaid and a provision for credit liability has been established. Thus the second set of journal entries necessary for the repayment of external debt is:

	Dr £	Cr £
Provision for credit liability	3,000	
Provision for capital discharged		3,000

There are also two sets for the changing revenue account with the repayment of debt. It is at the point that the revenue account is charged that the loan is assumed to be redeemed from the standpoint of the capital discharged – loans redeemed. The first entries will be:

	Dr £	Cr £
Revenue account	2,000	
Capital discharged – loans redeemed		2,000

This causes the provision for capital discharged to be used up, and charging the revenue account with principal repayment of debt has the effect of increasing the provision for credit liabilities, so the other two entries are:

	Dr £	Cr £
Provision for capital discharged	2,000	
Provision for credit liabilities		2,000

Most local authorities finance a proportion of capital expenditure direct from revenue. In this case the whole of the capital expenditure is met from revenue in the year in which it is incurred, instead of over a period. Projects may be financed partly from loan and partly from revenue.

Using the finances in the previous example, and assuming that the fixed asset is to be financed by direct revenue financing, the journal entries would be:

		Dr £	Cr £
1)	Fixed asset account	60,000	
	Creditor		60,000

Being capital expenditure on project

		Dr £	Cr £
2)	Creditor	60,000	
	Cash		60,000

Being payment of creditor

3)	Revenue account – direct revenue financing	60,000	
	Capital discharged – direct revenue financing		60,000

Being payment of creditor

Notice that in the example just given, the three transactions are in respect of:

- acquisition
- payment
- financing.

Each of the three transactions must be dealt with separately using the correct double entry.

After the project has been completed, the account in balance sheet form would be:

	£
Fixed asset	60,000
Less: Capital discharged – direct revenue financing	60,000
	—

You can see that when a fixed asset has been fully financed and paid off, the balance sheet shows the net fixed asset figure and the 'financed by' figure as nil.

If we assume in the loan financing example above that there was a £2,000 overspending in respect of the £60,000 project, which was financed from revenue, then the balance sheet at the end of year one would show:

	£	£
Fixed asset		62,000
Less: Capital discharged – loan repaid	3,000	
Capital discharged – direct revenue financing	2,000	
		5,000
Net fixed asset		57,000
Financed by:		
Loan outstanding		57,000

The next situation concerns the financing of capital expenditure from a repair and renewals account. This fund is built up from contributions from the various revenue accounts, investment income and miscellaneous receipts. It is a separate 'fund' and would have been entitled as such before the LGHA(1989) came into force. The main difference between financing capital expenditure from direct revenue as district from financing it from a repair and renewals fund is that the making of the contribution from revenue to the account is not directly related to the use of the money to meet capital expenditure.

Assume that a repair and renewals account has a balance of £200,000 and that annual contributions from revenue are £20,000. Expenditure to be met from the fund in the year will be £60,000. The journal entries would be:

	Dr £	Cr £
Revenue Account	20,000	
Repair and renewals account		20,000

Being annual contribution

	Dr	Cr
Fixed assets	60,000	
Creditors account		60,000

Being purchase of fixed assets

	Dr	Cr
Creditors account	60,000	
Cash		60,000

Being payment of creditor

	Dr	Cr
Repairs and renewals account	60,000	
Capital discharged – Repair and renewals Account applied		60,000

Being application of repairs and renewals fund to meet the cost of fixed assets

A fourth alternative source of finance used to be from a capital fund set up by an authority and built up by contributions from the revenue account. From 1 April 1990 the powers under which the capital fund was established were repealed. However, some accounting statements will still refer to 'capital discharged–capital fund applied account'. This reflects the fact that the purchase of a fixed asset was financed from the capital fund prior to 1 April 1990.

Lease finance

A mention should be made at this point of lease finance, which enables the local authority to use capital assets without purchasing them outright. The most popular example is local government being in respect of computers where use is important, but ownership is not. Lease rental charges appear in the revenue account.

Under a lease contract, the legal title does not pass to the lessee. Leases may be classified as either finance leases or operating leases. The distinction is important for local authorities as leases are included within the definition of credit arrangements referred to in the section above. The Secretary of State for the Environment is able to define by regulation descriptions of leases which are to be excluded from being credit arrangements. Thus, Regulation 6 of the *Local Authorities (Capital Finance) Regulations* exempts operating leases of any vehicles, vessel, plant machinery or apparatus from being a credit management. Finance leases are not exempt. The exemption of operating leases from the capital expenditure controls provides local authorities with an incentive to enter into operating leases provided the requirements of the legislation can be fulfilled.

The key characteristics that distinguish operating leases from finance leasing are as follows.

- the property in the asset must not pass to the local authority. Ownership of the asset must remain with the lessor. This must be the case both in the primary lease period and in any subsequent period where there is a renewal or continuation of the lease. There must be no option to purchase the asset at any time.
- operating leases are those which do not provide for an extension of the lease for a further period at less than open market rentals. This is frequently the case in finance leases where there is provision to extend the initial lease period of the asset at a peppercorn or nominal rate.
- the value of the asset at the lease expiry date must not accrue directly or indirectly to the local authority; the lease expiry date can be the end of both the primary and subsequent periods. This in practice means that the local authority cannot usually benefit from any sale proceeds. This contrasts with a finance lease where frequently a majority of the sale proceeds are kept by the local authority in return for acting as the lessor's agent in disposing of the asset.
- finally, the termination value of the asset under an operating lease at the end of the lease must equal or exceed 10 per cent of its value at the commencement of the lease. This termination value is estimated by the local authority on commencement of the lease. This figure is likely to be 10 per cent of the price at which the asset could be purchased at the commencement date of the lease.

Finance leases contrast with all the above criteria of operating leases in that a finance lease substantially transfers to the lessee all the risks and rewards of ownership of an asset. It is a lease of a long-term nature, i.e. it is intended that the lessee will have use of the asset for the greater part of the asset's useful life.

Capital ledger accounts

The points made so far can now be illustrated in ledger account form, as follows:

At 31 March 1993 the general fund balance sheet of a local authority showed the following balances:

	£
Fixed assets (of this £6m is buildings and £3m infrastructure)	9,000,000
Cash	60,000
Loans outstanding	6,600,000
Capital discharged – loans repaid	1,520,000
Capital discharged – direct revenue financing	510,000
Capital receipts unapplied	30,000
Provision for credit liabilities	400,000

During 1993/94 the following transactions took place.

1) Capital expenditure includes expenditure on projects totalling £93,500 met by revenue contribution.
2) Capital expenditure during the year was:

	£
Fixed assets – buildings	990,000
Fixed assets – infrastructure	715,000
	1,705,000

3) Loans raised amounted to £1,540,000.
4) Charge to the revenue account for debt repayment amounted to £440,000. There was no external repayment of debt.
5) A capital receipt of £55,000 was received. Note that 50 per cent of this, i.e. £27,500. will need to be transferred to the provision for credit liabilities.
6) Capital receipts totalling £50,000 were used to finance a buildings project, (already included in the above expenditure).

Example

Prepare ledger accounts to record the transactions and draw up the balance sheet as at 31 March 1994.

Solution

Loans outstanding account

		£			£
			Apr 1	Balance b/f	6,600,000
Mar 31	Balance c/f	8,140,000	1993–4	Cash account	1,540,000
		8,140,000			8,140,000

Capital discharged (loans redeemed) account

		£			£
			Apr 1	Balance b/f	1,520,000
Mar 31	Balance c/f	1,960,000	1993–4	Revenue account provision for repayment	440,000
		1,960,000			1,960,000

Capital discharged (DRF) account

		£			£
			Apr 1	Balance b/f	510,000
Mar 31	Balance c/f	603,500	1993–4	Revenue account contribution	93,500
		603,500			603,500

Capital discharged (capital receipts applied) account

		£			£
Mar 31	Balance c/f	50,000	1993–4	Capital receipts unapplied	50,000

Provision for capital discharged

		£			£
Mar 31	Balance c/f	440,000	Mar 31	Revenue account	

Provision for credit liabilities

		£			£
			Apr 1	Balance b/f	400,000
Mar 31	Balance c/f	867,500	1993–4	Provision for capital discharged	440,000
				Capital receipts unapplied	27,500
		867,500			867,500

Capital receipts unapplied account

			£			£
1993-94	Capital discharged (PCL)		27,500	Apr 1	Balance b/f	30,000
	(capital receipts applied account		50,000	1993-94	Cash account	55,000
Mar 31	Balance c/f		7,500			
			85,000			85,000

Fixed assets – Buildings

		£			£
Apr 1	Balance b/f	6,000,000			
1993-94	Cash account	990,000	Mar 31	Balance c/f	6,990,000
		6,990,000			6,990,000

Fixed assets – Infrastructure account

		£			£
Apr 1	Balance b/f	3,000,000			
	Cash account	715,000	Mar 31	Balance c/f	3,715,000
		3,715,000			3,715,000

Cash account (capital only)

		£			£
Apr 1	Balance b/f	60,000	Mar 31	Fixed assets account	1,705,000
	Revenue account				
1993-94	cash				
	transferred	93,500			
	Loans raised	1,540,000			
	Revenue account	440,000			
	Capital receipts a/c	55,000		Balance c/f	483,500
		2,188,500			2,188,500

The effect of the above transactions on the revenue accounts within the general fund would be as follows:

	£
Capital financing costs	
Loans – principal repayments	440,000 Dr
Direct revenue financing	93,500 Dr
	533,500 Dr
Reduction in revenue account cash (transferred to capital cash account)	533,500 Cr

Balance sheet as at 31 March 1994

	£	£
Fixed assets		10,705,000
Capital discharged		
Loans repaid	1,960,000	
Direct revenue financing	603,500	
Capital receipts applied	50,000	
Provision for capital discharged	(440,000)	
		2,173,500
Total long-term assets		8,531,500
Cash		483,500
		9,015,000
Financed by:		
Loans outstanding		8,140,000
Capital receipts unapplied		7,500
Provision for credit liabilities		867,500
		9,015,000

Writing down capital expenditure

Fixed assets recorded in the books of account at cost will remain as long as they exist and are of use. When they cease to exist, are sold or are scrapped they are written out or 'alienated'. Where there are deferred charges, these will be written out by a relevant amount each year to the extent that any capital liability incurred in respect of them has been discharged. Writing a fixed asset out of the books requires the establishment of the ledger balances existing in respect of the particular fixed asset. There are likely to be three aspects to this.

- the figure (at cost or market value) in the fixed asset account
- the amount financed relating to the fixed asset and included in one or more capital discharged accounts
- the amount of any loan outstanding in respect of the fixed asset (for fixed assets written off because they have reached the end of their loan period, this will be nil).

Where no liability exists, the fixed asset value (debit) and the total capital discharged (credit) will be equal, and thus the balance sheet figure of net fixed assets will be nil. Here, alienation will be achieved by crediting the fixed asset account and entering the corresponding debit in the capital discharged account (or accounts).

Earlier we considered a project that cost £62,000. £60,000 was financed from a loan repayable over 20 years and £2,000 from direct revenue financing. If the fixed asset is scrapped after the loan has been entirely repaid, the entries to write out the asset would be:

	Dr £	Cr £
Capital discharged – loan redeemed	60,000	
Capital discharged – direct revenue financing	2,000	
fixed asset		62,000

Being alienation of asset

Using capital receipts

Usable capital receipts can be used to repay outstanding debt:

- on the particular asset sold; or
- generally, i.e. debt outstanding on any fixed assets, other than the one giving rise to the capital receipt in line with government guidelines.

Remember that apart from housing, 50 per cent of capital receipts must be transferred to the provision for credit liabilities.

The following example is of an asset costing £20,000, which is sold for £28,000, and has a loan of £8,000 outstanding on it at the time of the sale. The outstanding loan is to be set up as a deferred charge but then paid off using part of the capital receipt.

	Dr £	Cr £
Cash	28,000	
Capital receipts unapplied		28,000
Capital receipts unapplied	14,000	
Provision for credit liabilities		14,000

Being capital receipt due on sale of asset

	Dr £	Cr £
Capital discharged – loans redeemed	12,000	
Deferred charge account	8,000	
Fixed asset account		20,000

Being alienation of fixed asset sold and raising of deferred charge

£14,000 of capital receipt remains unapplied. If this were used to pay off loans outstanding on the assets sold, the entries would be:

	Dr £	Cr £
Loans outstanding account	8,000	
Cash		8,000

Being repayment of loans outstanding

	Dr £	Cr £
Capital receipts unapplied	8,000	
Deferred charged		8,000

Being application of capital receipt to repay debt outstanding on fixed asset sold

The accounts in balance sheet form would now be:

	£
Cash £28,000 – 8,000	20,000
Capital receipts unapplied	6,000
Provision for credit liabilities	14,000
	20,000

There is no capital discharged–capital receipts applied account, because no new capital expenditure has been created.

Writing out deferred charges

Deferred charges should be written off as soon as possible as they show the extent of the liabilities of the local authority not balanced by equivalent assets. Therefore at the same time as loans are repaid, the deferred charges account should be written down.

Assume that £60,000 expenses had been incurred in promoting a local act and that the money had been borrowed over ten years. As loan repayments are made, the deferred charge will be written off to revenue account as follows:

	Dr £	Cr £
Loans outstanding	6,000	
Cash account		6,000
Being instalment of loan repaid		
Revenue account	6,000	
Deferred charges account		6,000
Being provision for repayment of an instalment of loan represented by a deferred charge		

Internal transfers and appropriations

Capital expenditure on purchase of assets can only be undertaken in accordance with statutory powers. These powers are usually specific to a service purpose or function. As a consequence, an authority may buy land or construct buildings for a service under legislation relating to that service, but with the passage of time and the changing needs of services, it very frequently happens that one service may cease to need one of its assets, but another service could very well use it. In these circumstances, the asset will be transferred. It is usual practice and sometimes a statutory requirement, to register the transfer between the account of the selling and buying services. Even though the overall position of the authority does not change, the transfers do enable the costs associated with each service to be properly maintained. Such transfers are called 'appropriations'. Land appropriations will normally require a formal resolution of the local authority, and in certain circumstances, i.e. where grant is involved, central government approval may also be required.

Accounting entries

Land or assets which are transferred within the same authority may be recorded in two main ways, according to the particular circumstances of the transfer.

1   Transfer at historic cost, i.e. where there has been capital value appreciation
The method for dealing with such a transfer involves firstly the need to draw up a balance sheet prior to transfer, and from it open up the appropriate ledger accounts, and then to

transfer the asset, loans and capital discharged to the new committee, after having reduced the former committee's balances to nil.

Example

A piece of land which originally cost £120,000 and which was financed partly from revenue (£10,000) and the balance from loan, on which £60,000 is outstanding, is transferred from Education to Social Services.

a) **In the books of the Education Committee:**
— Opening balance sheet

			£	£
Fixed asset				120,000
Less:	Capital discharged			
	Direct revenue financing	20,000		
	Loans repaid	40,000		
			60,000	
				60,000
				60,000
Financed by:				
Loans fund advances				60,000

— Journal entries required to eliminate asset
  from Education books

		Dr	Cr
		£	£
Loans fund advances		60,000	
Capital discharged			
Direct revenue financing		20,000	
Loans repaid		40,000	
Fixed assets			120,000

b) **In the books of the Social Services Committee**

	Dr	Cr
	£	£
Fixed assets	120,000	
Loans outstanding		60,000
DRF		20,000
Loans repaid		40,000

Thus, the journal entries 'mirror' each other and the balance sheet entries for Education now appear in the Social Services Committee accounts.

2   Transfer at enhanced value, i.e. where the asset to be transferred has increased in value

Using the figures in the previous example, assume that the land which cost £120,000 is now valued at £180,000, so that the Social Services Committee has to pay Education the 'appreciation' sum of £120,000, after allowing for the £60,000 outstanding loan to be taken over

The journal entries in each set of books are similar to those already set out, but in addition the cash adjustment needs to be recorded, as follows:

a) **In Education books**

	Dr £	Cr £
Debtors – Social Services Committee	120,000	
To revenue account – Income - Revenue appropriation adjustments		120,000

b) **In Social Services books**

	Dr £	Cr £
Revenue account – Capital financing Costs – revenue appropriation adjustments	120,000	
Creditors – Education Committee		120,000
Capital cash	120,000	
Capital discharged – Revenue appropriation adjustments		120,000

The first journal entry in each committee's books will be cleared to reflect the transfer of cash when the payment actually takes place. The second entry for Social Services has recorded the extent to which the transferred asset has been paid for.

Loans pooling

Introduction

The *Local Government Act 1972* gives general authority for local authorities to borrow money. An authority can therefore choose the type of borrowing which best suits its circumstances or the financial conditions at the time of borrowing.

Initially authorities borrowed specifically for each project or transaction, and loans were 'earmarked' to that expenditure. In some circumstances such as mortgages, these were made as a specific charge on the asset concerned. This procedure was very much like that of the general houseowner with a mortgage. With the expansion of local authority activity, and the size of even the smallest authority's asset holdings, this procedure became far too cumbersome, and the concept of loans pooling developed.

In support of this concept the *Local Government Act 1972* provided that all money borrowed by a local authority should be charged indifferently on all the revenues of the authority. This, therefore, supersedes the practice of specific mortgaging of property and gives the lender powers to enforce his rights, if an authority fails to meet its liabilities, by giving him powers to raise revenues similar to those bestowed on the authority.

Paragraph 15 of Schedule 13 to the *Local Government Act 1972* provides:

'A local authority may, in accordance with a scheme made by them, establish and operate a loans fund for defraying any expenditure which the authority are authorised by or under any enactment to meet out of monies borrowed …'

CIPFA originally produced a model 'consolidated loans fund' scheme and most authorities based their schemes on this model, although the word 'fund' can no longer be used legally and the term 'loans account' is used in the example below.

The concept of a loans account is very like the role of a building society, whereby the fund borrows money from any approved source at varying rates of interest and for varying periods, in order to lend to borrowing service accounts for fixed periods to finance their approved capital expenditure.

Repaying a loan (internally) is different from redeeming a debt (externally), and the loans account concept of pooling developed. Under the system of loans pooling, only the loans account is regarded as borrowing money, whether from one of the many external sources available or from funds internal to the authority. Cash is advanced from the account to other accounts of the authority to meet capital expenditure. These are the 'borrowing' accounts in loans account terminology; the annual sums provided from revenue to redeem debt are paid by the borrowing accounts back to the loans account where they are merged and become available, together with any external loans raised, for advancing to borrowing accounts. All interest on loans paid in a financial year is paid by the loans account in the first instance, and then recharged to the borrowing accounts at an average rate. Administrative costs are also recharged at an average rate.

As all the sums provided from revenue to redeem debt by the borrowing accounts are automatically available for new capital purposes, external debt is kept to a minimum. The operation of a loans account results in a cross-subsidisation, through the averaging arrangements for interest charge calculations between different accounts. Thus, if the housing committee borrows heavily when interest rates are higher than the average pool rate, it will benefit from the averaging process at the expense of other accounts.

The consolidated loans account therefore:

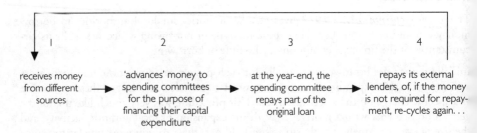

1	2	3	4
receives money from different sources	'advances' money to spending committees for the purpose of financing their capital expenditure	at the year-end, the spending committee repays part of the original loan	repays its external lenders, of, if the money is not required for repayment, re-cycles again…

Capital transactions of the loans account

The accounts of the loans account are split into two types of transaction – capital which deals with the movement of capital borrowings, advances and repayments – and revenue, which handles the interest and administrative costs and their recoupment from borrowing accounts.

The capital transactions section looks like this:

Capital transactions for the year ended 31 March 1994

£'000

Cash balance at 1 April 1993
(Invested)   X

Loan transactions during the year

	Amounts raised (1)	Amounts repaid (2)	Net change (3)	
(Analysis of individual	X	X	X	
types of borrowing)	X	X	(X)	
	X	X	(X)	
	—	—	—	
Net total raised by loans				X
		—	—	
Bank overdraft increase/decrease				X
				—
				X

Borrowing transactions during the year

	Advances (3)	Amounts repaid (4)	Net change (3-4)	
Housing	X	X	X	
Recreation	X	X	(X)	
Refuse collection	X	X	X	
Transport	X	X	X	
	—	—	—	
Net total of advances				X
	—	—	—	

Other capital transactions

Profit on purchase of stock		X
---------------------------		-
Capital receipts		X
		—
Cash balance at 31 March 1994		X
		—

Revenue transactions of the loans account

a) **Interest transactions**

£'000

Interest paid to external lenders (analysed by type of borrowing)   X
Less: Investment interest received   X
                                                                      —

Balance – net interest cost recharged to borrowing accounts   X
at an average rate of A % (see page 133)   X
   –
   –

b) **Debt management expenses**

£'000

Operating costs   – Salaries and on-costs   X
   – Running costs   X
   – Other   X

   X

Less: Miscellaneous income   X

   X

Balance – net management cost recharged to borrowing accounts
at an average rate of B % (see page 134)   X
   –
   –

The bases of recharging interest and administrative costs

● Interest – it is usual for net interest to be apportioned at the year end, pro rata to advances outstanding at the beginning of the year, plus an equated amount for advances during the year.
● Management expenses – the basis for interest is used, except that advances outstanding at the end of the year are used.

Having said that, authorities may employ their own method and need not follow these bases. Examples of each calculation are as follows:

Advances £'000

| Committee | Outstanding at 1 April | Advanced during year | | | Outstanding at 31 March |
		30 Sept	31 March	Repaid	31 March
Education	29,000	1,500	3,750	2,000	32,250
Recreation and Amenities	725	–	–	150	575
Environment	825	500	–	75	1,250
Transport	1,125	500	500	125	2,000
	31,675	2,500	4,250	2,350	36,075

Using an interest paid figure of £2,800,000, the basis of apportionment would be as follows:

Advances £'000

Committee	Outstanding at 1 April	During year	Equated to full year equivalent	Total equated outstanding during year
Education	29,000	1,500	750	29,750
Recreation and Amenities	725	–	–	725
Environment	825	500	250	1,075
Transport	1,125	500	250	1,375
	31,675	2,500	1,250	32,925

It is normal practice to convert the advances made during the year to a sum equivalent to that which would give the same interest if a full year rate was applied; for example interest on £1,000 for half a year is equivalent to annual interest on half £1,000 for a full year. Advances made on 31 March (i.e. at the year end) are ignored.

The basic calculation using the above information is therefore as follows:

	£
Advances at beginning of year	31,675,000
Advances during year converted or equated to a full year equivalent 1,000,000 ÷ 2	1,250,000
	32,925,000

$$\text{Average or 'pool' rate} = \frac{2,800,000}{32,925,000} = 8.5\%$$

Interest can therefore be apportioned to borrowing accounts on the basis of 8.5 per cent of their equated outstanding advances as follows:

	Equated advances o/s £'000	Interest @ 8.5% £'000
Education	29,750	2,530
Recreation and amenities	725	63
Environment	1,075	90
Transport	1,375	117
	32,925	2,800

On the basis of the above example, the apportionment of total debt management expenses of £240,000 would give an average percentage basis of apportionment of 0.66 per cent, calculated as follows:

Expenses to be apportioned   £240,000 (a)

Advances outstanding at 31 March   £36,075,000 (b)

$$\text{Average rate} \quad \frac{(a)}{(b)} = 0.66\%$$

The impact of the 1993 Accounting Code of Practice

At several places during this chapter reference has been made to dissatisfaction with the method of accounting for capital in local government. This debate has rumbled on for over twenty years and caused vigorous and at times bitter debate in the profession. At a time when various factors were combining to make local government more commercially accountable and its published financial information more directly comparable, the flexibility for treatment of capital finance and accounting left much to be desired.

Following the *1989 Local Government and Housing Act*, CIPFA, with positive support from the Department of the Environment, published consultative proposals on a new system of capital accounting to correct defects in the present system. These defects were:

- The way in which the expenditure on the fixed asset is financed is reflected in the service revenue account and may distort the performance of the service managers in a financial year. For example, if the purchase of a fixed asset was financed from loan there would be an annual charge to the revenue account, the principal repayment, as well as an annual charge for interest on the balance outstanding. On the other hand, if the purchase was financed directly from revenue, direct revenue financing, the impact of this may turn a revenue account surplus into a revenue account deficit in the year of purchase as the full cost of the purchase will be charged to the revenue account in that year.
- The fixed assets are recorded in the balance sheet at historic cost and so their current worth to the local authority is not reflected. The net fixed assets figure in the balance sheet becomes less as loans are repaid, i.e. as the capital discharged figure increases.
- The fact that there is no depreciation accounting in the local authority accounting system is not in line with accepted and recognised commercial practice.
- Financial management within local authority services is made difficult by the present system of capital accounting, because managers do not know the true cost of using local authority fixed assets. Charges for services may therefore be set too high or too low.

In the 1993 *Accounting Code of Practice*, CIPFA announced its recommendations for local authority capital accounting, expected to be in force for the 1994/95 financial year. The status of the code as a proper accounting practice under the 1989 Act is described in Chapter 3.

The main features of these proposals are:

- the use of accruals in capital accounting
- local authorities must compile fixed asset registers
- fixed assets will be shown in balance sheets at current cost and be revalued regularly
- depreciation will be charged on the current value of the assets
- a 'cost of capital' charge will be made on assets held in service.

Such an accounting system will improve on current practice by:

- separating the accounting for assets and the cost of using them from the way in which they are financed
- accounting for the full current cost of using assets to provide services
- recording the current value of assets under the control of the authority
- making services bear a cost of capital charge, whereas the actual cost of repaying principal and interest will be borne by the authority as a whole.

These proposals were subsequently formally set out in the September 1993 *Accounting Code of Practice*. The relevant capital paragraphs of the code are summarised below.

13   All expenditure on the acquisition, creation or enhancement of fixed assets should be capitalised on an accruals basis. The two basic requirements for classification as a fixed asset are that the expenditure should yield a benefit to the authority and provide a service for a period of more than one year.

14/15   Lists expenditure which should be capitalised and defines enhancement as expenditure which either lengthens the useful life of an asset or substantially increases its market value.

16   Improvement works and structural repairs should be capitalised but not jobbing maintenance, painting or decorating.

17/18   Assets acquired under finance leases or for other than a cash consideration should be capitalised.

19/21   Infrastructure assets should be included in the balance sheet at historical cost less any depreciation.

22/24   Assets included in the balance sheet at current value should be formally revalued at intervals of not more than five years. There is provision for an annual review of values where they may have materially changed and also the creation of a fixed asset restatement reserve to reflect the pluses/minuses of revaluations.

25/27   Income from the disposal of fixed assets should be credited to the usable capital receipts reserve and the book value of the assets written off against the fixed asset restatement reserve.

28/29   Depreciation on a realistic life basis should be provided for all fixed assets, except for freehold land or non-operational investment properties.

34/39   Revenue accounts should include a capital charge for all fixed assets used in the provision of a service. This should as a minimum cover the annual depreciation provision plus a capital financing charge at a specified notional rate of interest.

All expenditure on the repair and maintenance of fixed assets should be charged to the service revenue account.

An asset management revenue account should be created and this account will be:

- debited with interest payable and provision for depreciation
- credited with the capital charges for the use of a fixed asset appearing in service revenue accounts.

Main objectives of the code

CIPFA's principal objective is developing a new system of accounting for fixed assets by local authorities was to improve external financial reporting and thereby promote accountability by local authorities for the use of capital. It was also intended to provide current balance sheet information about assets held by an authority, by including a current cost for the use of capital in the revenue accounts of individual services.

The Code of Practice defines the basis on which both fixed assets should be included in the balance sheet and charges to service revenue accounts should be determined. CIPFA believes that within the framework and requirements of the Code, much is left to the discretion of individual authorities. In this respect, it is worth recalling that the code had its origins back in 1987, because of the need for self-regulation to head off detailed accounting prescription by the government. Uniformity is not what the code seeks to achieve. It is concerned with consistency and comparability.

Principles of the new system

The statement below sets out the current position, which shows the clear link between borrowing and accounting. Borrowing is the main source of finance for capital programmes and is also the basis of government spending controls, so a bias in that direction is understandable. The value of assets and their depiction in the balance sheet leaves much to be desired.

Traditional capital accounting methods

Charges to revenue for capital assets are determined by the method of financing the asset in question:

Financing method	Revenue charges
Directly from revenue budget	100 per cent of asset cost in that year's revenue account.
From capital receipts (i.e. reserves accumulated from past asset sales)	No revenue charge in any year
Borrowing	Annual charges of principal repayment (2 or 4 per cent of debt outstanding, known as minimum revenue provision), plus interest on debt outstanding

Balance sheet values are based on historical cost or debt outstanding

To deal with the unsatisfactory asset position, four categories of asset, each with its own rules on valuation and capital charging have been devised. The new categories of capital asset are as follows:

- operational assets: held, occupied or consumed by the council in the direct delivery of services for which it has a statutory or discretionary responsibility; they include council houses, schools, vehicles and computers
- non-operational assets: fixed assets held by the council but not used directly for service delivery; they include commercial and investment property
- infrastructure: inalienable (cannot be transferred out of the council's possession) fixed assets, expenditure on which is recoverable only by continued use of the asset created, for example highways, footpaths, sea defences
- community assets: held in perpetuity with no determinable useful life, often with use restrictions; these include parks or historic buildings.

These categories will be reported separately in the balance sheet and, of course, categorisation affects the basis of valuation and the capital charge to service revenue accounts. These capital charges are a combination of depreciation and notional interest. This is a compromise as, if 'pure' depreciation had been employed, services would have borne no charges for land and similar non-depreciating assets. The valuation bases and capital charges for the different categories of asset are as follows:

Type of asset	Balance sheet valuation	Capital charge (to revenue)
Operational	The lesser of: * Net current replacement cost Net realisable value in existing use	Depreciation plus notional interest (a) Some operational assets are exempt or from depreciation including: * Freehold land * If the council can demonstrate it carries out regular repairs and maintenance to extend the asset's life
Non-operational	As operational If land has planning permission for an alternative use which raises its value, this should be used for the net realisable value.	Notional interest (a), but no depreciation
Infrastructure	Depreciated historical cost	Depreciation plus notional interest (b)
Community assets	Historical cost	Notional interest (b), but no depreciation

Interest rates

The rate used for operational and non-operational assets is the government-set rate of return for council direct service organisations (DSOs). This is currently 6 per cent.

For infrastructure and community assets, a borrowing rate charged by the government-backed Public Works Loan Board is used. This is the rate charged on 1 October preceding the financial year for 25-year loans.

As the final statement shows, there is a system to 'reverse' the new capital charged back to traditional debt charges so that there is no impact on council taxpayers. This example takes an asset on which the annual depreciation has been calculated as £50, along with notional interest of £30. Under the old system, the charge for this asset would have been actual interest on debt outstanding of £20 plus a minimum revenue provision of £10 (see the table on page 136 for minimum revenue provision definition).

The new system credits capital charges to the asset management revenue account (AMRA). This is, in effect, a central property holding account. It earns asset income (the new capital charges), and pays for depreciation and interest (actual, not notional!).

Higher service charges

In a council's consolidated revenue account, individual service costs (education, housing, etc.) will be higher than under the old system, because many assets were charge-free under traditional methods.

But there is also likely to be a considerable credit on the asset management revenue account (many of the assets on which notional interest arises will, in reality, be debt-free), so the increased service costs will be offset by the property holding surplus, before calculating net operating cost. In our example this is a £10 adjustment.

Even with that adjustment, the new property charges will be higher. The depreciation on assets will usually be much greater than the minimum revenue provision, so that surplus, too, needs to be credited back to taxpayers before reporting the cost to taxpayers (in our example, a further £40 adjustment)

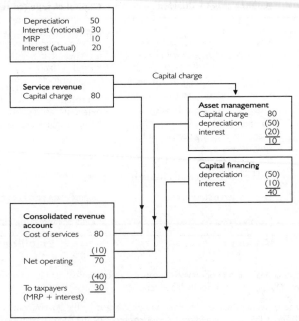

Individual services include the new capital charges; traditional costs are council-wide.

The deadline for the introduction of the new system is the 1994/95 final accounts, though councils which are being reorganised are exempt from this requirement.

6 Balance sheets and supporting statements

This chapter first examines the general purpose and structure of balance sheets. It then considers (a) the statutory requirements so far as they affect the balance sheets of local authorities; (b) horizontal and vertical balance sheets; (c) fund balance sheets and consolidated balance sheets; (d) national recommendations to support and provide more detailed information about the picture shown by a balance sheet; (e) the Consolidated Statement of Revenue and Capital Movements; and (f) items excluded by law from a local authority's balance sheet.

What is a balance sheet?

The balance sheet is a statement of the local authority's values at a particular point in time, usually the 31 March at the end of each financial year. It shows on one side the valuables owned by the authority (its 'assets') and on the other, amounts owed to other people (its 'liabilities'). To this extent, the balance sheet of a local authority is no different from that of a business, but some of the terminology, particularly that relating to capital accounting, is unique to local government. There will be no heading for capital, as would apply for a business or a limited company, and the analysis of fixed assets (extensively revised in the *1993 Accounting Code of Practice*) will be different from that normally met in accounting exercises. Apart from that, the traditional principles of balance sheet preparation apply and these principles underpin the recommended balance sheet layout in the *1993 Accounting Code*.

To recap, the simplified balance sheet of a limited company, will look, in its traditional 'two-sided' format like this:

Example ————————————————————————————————

Assets		Liabilities	
Property	155,000	Capital	202,250
Stock	120,500	Loan	106,000
Debtors	17,000	Creditors	16,000
Cash at bank	31,750		
	£324,250		£324,250

Or, using the vertical format, which focuses on shareholders equity:

Example

	£	£
Assets:		
Property		155,000
Current assets:		
Stock	120,500	
Debtors	17,000	
Cash	31,750	
	169,250	
Less: Current liabilities:		
Creditors	16,000	
Net current assets		153,250
Less: Long term liabilities:		
Bank loan		(106,000)
Net total assets		202,250
Capital:		
Ordinary shares		150,000
Retained profits		52,250
		202,250

This total of 'Capital' is equivalent to the equity of the business and represents the owners claims upon the business. It is an integral part of what is termed the balance sheet equation:

Assets = Liabilities + Equity

Local authority statutory requirements

The *Local Government, Planning and Land Act 1980*, requires that each local authority must produce an annual report and that the report shall contain relevant accounts. The local authority will finalise its financial year after each 31 March and there is a requirement to prepare accounts by 30 September and publish them by 31 December. The extent of publication will be determined by each authority and is considered further in Chapter 3 and Chapter 11. The *Accounts and Audit Regulations 1983*, require that the annual statement of accounts, produced by a local authority should include:

- a summary of the income and expenditure of each fund or undertaking
- a summary statement of capital expenditure and how financed
- a consolidated balance sheet.

The balance sheet is a different type of financial statement to the revenue account, which accounts for a year's transactions and shows the resulting surplus or deficit on an account.

A balance sheet depicts the state of the local authority, or an account thereof, at one moment in time, i.e. the 31 March in each year. The balance sheet lists the assets (amounts owned) and liabilities (amounts owed) as at that particular date.

Prior to the *Local Government and Housing Act 1989* there was a statutory requirement for a separate fund accounting system to be maintained for each function, activity or service provided and administered by a local authority. A fund balance sheet was produced for each function, activity or service, but this was not published. A consolidated balance sheet was and continues to be produced for the authority as a whole. This is included with the other published financial statements in the annual report.

The *Local Government and Housing Act 1989* repealed existing statutory provisions to set up separate funds. However, local authorities may continue to produce revenue accounts and balance sheets of service committees on 31 March each year as part of the system of financial management and control within a local authority.

The balance sheet is required, to comply with the Regulations, to show any corresponding amounts for the previous financial year or accounting period.

The *1993 Code of Practice on Local Authority Accounting for Great Britain* (ACOP) published by CIPFA states that a local authority's published statement of accounts shall include a consolidated balance sheet. It describes the consolidated balance sheet thus:

> this statement is fundamental to the understanding of an authority's year end financial position. It shows the balances and reserves at an authority's disposal and its long-term indebtedness, the fixed and current assets employed in its operations, together with summarised information on the fixed assets held. It excludes the superannuation fund, trust funds, and similar funds administered for third parties.

The Code does not specify that balance sheets of service committees, or of the general fund, need to be published. Local authorities have the discretion to publish summarised statements relating to service committees. The production of a consolidated balance sheet, involves the consolidation of various fund balance sheets maintained by a local authority. The format for both a fund balance sheet and a consolidated balance sheet can, of course, be the same.

Types of balance sheet – horizontal and vertical

Balance sheets, employed in local government, are those recommended from time to time by CIPFA and, at present, two types of balance sheet may be prepared – tabular or narrative. Tabular or traditional 'two-sided' balance sheets are often used for service or specific accounts. Narrative balance sheets are employed for those areas of work that have a trading connotation. That, however, is not a hard and fast rule. The published consolidated balance sheet, is now invariably produced in a narrative format and this style is recommended in CIPFA's Standard Form and in the 1993 ACOP. These types of balance sheet may also be referred to as 'horizontal' and 'vertical' respectively.

Example _____

Structure of a 'horizontal' balance sheet

	£	£		£	£
Long-term liabilities			Fixed assets		
	X			X	
	X			X	
	X			X	
	X			X	
	—			—	
		X			X
Current liabilities			Current assets		
	X			X	
	X			X	
	X			X	
	X			X	
	—			—	
		X			X
Provisions					
	X				
	X				
	X				
	—				
		X			
Other balances		X	Other balances		X
		X			X
		—			—

_____

Example _____

Structure of a 'narrative' balance sheet

	£	£	£
Fixed assets			
		X	
		X	
		X	
		X	
		—	
			X
Current assets			
		X	
		X	
		X	

$$\begin{array}{r} X \\ \hline X \end{array}$$

Less: Current liabilities

$$\begin{array}{r} X \\ X \\ X \\ \hline X \end{array}$$

$$\overline{X}$$

Net current assets/liabilities

$$\begin{array}{r} X \\ \hline X \end{array}$$

Long term liabilities

$$\begin{array}{r} X \\ X \\ X \\ X \\ \hline X \end{array}$$

Because of the wide diversity of services and undertakings run by local authorities, it is usual to split the final accounts into the following distinct sections:

- *General or county funds* – general fund (district council) and county fund (county council) services are those services provided by a local authority which are financed from council tax, business rates and government grant. The fund accounting system operated within an individual local authority produces information so that the expenditure and income in relation to each service provided can be identified within the general fund for each financial year.
- *Trading undertakings* – trading undertakings or trading services relate to services where the local authority decides overall policy on charging, etc., and where the aim of the service is to break even, i.e., raise sufficient income to cover expenditure.

Each undertaking produces an annual trading account based on the CIPFA standard form, a balance sheet and supporting capital statements (see Chapter 7).

- *Direct service organisations* – these organisations carry out a variety of work on a commercial basis. Annual accounts are based on CIPFA's 1993 ACOP as detailed in Chapter 7.
- *Collection funds* – the fund accounts for the proceeds of the council tax and the business rate. Annual accounts are based on CIPFA recommendations, contained in the 1993 ACOP and are detailed in Chapter 7.
- *Trust funds* – trust funds are those funds operated but not owned by a local authority. The superannuation fund is the most common example and there may be other monies where the local authority acts as a trustee. Annual accounts, comprising a revenue account and a statement of net assets are recommended by CIPFA in the 1993 ACOP (see Chapter 7).

In addition and pending the full implementation of the capital accounting requirements of CIPFA's 1993 Accounting Code, some authorities still maintain a consolidated loans account. Loans accounts relate to the funds managed by a local authority to finance capital expenditure and the repair, replacement or renewal of plant, machinery, vehicles and equipment. Annual accounts are produced based on CIPFA recommendations, and are covered in detail in Chapter 5.

Fund balance sheets

Each of these types of fund or account will have its own format of balance sheet which, as indicated, are described and depicted in more detail in other chapters of this book.

Where a fund balance sheet is prepared for an individual service, e.g. education, it can be produced on either the tabular or narrative basis. Invariably, for published purposes, the narrative format will be used, but if more traditional methods are employed, the broad structure of the balance sheet will be as follows with figures for the previous year also shown for purposes of broad comparison:

Example _____

Local authority fund balance sheet as at 31 March 1994

	£	£		£	£
Long term liabilities			Fixed assets		
Loans outstanding			(detailed in statement		
Consolidated loans			of fixed assets)*		X
account	X				
Stock	X				
Mortgages	X				
Superannuation fund loans	X				
Other internal loans	X				
	X				
Current liabilities			Current assets		
Temporary borrowing	X		Work in progress	X	
Creditors	X		Stocks	X	
Internal advances	X		Investments	X	
Cash overdrawn	X		Debtors – deferred	X	
			– others	X	
		X	Cash	X	
					X
Provisions	X				
Other balances			Other balances		
Capital discharged			Deferred charges		
(detailed in statement			(detailed in statement		
of capital discharged)*	X		of deferred charges)*	X	

Capital receipts unapplied	X		Revenue accounts	
Revenue account surplus	X		deficiency	X
		X		X
		XX		XX

*See Appendix 6.1

This balance sheet will appear unfamiliar to many readers not used to the particular terminology of local government accounting. Such terms are explained in Chapters 4 and 5, and are defined in the Glossary.

The next example is of a district council general fund balance sheet which is produced on the vertical, or narrative format. It contains the same main headings as the tabular balance sheet that we have just examined.

Example —————————————————————————————

Local authority general fund
balance sheet as at 31 March 1994

	1994 £'000	£'000	1993 £'000
Net fixed assets		X	X
Council dwellings		X	X
Other land and buildings		X	X
Infrastructure		X	X
Vehicles, plant, furniture and equipment		X	X
Deferred charges		X	X
Investments (long term)		X	X
Long term debtors		X	X
Total long term assets		X	X
Current assets	X		X
Stocks and work in progress	X		X
Debtors	X		X
Investments (short term)	X		X
Cash at bank	X		X
Cash in hand	X		X
	X		X
Current liabilities			
Temporary borrowing	X		X
Creditors	X		X
Bank overdraft	X		X
	X		X

Net current assets	X	
	X	X

Financed by:

Provisions	X	X
Borrowing	X	X
Deferred liabilities	X	X
Deferred credits	X	X
Provision for credit liabilities	X	X
Fund balances and reserves	X	X
	X	X

Consolidated Balance Sheets

The broad arrangements for the consolidation of individual funds are shown below:

Example

Shire County Council

Type of fund	Detail	
1 County	Education Fire and public protection Highways Libraries Planning Police Social services Waste disposal	Consolidated
2 Enterprise	Direct service organisation	Consolidated
3 Loans and renewals	Consolidated loans pool Repairs and renewals fund	Consolidated
4 Special	Superannuation fund	Not consolidated

District Council

1 General	Environmental services Housing Leisure and recreation Planning and transportation committee	Consolidated

2 Enterprise	Direct service organisation Markets	Consolidated
3 Loans and renewals	Consolidated loans pool Repairs and renewals fund }	Consolidated
4 Special	Trust funds*	Not consolidated
5 Collection Fund		Not consolidated

* Some councils act as trustees for legacies left by inhabitants of the area. A legacy is paid into a specific trust fund, the money is invested and the investment income received is used to finance or part finance the running of an establishment or facility. These balance sheets are not consolidated as they represent assets and liabilities of funds administered by a local authority on behalf of others or on behalf of the owners of the fund.

The process of consolidation of fund balance sheets involves:

- the exclusion of funds which are not owned by the authority
- the elimination of inter-fund debtors and creditors
- the elimination of inter-fund investments
- the summation of all remaining balances.

The elimination of inter-authority indebtedness is necessary to remove accounts which appear in more than one balance sheet and which relate to internal transfers or adjustments between accounts. These are cancelled out so that only the external assets and liabilities of an authority are shown in the consolidated balance sheet.

Investments of surplus funds by the consolidated loans fund in the superannuation fund are, of course, treated as external investments, as the superannuation fund is outside the scope of consolidation.

An example of a consolidated balance sheet involving inter-fund investments is now shown:

Example ——————————————————————————

Highways balance sheet

	£'000	£'000
Fixed assets		29,079
Current assets		
Investments	2,247	
Debtors	225	
		2,472

Other balances
Deferred charges   1,875
                                                            ───────
                                                             33,426
                                                            ═══════

Long-term liabilities
Loans outstanding:
Consolidated loans account   17,922

Current liabilities
Creditors   1,425

Provisions
Renewals and repairs account   4,944

Other balances
Capital discharged   9,135
                                                            ───────
                                                             33,426
                                                            ═══════

Example ───

Consolidated loans account balance sheet

                                                              £'000
Assets
Advances to borrowing accounts   284,238
Debtors   1,425
                                                            ───────
                                                            285,663
                                                            ═══════

Liabilities
Long term loans   282,870
Internal loans   2,247
Creditors   225
Cash overdrawn   321
                                                            ───────
                                                            285,663
                                                            ═══════

Notes
a) Highways committee renewals and repairs account has invested £2,247,000 surplus funds in the consolidated loans account.
b) Highways creditors are in respect of sums due to the consolidated loans fund.

c) Consolidated loans account creditors are in respect of investment interest due to the highways committee.

For illustration purposes only the two balance sheets are consolidated. In practice the consolidation process is one large exercise, with all service committee fund balance sheets, enterprise fund balance sheets and so on, being consolidated.

Example

Consolidated balance sheet

	£'000
Fixed assets	29,079
Current assets	
Advances to borrowing accounts	266,316
Other balances	
Deferred charges	1,875
	297,270
Long-term liabilities	
Long-term loans	282,870
Current liabilities	
Cash overdrawn	321
Provisions	
Repairs and renewals fund	4,944
Other balances	
Capital discharged	9,135
	297,270

Workings

All inter fund debtors and creditors are eliminated.

a) Highways creditor £1,425,000 = consolidated loans fund debtor £1,425,000, so the balances are eliminated.
b) Consolidated loans account creditor £225,000 = highways committee debtor £225,000, so the balances are eliminated.
c) The consolidated loans account has advanced £17,922,000 to the highways committee. As this is an internal transaction the liability is eliminated in the highways committee balance sheet and the asset in the consolidated loans account balance sheet is reduced: £284,238,000 – £17,922,000 = £266,316,000.*

* Note. In the total consolidation of the fund balance sheets this figure would be eliminated.

2   All inter-fund investments are eliminated.

Highways balance sheet investments of £2,247,000 = consolidated loans account balance sheet internal loans of £2,247,000.

The next example illustrates the process of consolidation in respect of a wider range of activities of the local authority.

The following balances were extracted from the accounts of X City Council on 31 March 1994.

Example

	Service committees	Enterprise funds	Consolidated loans account
	£'000	£'000	£'000
Fixed assets	459,652	17,970	
Advances to service committees and enterprise funds			226,016
Renewals and repairs fund	11,152	3,912	
Revenue account surplus	4,038 (Cr)	14 (Cr)	
Creditors	12,776	404	
Stocks	3,452	490	
Debtors	15,858	660	
Investments (short term)	35,202	3,686	
Cash in hand	18 (Dr)	24 (Dr)	
Bank balance in hand			8,400 (Dr)
Bank balance overdrawn	6,024 (Cr)	654 (Cr)	
Loans outstanding:			
external			202,490
internal			31,926
Deferred charges	444		
Capital discharged	182,838	16,544	
Advances from the consolidated loans fund	224,794	1,222	
Temporary loans	45,898		
Capital receipts unapplied			

Notes
a) The debtors/creditors balances include £146,000 owed by one of the service committees to one of the enterprise funds.
b) Service committees have investments of £31,926,000 in the consolidated loan fund.

Required
A consolidated balance sheet for X City Council as at 31 March 1994 is set out below.

Solution

Consolidated balance sheet as at 31 March 1994

	£'000	£'000
Fixed assets		477,622
Current assets		
Stocks	3,942	
Investments	6,962	
Debtors	16,372	
Cash at bank	1,722	
Cash in hand	42	
		29,040
Other balances		
Deferred charges		444
		507,106
Long-term liabilities		
Loans outstanding		202,490
Current liabilities		
Temporary loans	45,898	
Creditors	13,114	
		59,012
Provisions		
Renewals and repairs fund		15,064
Other balances		
Capital discharged	199,382	
Capital receipts unapplied	27,106	
Surplus	4,052	
		230,540
		507,106

Workings

1 All inter fund debtors and creditors are eliminated.

a) Service committees' creditors £12,776,000 – £146,000 = £12,630,000. Enterprise funds' debtors £660,000 – £146,000 = £514,000.

b) The consolidated loans account has advanced £226,016,000 to the service committees and the enterprise funds. As this is an internal transaction the liability is eliminated in the service committees' and enterprise funds' balance sheet and the asset in the consolidated loans is also eliminated:

£224,794,000 + £1,222,000 = £226,016,000.

2   All inter-fund investments are eliminated.

Service committee balance sheet investments = £35,202,000 – £31,926,000 = £3,276,000.

Consolidated loans account balance sheet external loans outstanding = £31,926,000 – £31,926,000 = Nil.

The published format of the consolidated balance sheet

The *Accounts and Audit Regulations 1983*, require local authorities to publish an annual statement of account showing the financial position of the authority as at 31 March each year. This statement is to be included in the published Annual Report.

The 1993 ACOP provides that, so far as balance sheets are concerned, an authority's statement of accounts shall include a consolidated balance sheet. It comments that:

> This statement is fundamental to the understanding of an authority's financial position at the year end. It shows the balances and reserves at an authority's disposal and its long-term indebtedness, and the fixed and net current assets employed in its operations, together with summarised information on the fixed assets held.

> The Consolidated Balance Sheet should include the assets and liabilities of all activities of the authority, excluding the superannuation, trust, common good (in Scotland), and similar funds administered for third parties.

> Further analysis of any of the items below should be given if it is necessary to ensure fair presentation.

ACOP further provides that the following information should be included to support the consolidated balance sheet:

● Fixed assets
● Operational assets
  – Council dwellings
  – Other land and buildings
  – Vehicles, plant, furniture and equipment
  – Infrastructure assets
  – Community assets
● Non-operational assets
● Deferred charges
  – Improvement grants
  – Other
● Long-term investments
● Long-term debtors
● Current assets
  – Stocks and work in progress
  – Debtors (net of provision for bad and doubtful debts, to be disclosed separately if material)
  – Investments
  – Cash and bank

- Current liabilities
  - Borrowing repayable on demand or within 12 months
  - Creditors
  - Bank overdraft
- Borrowing repayable within a period in excess of 12 months
- Deferred liabilities
- Government grants-deferred
- Deferred credits (including deferred capital receipts in England and Wales)
- Fixed asset restatement reserve*
- Capital financing reserve*
- Usable capital receipts reserve
- Fund balances and reserves

* these are new terms arising from the new capital accounting requirements of the 1993 ACOP and are further considered in Chapter 5.

Supplementary information to the consolidated balance sheet

It is a key feature of CIPFA's accounting recommendations, that published statements should be supplemented with such additional information as will aid their usefulness and understanding. For the consolidated balance sheet, the 1993 Code supplementary information requirements are given in Appendix 6.1, together with practical comments where considered necessary.

Cash flow statement

Introduction

This consolidated statement summarises the inflows and outflows arising from transactions with third parties (i.e. external to the authority) for both revenue and capital purposes. The statement is designated in the 1993 ACOP as 'The Cash Flow Statement'.

Local authorities are required to produce such a statement by the *Accounts and Audit Regulations 1983*. CIPFA also categorises SSAP10 on sources and applications of funds statements as relevant to the local authorities. In order to obtain greater comparability between local authorities the *1993 Accounting Code of Practice* gives more detailed guidance on the statement and specifies which items are to be included.

Purpose of the statement

The financial transactions of the local authority are already completely summarised in the consolidated balance sheet and the general county fund summary revenue account. However there is certain information which is not revealed by this method of summarising the financial transactions of the authority.

The following additional items of information are shown in the statement.

- A subjective analysis of revenue expenditure. This is not available in the general fund summary account which analyses expenditure in terms of service committees, not in terms of what items the money was spent on.
- The gross expenditure on fixed assets. This information is not readily available from the balance sheet, although it could be obtained from the notes on the balance sheet.
- The proceeds from the sale of fixed assets. This information can also only be obtained by looking at the notes on the balance sheet.
- Capital and revenue expenditure are brought together in one statement to show the gross expenditure. Capital and revenue income are also brought together in this statement to show the net shortfall or excess of income to cover the total expenditure of the authority for the year.
- The second part of the statement shows how this shortfall or excess has been dealt with, i.e. by a change in long-term borrowing, in short-term indebtedness or in net current assets.

The format of the statement

The format as set out in the 1993 Accounting Code of Practice is as follows.

Example

Information to be included in the accounting statement

Revenue activities

Expenditure

Cash paid to and on behalf of employees	X
Other operating costs	X
Housing benefit paid out	X
	X

Income

Rents (after rebates)	X
Council tax income	X
Disbursements from the collection fund (England and Wales)	X
Non-domestic rate income	X
Revenue Support Grant	X
DSS grants for rebates	X
Other government grants	X
Cash received for goods and services	X
Other revenue cash payments/income	X
	X

Servicing of finance

Expenditure

Interest paid	X

Interest element of finance lease rental payments	X	
		X
Income		
Interest received		X
		X
Capital activities		
Expenditure		
Purchase of fixed assets	X	
Purchase of long-term investments	X	
		X
Income		
Sale of fixed assets	X	
Capital grants received	X	
Other capital cash payments/income	X	
		X
Net cash inflow/outflow before financing		X
Financing		
Expenditure		
Repayments of amounts borrowed	X	
Capital element of finance lease rental payments	X	
		X
Income		
New loans raised	X	
New short-term loans	X	
		X
Increase/decrease in cash and cash equivalents		X

Information to be disclosed in notes to the cash flow statement

- A reconciliation between the net surplus or deficit on the income and expenditure account to the revenue activities net cash flow.
- The movement of cash and cash equivalents and the items shown within the financing

section of the cash flow statement should be reconciled to the related items in the opening and closing balance sheets for the period.
- Any further narrative or analysis that may assist in interpreting the statement.
- Analysis of government grants.

Appendix 6.1

Information to be disclosed in notes to the consolidated balance sheet

- Summary of capital expenditure and disposals during the year, including assets acquired under finance leases, analysed for each category of fixed assets, together with the sources of finance.
- Summary of movements of deferred charges during the year.
- Details of any significant commitments under capital contracts.
- Information on assets held, appropriately classified to provide a straightforward but informative picture of the fixed assets of the authority.
- The gross amounts of fixed assets that are held under finance leases together with the related accumulated depreciation, for each category of asset.
- For each category of fixed assets included in the balance sheet at current value the following information should be disclosed:
  a) the date of the last valuation
  b) the basis of the valuation
  c) where there is a rolling programme of revaluations, an explanation of the method used
  d) in the period in which a valuation is carried out, the names of the valuers and details of their qualifications.
- Details of movements in capital reserves, including the fixed asset restatement reserve, the capital financing reserve and usable capital receipts.
- Details of movements in the provision for credit liabilities (PCL), in compliance with statutory requirements (England and Wales).
- An analysis of net assets employed by the general or county fund, HRA, DSOs and other trading undertakings.
- Details of the name, business, shareholding, net assets and results of operations and other financial transactions of any related companies, including reference to where the accounts of the related companies may be acquired and whether there has been any qualification to the audit opinion in respect of those accounts.
- Analysis of borrowing repayable within a period in excess of 12 months, by lender category and maturity.
- The amount and nature of any significant contingent liabilities.
- Details of material post balance sheet events not reflected in the financial statements.
- An indication of the overall nature and amount of trust funds and other third party funds administered by the authority.
- The amounts included in reserves and balances which are held by schools under delegated schemes, where not disclosed in the statement, together with a statement that such

balances are committed to be spent on the education service and not available to the authority for general use.

● Details of insurance provisions created by the authority together with an explanation of the balance and the nature of the risk covered. Also details of any material risk which is unfunded.

Some of the headings used in this consolidated balance sheet and disclosure information are new to local government accounting terminology. They arise from the new capital accounting requirements of the 1993 ACOP, which are described in more detail in Chapter 6.

These new headings in the balance sheet are:

Fixed asset restatement reserve
Capital financing reserve

and in the information to be disclosed, sections (6) and (7).

Memorandum capital statements are prepared to support the balance sheet figures and detail changes in the financial year in respect of fixed assets, capital discharged, deferred charges and capital projects in progress. Although in practice the format of the statements produced varies between authorities, the following layouts are not unusual.

Statement of fixed assets			
	Total at 31.3.93 £	Expenditure during year £	Written off during year £	Total at 31.3.94 £
Council dwellings				
Other land and buildings				
Infrastructure				
Vehicles, plant, furniture and equipment				
Totals				

Statement of capital discharged				
	Total at 31.3.93 £	Expenditure discharged during year £	Written off during year £	Total at 31.3.94 £
Loans redeemed				
Sales and other capital receipts applied				
Gifts and bequests applied				
Revenue contributions to capital outlay				
Reserve funds applied				
Totals				

Statement of deferred charges				
	Total at 31.3.93 £	Expenditure during year £	Written off during year £	Total at 31.3.94 £
(a) Non-tangible assets financed from loan				
(b) Loans outstanding on assets disposed of				
(c) Expenses of local Acts				
(d) Expenses of stock issues				
(e) Discounts on stock issued				
Totals				

Statement of capital projects in progress			
Committee and project	**Total at 31.3.93 £**	**Expenditure during year £**	**Total at 31.3.94 £**
Education detail			
Environmental health detail			
Etc			
Totals			

7 Special accounts

This chapter deals with some of those accounts that are published separately from the general or county fund, as required by the *1993 Accounting Code of Practice* or by local custom and practice, as being an important, or unusual, local service of the authority concerned.

Collection fund

Introduction

District councils or London boroughs have the statutory duty to collect the council tax and business rates in their administrative area. Local authorities who do not have this statutory authority precept the district council. This process involves county councils and parish councils calculating the amount required from this source to finance expenditure and the district council or London borough collects the sums on their behalf and then pays it over to the precepting authority.

The collection fund is kept quite distinct from the other assets and liabilities of the billing authority.

Main features

The main features of the operation of a collection fund from 1 April 1993 are:

- It is operated on an accruals basis.
- The major precepting authorities and the billing authority demands on the fund for a year have to be met in full by the fund in the course of the year.
- Payments during the year in respect of each demand have to be made in accordance with a schedule drawn up by the billing authority after consultation with the major precepting authorities.
- Revenue Support Grant, National Non-Domestic Rate (NNDR) and additional grant are to be payable to all billing and major precepting authorities, and in the case of a billing authority are to be paid into its general fund, not, as under the community charge in England, its collection fund.

- Precepts of local precepting authorities are to be met from a billing authority's general fund, not as under the community charge, its collection fund.
- All interest receivable in respect of the temporary investment of collection fund sums, and all interest payable in respect of any temporary borrowing to meet collection fund liabilities, is to be credited or debited to the billing authority's general fund, not its collection fund, and hence is to be taken into account by the billing authority when calculating its budget requirement for 1993/94 and subsequent years.
- Any estimated surplus or deficit on the fund for the year is not to remain in the collection fund, but is to be shared so as to benefit or be borne by the billing authority and its major precepting authorities in the following year.
- In England any estimated deficit or surplus at 31 March 1993 benefited or was borne solely by the billing authority in 1993/94.
- Amounts to be shared or borne by authorities will be transferable to, or payable from, the collection fund, in instalments in the financial year following the year for which the surplus/deficit has been estimated.
- Any surplus/deficit in respect of community charges, has to be transferred to/from the billing authority's general fund within the financial year.
- There is only one collection fund in respect of both council tax and community charge items. Sums received or payments made after 1 April 1993 in respect of community charges continue to be paid into or met out of the billing authority's collection fund. It is necessary for the purposes of making certain prescribed transfers to or from the general fund in respect of community charge transactions and for estimating surpluses and deficits, to separately identify community charge items within the collection fund.

Operation of fund

Throughout a financial year each billing authority makes payments and transfers into and out of its collection fund.

Section 90(1) of the *Local Government Finance Act 1988* (as amended) states that the following items have to be paid into the collection fund:

- income from council taxpayers (not penalties)
- sums received from major precepting authorities to meet estimated previous year's deficit on the collection fund
- non-domestic rate income collected from own ratepayers
- refund of NNDR income paid to the central pool
- any other sums specified by the Secretary of State.

Section 90(2) of the *Local Government Finance Act 1988* (as amended) states that the following items have to paid out of the collection fund:

- precept payments to major precepting authorities (but not interest on any late payment)
- sums paid to major precepting authorities as their share of the estimated previous year's surplus on the collection fund
- contributions to the NNDR pool
- refunds of NNDR and council tax
- any other sums specified by the Secretary of State.

Format of the fund

Example ————————————————————————————————

The collection fund
Accounting statement

	Note	£'000
Income		
Council tax	2	11,300
Transfers from general fund		
– Council tax benefits		1,550
– Transitional relief		130
– Discounts for prompt payment		20
Income from business ratepayers	3	14,500
Contributions		
– Towards previous year's collection fund deficit		100
		27,600
Expenditure		
Precepts and demands	4	12,500
Business rate		
– Payment to national pool		14,300
– Costs of collection		200
Provision for bad and doubtful debts		400
Contributions		
– Adjustment of previous year's community charges		100
		27,500
Movement on fund balance		100

Notes to the accounts

General

This account represents the statutory requirement for billing authorities to maintain a separate collection fund. The account is not consolidated with the council's accounts.

Note 2: Council tax

The council's tax base, i.e. the number of chargeable dwellings in each valuation band (adjusted for dwellings where discounts apply) converted to an equivalent number of band D dwellings, was calculated as follows:

Band	Estimated number of taxable properties after effect of discounts	Ratio	Band D equivalent dwellings
A	4,276	6/9	2,851
B	5,116	7/9	3,979
C	7,027	8/9	6,246
D	6,211	9/9	6,211
E	2,579	11/9	3,152
F	1,843	13/9	2,662
G	620	15/9	1,033
H	412	18/9	824
	28,084		26,958

Less: Adjustment for collection rates and for anticipated changes during the year for successful appeals against valuation banding, new properties, demolitions, disabled persons relief and exempt properties	674
Council tax base	26,284

Note 3: Income from business ratepayers

Under the arrangements for uniform business rates, the council collects non-domestic rates for its area which are based on local rateable values multiplied by a uniform rate. The total amount, less certain reliefs and other deductions, is paid to a central pool (the NNDR pool) managed by central government, which in turn pays back to authorities their share of the pool based on a standard amount per head of resident population.

Note 4: Precepts and demands

	£'000
Trumpton County Council	10,000
Greendale District Council	2,500
	12,500

Information to be disclosed in notes to the account

The *1993 Accounting Code of Practice* requires:

● the total non-domestic rateable value at the year end and the national non-domestic rate

multiplier for the year;
- the calculation of the tax base (as note 2 above);
- the name of each authority which made a significant precept or demand on the Fund and the amount of that demand.

Housing Revenue Account

Introduction

Housing services are the responsibility of the housing authorities which are the London borough councils, metropolitan district councils and district councils.

The major services for which housing authorities have responsibility are the provision of council houses or flats for rent and their subsequent maintenance. There are, however, many other activities which are undertaken in connection with housing in both the public and the private sector, and brief details of these are given below.

- *Area improvement initiatives* – areas are designated as general improvement areas and housing action areas. The effect of this is that the local authority receives extra funds from the government towards the costs of improving the local authority property in the area and towards the costs of lending or granting money to owners of private sector buildings in the area.
- *Caravan sites* – provision of caravan sites for travelling people.
- *Homelessness* – this relates to provision for the homeless in the private or other parts of the public sector.
- *Home insulation grants* – central government operates a system of grants to occupiers of houses for insulation. The local authority administers this scheme and thus incurs the cost of its administration.
- *House renovation grants* – these grants are available to renovate houses in specific categories, for example pre-1914 houses or those in housing action areas. A 100 per cent grant is available from the government in these cases, so costs recorded here are administrative costs only.
- *Housing advances* – local authorities have the power under the *Housing (Financial Provisions) Act 1958* to provide mortgages for the purpose of house purchases. The local authority incurs the cost of administering this scheme. Any losses due to defaults on repayments are also included here.
- *Housing aid and advice centres* – these provide information and advice on many aspects of housing to both public and private sector tenants and to owner occupiers.
- *Housing associations* – loans and grants are made to housing associations for the provision of special types of housing, for example for the elderly. Administration and interest payments are recorded here.
- *Housing benefits* – rent rebates are given to local authority tenants and rent allowances to private sector tenants on low income. The local authority incurs administrative expenses in running these schemes and receives a grant from central government to cover a significant part of the rebates and allowances given to tenants. The local authority must bear the cost of the remaining part of the rebates and allowances.
- *Overspill agreements* – the council may 'purchase' the right to place their council in cer-

tain properties of neighbouring councils and a small fee is paid to the neighbouring council for that right.

- *Slum clearance* – local authorities are responsible for slum clearance in their area and receive some grants from central government towards the cost of this activity.
- *Town development* – this covers other aspects of agreements with neighbouring councils which are not covered by the overspill agreements.
- *Unfit private sector housing* – compensation is paid to owners if their property is designated unfit by the council.

All of these activities, with the exception of the provision of council housing, are known as 'general fund housing activities' and appear in the general fund section of the accounts. This is to distinguish them from the provision of council housing which is accounted for separately in the Housing Revenue Account.

Housing Revenue Account

Under the *Housing Finance Act 1972* each local authority is required to keep a separate revenue account for the income and expenditure relating to the provision of council houses. The debits and credits which must be included in this account are laid down in this Act and in the *Manual on Local Authorities Housing Subsidies and Accounting* published by the Department of the Environment.

The CIPFA 1985 Standard Classification includes a standard form for the Housing Revenue Account (HRA) which is based on the standard subjective classification used for other services. The two main items in this account are the expenditure on the maintenance of council houses and the administration of the council house system. Separate holding accounts are usually kept to deal with these two items.

The standard form of the housing revenue account is shown below.

Housing Revenue Account for the year ended 31 March 1994

	£	£
Expenditure		
Premises related expenses		
Recharge from repairs and maintenance holding account	X	
Premises insurance	X	
		X
Supplies and services		
Bad debt provision		X
Central departmental and technical support		
Recharge from supervision and management holding account		X
Capital financing costs		
Principal repayments	X	
Interest payments	X	
Finance leasing charges	X	
Direct revenue financing	X	

Debt management expenses   X

Total expenditure   X

Income

Housing subsidy   X
Receipts from general fund   X
Rents   X
Interest on: capital and revenue balances   X
               sale of council houses   X   X
                                                                                X
                                                                                X

Surplus or deficiency for the year   X

The following information should be provided in notes (1993 ACOP requirement)

1) Number and types of dwellings in the authority's housing stock.
2) The amount of rent arrears (excluding amounts collectable on behalf of other agencies) and the aggregate balance sheet provision in respect of uncollectable debts.
3) The nature and amount of any exceptional or prior year items not disclosed in the statement.
4) Analysis of movement on the housing repairs account, if one is kept.

Since the *Local Government and Housing Act 1989* the housing revenue account has been 'ring fenced' in that local authorities no longer have general powers to make transfers between the HRA and the general fund. Prior to this, it was common for local authorities to keep rents low by subsidising them from the rate income.

The authority must not budget for a deficit on the HRA. If a deficit occurs, this is either carried forward into the next year, or the Secretary of State may give permission for a transfer from the general fund, or he may give a supplementary housing subsidy, depending on the circumstances.

The authority may budget for a surplus on the HRA and if this occurs it will be carried forward to the next year to be used to offset deficits.

Transfers from the general fund to the HRA occur in the following circumstances:

● for any communal service charged to HRA, for example estate lighting (this transfer is required by law)
● to make good any deficit, by permission of the Secretary of State.

The following transfers will be made to the general fund from the HRA:

● a mandatory amount equivalent to the housing subsidy, if this is negative, irrespective of whether there is an actual surplus on the HRA
● if the housing subsidy is negative and there is still an actual surplus after the mandatory transfer has been made, the authority has power to transfer the remaining surplus to the general fund.

Superannuation fund

Introduction

This fund is concerned only with the local government superannuation scheme and not with separate schemes provided for other public sector employees, e.g. police officers, fire fighters and teachers who are on the local government payroll.

Administering and employing authorities

An administering authority, i.e. one with the power to maintain a superannuation fund (basically county councils, metropolitan district councils and London borough councils) acts as a trustee on behalf of the employees for whom the fund is intended to provide pensions and related benefits. Thus, in Cambridgeshire, the county council is the administering authority for the superannuation fund which covers the employees of the county council and those of the five district councils within the county, termed 'employing authorities', for superannuation purposes.

Format of the accounts

A superannuation fund revenue account and a balance sheet (termed a 'net assets statement') is prepared, but the balance sheet is not incorporated into the consolidated balance sheet of the local authority.

The revenue account and balance sheet illustrate the debits and credits of the fund, as follows:

Items debited from the fund

- Pensions and annuities
- Retirement grants and death grants
- Return of contributions
- Loss on the realisation of investments
- Outgoing transfer values
- Investment management fees
- Support services costs

Items credited to the fund

- Contributions by employees admitted to the scheme
- Contributions by the employer
- Interest and commission on investments
- Profit on the realisation of investments
- Incoming transfer valuesItems credited to the fund

Although certain items may initially be paid out of the fund, they are not a charge on the fund and are recovered from the department that formerly employed the pensioner. These items are:

- additional retirement pensions
- pension increases
- additional retirement grants
- additional death grants
- additional widow's pensions.

An example of a superannuation fund revenue account and net assets statement now follows. Information supporting the final accounts will also be published.

Format of the revenue account

1993-94 £'000	Revenue account	1994–95 £'000
	Income	
6,992	Contributions from: Employees	7,729
7,011	Employers	7,600
14,003		15,329
4,554	Transfer values from employers of contributors joining the fund	4,218
16,728	Investment income	13,903
33	Commission and other income	35
35,318	**Total income**	**33,485**
	Expenditure	
	Superannuation benefits	
15,710	– Pensions	18,026
3,244	– Lump-sum benefits	2,860
18,954		20,886
6,148	Transfer values to employers of contributors leaving the fund	5,641
182	Refunds of contributions	191
510	Administrative and other expenses	454
25,794	**Total expenditure**	**27,172**
9,524	**Net income available for investment**	**6,313**

Format of the net assets statement

At 31 March 1994 £'000	Net assets statement	At 31 March 1995 £'000
	Investments at Market Value	
	Fixed-interest securities	
19,055	– UK	8,909
7,890	– Overseas	23,666
–	Index Linked	27,946
	Equities	
166,697	– UK	137,470
55,514	– Overseas	57,989
18,400	Direct property	17,970
267,556		273,950
23,307	Temporary investments	22,919
290,863	**Total invested**	**296,869**
	Current assets	
2,987	– Debtors	1,880
	Less: Current liabilities	
2,188	– Creditors	3,698
799	**Net current assets (+) / liabilities (–)**	**–1,818**
291,662	**Net assets – Balance of Fund**	**295,051**

Reconciliation of net movements of assets of the fund

At 31 March 1994 £'000	Reconciliation of the net movements of assets of the fund	At 31 March 1995 £'000
282,239	Opening net assets	291,662
9,524	Net income available for investment	6,313
−101	Change in market value of investments*	−2,924
291,662	Closing net assets	295,051

> *   The change in the market value of investments includes the annual movement in all securities held by the superannuation fund, including temporary investment of cash and movement in net current assets.

Trading accounts

Introduction

These are accounts for services and undertakings of a commercial nature which are, or could be, substantially financed by charges made upon the users of the services.

Trading accounts may be kept in two ways, according to local circumstances.

● As part of the general fund, and balanced annually by a transfer to or from the general fund.
● As separate undertakings with separate trading accounts. Surpluses from trading will be retained, i.e. not transferred to the general fund, and may be transferred to a reserve fund. Any loss will be financed by any accumulated surplus in that fund.

Trading services operate to cover their costs and preferably to earn an acceptable surplus. Where the trading service is accounted for as a separate 'fund' the surplus will be used to maintain and expand the service.

Trading services vary between local authorities because of differences in local policies, customs and Local Act powers.

Trading services include the following:

● Markets and abattoirs
● Car parks and spaces
● Cemeteries and crematoria
● Catering units
● Theatres, piers and entertainments
● Harbours, docks and airports.

Revenue accounts and balance sheets of trading services

The revenue accounts of trading services should be drawn up in accordance with the 1985 standard classification, described elsewhere, but with certain refinements.

- Income should be presented first. Trading income should be separately identified and come before non-trading income in order of presentation.
- A net revenue account and appropriation account should be used in order to achieve the following:
  - The separation of operating income and expenditure from non-operating income and expenditure, and the production of two key figures.

    1) Operating income less operating expenditure equals operating surplus or deficit;
    2) Operating surplus or deficit plus non-operating income, less non-operating expenditure equals total surplus or deficit for the year.
  - To show how the surplus or deficit for the year, plus the balance brought forward from the previous year, are dealt with (appropriated).

Balance sheets should be presented in the format prescribed by CIPFA and are dealt with in Chapter 6.

The standard format for the financial accounts of a trading undertaking is shown below.

Example ───

Trading undertaking

Revenue account for the year ended 31 March 1994

	£'000	£'000
Income		
Customer and client receipts		
Sales	X	
Fees and charges	X	
Rents	X	
	───	
		X
		───
Total income		X
		───
Expenditure		
Employees	X	
Premises-related expenses		
General	X	
Contribution to repair and renewals account	X	
	───	
		X
		───
Transport related expenses	X	
Supplies and services		

General	X	
Establishment expenses	X	
Miscellaneous	X	
		X
Total expenditure		X
Surplus from trading		X
Less: Capital financing costs		
Principal repayments	X	
Interest payments	X	
		X
Surplus for the year		X
Reserve fund brought forward at 1 April 1993		X
Reserve fund carried forward at 31 March 1994		X

Example

Balance sheet as at 31 March 1994

	£'000	£'000
Fixed assets	X	
Less: Capital discharged	X	
		X
Deferred charges		X
		X
Current assets		
Stocks	X	
Debtors	X	
Cash	X	
	X	
Current liabilities		
Creditors	X	
		X
		X
Financed by:		
Provisions – repair and renewals account		X
Loans account advances		X

Fund balances and reserves
  Reserve fund

$$\frac{\text{X}}{\text{X}}$$

Direct Labour/Direct Service Organisation Accounts

Introduction

The operation of the Direct Labour and Direct Service organisations (DLO and DSO), is strictly controlled by the *Local Government, Planning and Land Act 1980* and the *Local Government Act 1988*. They may be responsible for a variety of work ranging from maintenance or general construction work to providing a service. Many authorities have more than one of this type of organisation and a separate account must be maintained for each type.

The controls require them to act in a commercial manner and to make a required rate of return on their capital. Should they fail to do so then the government can order them to be wound up. Under the 1988 Act the government can prescribe work that must be subject to competitive tendering and no favouritism can be shown to the in-house organisation in awarding tenders even if an unsuccessful tender means the in-house organisation can go out of business. In recent years the awarding of contracts in-house has been subject to strict scrutiny by government who, in some cases, have ordered authorities to retender. There is a code of rules about what can and what cannot be taken into account in comparing in-house and external tenders. These organisations also have to produce an annual report which can be a fruitful source of information to potential competitors.

Despite the strict government rules which DLO and DSO managers claim put them at a disadvantage in competing with the private sector the majority of tenders have been won by in-house bids. Some organisations have also sought to provide themselves with a wider base by tendering for work for private sector bodies and local authorities outside their area. Advice given by the Audit Commission suggests that such 'trading' is illegal, unless it is only a small proportion of the total work and can be achieved as part of normal trading, without specific or additional expenditure.

Scope of the legislation

Local authorities have in the past carried out much of their building and engineering work by the use of direct labour, i.e. by staff employed by the local authorities themselves rather than by outside contractors. Questions arose as to whether these were the most efficient arrangements, and as a result of this the *Local Government Planning and Land Act 1980* introduced an element of competition into this area.

For this purpose, the Act required that the section of each local authority responsible for building and engineering work should be formed into a trading organisation known as a Direct Labour Organisation (DLO) and that the DLO should be required to tender for certain categories of the local authority's building and engineering work, in competition with private contractors.

Under the *Local Government Act 1988* the requirement to subject work to competition has been extended to cover a range of other activities. The collective term Direct Service Organisation (DSO) is now used to describe all such activities, irrespective of whether they were set up under the 1980 or the 1988 Act.

Each DSO is required to achieve a certain rate of return on assets employed for each category of work. If a DSO fails to achieve this rate of return over a three year period, the Secretary of State may require it to cease operating.

The 1980 Act requires DLOs to be set up to cover construction and maintenance on buildings, land and other structures. 'Land' includes all paved areas such as roads and pavements but excludes open spaces such as parks and allotments, which are exempt. 'Other structures' includes sewers, public lighting, sea defences, bridges and land drainage work. Any work not carried out by building and engineering tradesmen is excluded, which means that horticultural work, cleaning and caretaking work are excluded (painting and decorating are not excluded).

This work is divided into a number of categories, dependent upon type and contract value and if a local authority has less than 15 employees engaged in building and engineering work there is no statutory obligation to set up a DLO.

Under the 1988 Act work in the following categories must also be put out to tender and a DSO set up to carry out any work awarded to the local authority. The categories are periodically extended by the government.

- Refuse collection
- Building cleaning
- Other cleaning, such as roads
- Catering: schools and welfare
- Catering: other
- Maintenance of grounds
- Repair and maintenance of vehicles
- Management of sports and leisure centres (local authorities will maintain control of pricing admissions and opening hours).

The government has plans to increase the scope of DSOs to cover finance and other central support services, and a guideline note issued in January 1995 by the DoE produced a detailed timetable up to April 1999 for CCT, covering further manual services, legal, construction, property, finance, personnel and IT services.

DSO final accounts

DSOs are require to prepare the following documents for their final accounts.

- A historic cost balance sheet showing a true and fair view of the state of affairs of the DSO at the end of the financial year.
- A revenue account showing a true and fair view of the financial result for each of the categories of work defined. If there are less than 30 employees in any category then that category may be combined with another.
- A statement showing whether the required rate of return has been achieved in each category.
- A published report of the activities of the DSO during the year.

The accounts must be completed by 30 September each year and submitted to the Secretary of State.

CIPFA Code of Practice for Compulsory Competitive Tendering (1989)

The Secretary of State has extensive powers under the Acts to specify the way in which the accounts will be prepared. Instead of exercising these powers, the Secretary of State has supported the use of CIPFA's *Code of Practice for Compulsory Competitive Tendering (1989)* as a basis of preparing the accounts of DLOs. This Code sets out the requirements of the law as CIPFA understands and interprets them and recommends ways in which these should be met.

Adherence to the Code is voluntary, but the Secretary of State has said that he expects local authorities to follow the code, and external auditors use the Code to compare the local authority's preparation of the accounts with accepted best practice.

The Code covers the following topics:

- Scope of Acts
- Tendering
- Contracts
- Non-competitive work under the 1980 Act
- Revenue accounts
- The accounting treatment of work done by DSO staff
- The expenditure chargeable to DSO accounts
- The return on capital employed for direct service work
- Financial reports.

A separate revenue account must be kept for each category of work. The precise format of the account will vary depending on the category of work.

An example of a format revenue account for construction work is shown below.

Example _____

DSO revenue account

	£
Income	
Charges to other accounts of the council	X
Charges under agency agreements	X
Charges under works contracts	X
Miscellaneous income	X
Provision for future at end of previous year written back	X
Total income	X
Expenditure	
Labour	X
Direct purchases	X
Stores	X
Subcontractors	X
Transport and plant	X

Overheads	X
Provision for future losses	X
Cost of work in progress at beginning of year	
less cost of work in progress at end of year	X
Total expenditure	X
Surplus for the year (see Current Cost Accounting note below)	X

Details of the individual items in this account will be given below.

Charges to other accounts of the authority are the charges made to committees and departments of the DSO's own local authority for work done by the DSO on their behalf. This will include the work which the DSO has successfully tendered for and the work which has been automatically allocated to the DSO by other committees and departments.

A district council may carry out sewerage work on an agency basis on behalf of the water company in its area. In this case the district council is the agent and the DSO may do work on its behalf. The income from this source appears under 'charges under agency agreements'.

Direct labour is the productive labour for a particular category of work and it will be recorded directly in the revenue account of that category. This also applies to direct materials and contractors' services, which are purchased for jobs in a particular category of work, and stores issues.

The costs of transport, plant and overheads are normally recorded in a holding account in the first instance for the whole DSO and the total expenditure is then transferred to the revenue accounts for each category of work using an appropriate method of apportionment.

Support service costs of a local authority include the costs of democracy (briefing councillors, servicing committees and so on), which would still be incurred if the DSO work was undertaken by an outside company. These costs will not be included in the support costs of the DSO.

Current cost operating surplus

Return on capital employed (ROCE)
Return on capital employed is a ratio used to measure the financial performance of DSOs. The appropriate legislation specifies target minimum rates of return to be achieved by each type of DSO calculated in a prescribed way.

The return (current cost operating surplus) is calculated by adjusting the conventionally calculated surplus or deficit earned during the year by the DSO. These adjustments include the removal of financing charges and interest credits and the introduction of depreciation charges and stock adjustments.

The capital employed figure is calculated as the average aggregate depreciated replacement cost of capital assets and replacement value of stock held.

Comparison with private sector and other parts of local authority
Private sector financial performance is measured in a variety of ways, including return on

capital employed. Care needs to be exercised, however, in the use of this and other ratios in the private sector, as the method of calculation is generally not prescribed and will vary. In the case of ROCE, for example, it is common to see this calculated on a historic, rather than current, cost basis.

In other parts of a local authority, the lack of a profit objective means that there is not an obvious single financial performance measure. Assessment of performance normally relies on comparisons of unit costs, activity against budget, value for money studies, and so on.

Unacceptably low return on capital
Annual accounts have to be produced in respect of a DSO, showing a true and fair view of performance. Where the target rate of return is not achieved, the Secretary of State has the power to order the closure of the unit. If the low return is actually a loss, this will need to be charged to an appropriate DSO reserve, and if this proves insufficient, to the General Fund.

Balance sheet

A separate balance sheet may be produced for each category of work or one balance sheet may be produced for all DSO activities. The balance sheet will follow the same format as other local authority balance sheets. The format is shown below.

The surplus achieved on a historic cost basis must be corrected to a current cost basis, by first valuing the fixed assets used on the service (as shown in the balance sheet) and then deducting depreciation in respect of those assets from the historical cost surplus to show the surplus on a current cost basis.

Example

DSO balance sheet

	£	£
Capital employed		
Fixed assets		X
Less: Capital discharged		X
		X
Current assets		
Stocks and work in progress	X	
Debtors and prepayments	X	
Bank balances and cash	X	
		X
Current liabilities		
Creditors	X	
	X	

        X

Net current assets   X

Sources of capital

Loans outstanding   X
Repairs and renewals fund   X
Appropriation accounts   X
Reserve fund   X

        X

Information to be disclosed in notes to the account (1993 ACOP requirement)

- The turnover and rates of return on a current cost basis for each DSO.
- The prescribed financial objective of each DSO.
- Where further accounting information may be obtained.

Passenger transport authorities

Under the *Local Government Act 1972*, county councils and the then metropolitan county councils were made responsible for public transport. The passenger transport executives (PTEs) operated bus services and had powers to procure other services by agreement with the National Bus Company and British Rail thus bringing an integrated approach to local transport, while county councils merely 'promoted the provision of a co-ordinated system of public transport'. The 45 district councils who had provided a municipal bus service before 1972 were allowed to continue. Local authorities were able to subsidise services and in metropolitan areas, subsidies were often high and fares low, which brought some councils into conflict with the central government, because of the rapid increase in costs falling on local budgets at a time when the government was restraining local authority expenditure.

This position was significantly altered by the *Transport Act 1985* and the abolition of the Greater London Council and the six metropolitan county councils in 1986 (see Chapter 2). Following abolition, the passenger transport authorities became joint boards whose members were appointed by the district councils. PTEs continued although their role was radically changed by the *1985 Transport Act*. In London, responsibility for buses and tubes passed to London Regional Transport, a body established by the government.

The *Transport Act 1985* brought about the major changes in approach. The Act is based on the principle that local bus services should be provided by the free market, with local authorities responsible not for planning a comprehensive network, but for securing socially necessary services which the market has not provided. The cost of the service should in the main not be reduced by subsidies but by completion.

In order to permit competition, bus services are deregulated, thereby allowing any number of operators to run on a particular route. Anyone wishing to provide a bus service is merely required to obtain a Public Service Operators Licence from the Traffic Commissioners. This shows that the operator is competent to run buses. The Traffic Commissioners comprise a permanent chairman (appointed by the Secretary of State) and two commissioners selected from a panel nominated by county and district councils in the area. Route or routes which are to be run commercially have to be registered with The Traffic Commissioners. Deregulation was set for October 1986. With this new procedure it is not possible for existing operators to object and prevent a new operator providing a service.

The metropolitan counties became passenger transport authorities (PTAs). PTAs had already been established along with passenger transport executives under the *1968 Transport Act* in four of the new metropolitan county areas (Greater Manchester, Merseyside, Tyne and Wear, and West Midlands) and two more (South and West Yorkshire) were created.

As a result of the registration of the routes, county councils and joint boards know which routes are not covered commercially, and can decide which additional routes they wish to subsidise. These routes are put out to competitive tender to get the best value for money – in other words, an operator who will provide an acceptable service with the lowest subsidy.

Once the routes have been registered, the operators have to give the Traffic Commissioner notice of variations or cancellation of services. Action can be taken against operators who run an unreliable service.

Municipal bus services have had to be transferred from local authorities to separate companies under the *Companies Act*, with their own directors, and they have to compete with private operators in the market. Local authorities (usually district councils) may provide concessionary bus fare schemes for the elderly or disabled, provided all operators can participate and they compensate operators for the loss of revenue and any increased costs arising from the scheme.

The position in London is different from the rest of the country. In 1985, responsibility for the buses and underground was removed from the GLC and given to London Regional Transport (*London Regional Transport Act 1984*). London Regional Transport is a quango with members appointed by and responsible to the Secretary of State. LRT is required under the Act to contract out work wherever suitable, and to get greater involvement by the private sector.

Airports and docks

District councils, county councils and joint boards may also provide and run airports and docks. Joint committees may be set up for this purpose. Examples of such provision include Luton, Manchester and Leeds/Bradford airports and Portsmouth's ferry terminal. These have also been turned into companies, some in the public and others in the private sector.

Taxis

Taxis are licensed outside London by district and metropolitan district councils who also set the fare structure. Their powers to refuse granting a licence have been reduced by the *Transport Act 1985*.

The passenger transport executive

Responsibility for ensuring that the former metropolitan county areas' public transport meets the needs of the area rests with the PTA which is primarily a policy making body. Responsibility for the implementation of the authority's policies lies with the passenger transport executive (PTE) whose budget is determined by the authority. The PTE appoints its own professional and supporting staff.

The authority's policies were previously financed through a precept on the rates bill of all the districts and by funding from central government. However, from the beginning of 1990/91, in accordance with the *Local Government Finance Act 1988*, the authority no longer precepts but instead raises a levy on each district council directly for its share of planned expenditure in the coming year. The levy is apportioned between the districts pro-rata to 'relevant' population, that is the population data used by central government in its Revenue Support Grant settlement.

The role of the PTE, under the policy direction of the authority is to:

- support and develop the local rail network
- administer and fund the concessionary travel scheme
- fund socially necessary bus services through competitive tender
- support various services throughout the area for the special transport needs of mobility impaired people
- maintain and promote public transport services by the provision and maintenance of bus stations, local rail stations, bus/rail interchanges and passenger shelter facilities
- promote and provide information and publicity for public transport services
- plan and implement new investments, e.g. LRT, new rail lines.

The PTE is obliged, under the *1983 Transport Act*, to prepare an annual financial plan containing proposals for the following three years. This plan is approved by the PTA.

PTA accounts

The PTA as a local authority in its own right, is required to prepare its accounts in accordance with the *Accounts and Audit Regulations 1983* and the CIPFA recommendations relating to the final accounts and their publication, including the *1993 Accounting Code of Practice*. Its accounts are subject to certification by the Audit Commission.

The final accounts of the PTA consist of:

- a summary of revenue expenditure
- a consolidated balance sheet
- notes to the balance sheet
- cash flow statement
- the capital and revenue transactions of the loans account (see Chapter 5).

The more important requirements of the *Transport Act 1968* and *1983* and *Local Government Finance Act 1982* in respect of the annual statement of accounts for PTEs include the following:

- A PTE must not incur a deficit in respect of its consolidated revenue account for an year; if this proves not to be practicable the deficit must be made good in the following year.

- In calculating the amount of any deficit a PTE may credit such appropriations of reserves as have been proposed in a plan prepared under Section 4 of the *Transport Act 1983.*
- Charges to revenue account must make proper provision for depreciation or renewal of assets.

The form in which the PTE's account are presented satisfies the requirements of the *Local Government Finance Act 1982,* and the *Accounts and Audit (Passenger Transport Executives and the London Transport Executive) Regulations 1983.*

The final accounts of the PTE consist of:

- a revenue account
- a summary of operating income and expenditure
- a balance sheet
- a consolidated source and application of funds statement
- notes to the accounts.

Support services

Definition of support services

The term 'support service' is a comparatively recent one in local government and covers the internal professional, technical and administrative activities, that are not direct local authority services to the public. These services may be provided by central departments such as finance, legal, computing or personnel, or by sections within non-central departments, but in either case the support services should be identified and made more accountable to their users.

Support services can also be provided by external suppliers and make up one of the two main types of overhead in local government. The other overhead cost is that part of the central management of the authority which comprises direction, supervision and guidance by elected members, their committees and the chief officers management team. Management and support services are not mutually exclusive.

Support services include the functions of accountants, cashiers, committee administration, internal audit, printing and purchasing, surveyors, which are located within the central, as opposed to the service departments of a local authority.

Recent changes in terminology

The term support service is a recent one, because of the changing terminology used to describe these costs over the past twenty or so years.

Before the impact of competition in local government, beginning with the *Local Government, Planning and Land Act 1980,* these central costs were termed 'central establishment charges' or 'CECs'. Thus, in rate estimates or published accounts, the costs of the central departments would be shown and then the whole of those costs would be re-allocated to user service departments, based on broad estimates of time spent (for employees costs), or square footage (for accommodation costs), or other imprecise but solid methods, e.g. numbers of telephone extensions, as a basis on which to allocate the costs of a central switchboard. Thus, central departments would have a net nil cost and allocations to spending departments would be shown in their estimates/final accounts as 'central establishment charges'.

The title central establishment charges was then changed in the mid 1980s to 'costs of management and administration' (CMAs) and then again, two or three years later to 'support services' in CIPFA guidance booklets to the profession, to reflect more accurately what these costs were intended to do in the financial management of the local authority.

Allocation and recharging

CIPFA's advice restates the principles of full allocation of support services costs, but says that support services' users should specify as far as possible their requirements in advance, rather than be given (and charged for) what the support service provider thinks is needed.

Implementing CIPFA's *Accounting for Support Services* concentrated attention on the contribution and relevance of support services to an authority's corporate objectives and particularly the following aspects:

a) Evaluation of the various support services required by clients and DSOs. Finance departments should assess the adequacy of their financial systems and services for direct service managers and be responsive to demands.
b) The collection, classification, apportionment and review of support services costs and the development of improved charging systems.
c) The drawing up of service level agreements (SLAs) between support services and their clients.
d) Setting up support services as trading accounts and including the full costs of employees, running expenses and financing charges.
e) Arrangements to encourage the joint responsibility of all managers for the cost-effectiveness of all support services.
f) The comparison of support service recharges with commercial costs, e.g. accounting services and commercial rents.

Support services can be provided in-house or contracted out, but in either case their cost will be fully recharged to direct services. This will help direct service managers provide realistic tenders for their services.

Service level agreements

The reference to SLAs in (c) above is significant. It refers to the fact that, as more units of local government become subject to compulsory or voluntary competitive tendering, so managers have become much more critical of the traditional allocation methods of chief financial officers – that is broadly based on estimates of time spent on a particular service or function. Managers of services, at the sharp end, increasingly refused to accept such broad estimates, automatically debited to their (trading) accounts. SLAs therefore developed to put in place a system of internal 'contracts', under which service managers first decide what support services they wish to buy in and set those requirements down in a tender document to be costed by potential suppliers, including their own local authority's central support departments. If a central department is successful in its tender, those costs will then be recharged to the service user, under the terms of the service local agreement. If a central department is, therefore, not able to recharge all of its costs then its own budget must be reduced, as people do not want to buy in their services.

Thus, the significant changes in accounting for central costs, can be shown in the following statements:

Under the CEC regime

Borough Treasurer's Department

	£
Employees	520,000
Running costs, etc. (as CIPFA Standard Form)	175,000
...	
...	
	695,000
Less: Allocated to other services	695,000
Central cost	–

Under a SLA

Borough Treasurer's Department

	£
Expenditure as above	695,000
Less: Charged to other services and functions	
under Agreements	650,000
Central cost not recharged	45,000

With all local government costs, and particularly those of central departments under close scrutiny, the £45,000 that has not been able to be 'sold', will be critically examined by councillors, since it would otherwise be a direct charge on the authority's council tax.

Statements of support service costs

In its November 1991 consultation paper *Competing for Quality*, the government made it clear that as well as extending CCT to support services, local authorities would be required to produce internal trading accounts for support services, as a precursor to CCT. These accounts would have to be maintained whether or not a particular service was subject to competition.

CIPFA's reaction was to propose a system of self regulation on the basis of a code of practice rather than a legislative requirement to produce trading accounts. In October 1992 CIPFA issued a draft code of practice and established a trading accounts working party.

In November 1992 the government announced that it would rely upon regulations, rather than primary legislation, to produce an internal accounting framework for support services. At that time it appeared that CIPFA's draft code would form the basis of these requirements.

Subsequently it became clear that the government would not require local authorities to introduce and maintain trading accounts for support services. Instead, councils would have to produce statements of support service costs (SSSCs). Given this changed approach, CIPFA updated its code of practice and changed its status to that of a guidance note. It also published a further discussion document *The competitive environment, internal trading accounts for support services in local authorities*. CIPFA's view was that the introduction of trading accounts was still important despite the change in the government's position.

In February 1994 the Environment Minister issued the government's proposals for the statutory accounting framework that was promised for competition in local authorities' professional support services. The document, entitled *Statement of Support Service Costs (SSSC)*, will apply to all accounts published after April 1994, as a memorandum statement. It will apply to all white collar services which are subject to CCT.

The statement will break down the full cost of each service, including overheads, regardless of the percentage that has to be contracted out. In 1994/95, statements will cover legal and construction related services and the following year will be extended to finance, information technology, personnel and corporate administration. Councils facing reorganisation have a year's amnesty. All six support services will therefore be covered.

An example of what is to be contained in a proposed SSSC is set out below.

Example

The Proposed SSSC: An example of what it shows

		Legal services £	Construction and property services £
1	Specified support service activity		
2	Direct cost of activity, excluding recharges from other specified activity	420,000	540,000
3	Plus: Recharges from other specified activity	30,000	60,000
4	Cost of activity	450,000	600,000
5	Less: Recharges to other specified activity	60,000	30,000
6	Net cost of activity	390,000	570,000
7	Less: Recharges to DSO/DLOs	120,000	180,000
8	Less: Recharges to capitalised costs	30,000	80,000
9	Less: Recharges relating to functions performed for or other authorities under Section 101 agency agreements	30,000	50,000
10	Less: Other recharges to front-line services	270,000	300,000
11	Appropriation (surplus + / deficit −)	(+) 60,000	(+) 40,000

12	Analysis of other recharges to front-line services:*		
	Nursery, primary, secondary and special education	26,000	49,000
	Continuing education, education support services which are not defined activities under Section 2(3) of the 1988 Act, youth and community services	13,000	8,000
	Housing functions	72,000	95,000
	Social services functions	31,000	22,000
	Waste collection	25,000	29,000
	Public transport, parking and highways	18,000	23,000
	Environmental health, sport and recreating, parks and open spaces, cemeteries and crematorium, port health	21,000	21,000
	Planning functions and economic development	37,000	32,000
	Electoral registration, registration of births, marriages and deaths, revenue collection, corporate management	12,000	8,000
	Fire, civil defence, probation and magistrates' court services	9,000	9,000
	Flood defence, libraries, museums and galleries and Section 137 matters	6,000	4,000
Total		270,000	300,000

* Service heads for London boroughs and metropolitan authorities. Different lists will apply to county councils and to district councils.

CIPFA's latest guidance

In the light of this government requirement, CIPFA revised guidance issued to the profession in 1991 with a *Statement of Best Practice* dated January 1995.

A copy of that statement is set out below.

The reasons for change
This statement replaces the Institute Statement on accounting for overheads, issued in 1991. The three changes since 1991 are that:

1 service strategy has been separately identified, as in more recent Institute guides to accounting for education, social services and housing;
2 the definition of corporate management has been clarified, and the headings for corporate management and civic ceremonials have been combined to form a single heading, entitled 'the corporate and democratic core';
3 a further heading entitled 'unapportionable central overheads' has been established for four types of expenditure which may arise in special circumstances.

Accounting requirements
The Institute Council recommends that:

1 charges or apportionments covering all support service costs should be made to all their users;
2 the cost of service management should be apportioned to the accounts representing the activities managed;

3 the costs of the corporate and democratic core, service strategy and regulation and unapportionable central overheads should be allocated to separate objective heads kept for the purpose and should not be apportioned to any other head.

The principle and extent of apportionment

Support services

The *Code of Practice on Local Authority Accounting*, specifies the accounting principles and practices required to prepare statements of accounts which present fairly the financial position and transactions of local authorities. One of the requirements of the code is that all users should invariably pay for the support services that they use. Users may include services to the public, divisions or smaller units of services, DSOs, the corporate and democratic core and other support services.

The Institute remains fully committed to the principle that there are no grounds for making apportionments or charges for support services otherwise than to their users, either in statements of account or in lower level accounting records. Full costs should be taken into account when fixing charges for support services operating in a trading environment.

Service management

The cost of service management should be apportioned to the services, DSOs or support services managed, in the same way as support service costs.

Service strategy and regulation

The cost of strategy and regulation of any service to the public should be allocated to a separate objective expenditure head in the accounts of the service, and should not be apportioned to divisions or units of service.

The corporate and democratic core

The costs of the corporate and democratic core should be allocated to a separate objective expenditure head, and should not be apportioned to other expenditure heads.

Unapportionable central overheads

The cost of apportionable central overheads should not be apportioned or charged because they currently have no users to whom apportionments could logically be made.

Definitions

Support services – services which support the provision of services to the public, other support services and the corporate and democratic core, as now defined. They are either obtained from support service units within the authority or bought in from external suppliers, to help their users to carry out those users' own main functions.

Management – comprises direction, supervision and guidance by members of the organisation superior to those whose overheads are under consideration. Local authorities and their committees comprise the two top levels of management in local government. Management is of the following two main types; service management and corporate management within the corporate rate and democratic core.

Service management – the management of specific services to the public, DSOs and support services. The management of services to the public comprises service strategy and operational management.

Operational management – comprises the whole of service management except service strategy.

Service strategy – that part of management which would remain even if all units of service were to be contracted out or sold, or if any part of their management were to be delegated. It includes, for example, apportioning available funds between units of service, and deciding their various objectives.

Regulation – comprises:

1   all the duties which local authorities are required by statute to carry out in order to maintain the standard of services provided to the public, whether through their own employees or third parties;
2   shadow regulation, which comprises the management of directly managed service units, to the extent that it would continue in the form of regulation, as just described, if the service units were to be sold, or if any part of their management were to be delegated;
3   service chief officers, such as chief education officers, whose apportionment is a statutory requirement.

The corporate and democratic core – comprises:

1   the back-funding of pensions increases;
2   unused shares of IT facilities;
3   shares of other long-term unused but unrealisable assets; and
4   deficiency on asset rents where cheaper accommodation would have been satisfactory.

Date of application

The Institute Council recommends that this statement should apply to all local authority financial statements for accounting periods beginning on or after 1 April 1996, and where practicable in earlier statements. Authorities that will cease to exist as a result of local government reorganisation in the period up to 1 April 1997 are exempted from this requirement. The requirement will apply to the new local authorities.

Parish councils

Chapter 2 of this book set out the position and duties of parish councils within the present local government structure. A large district council, covering a rural area, may have 60 or 70 parish councils to liaise with.

In essence, each parish decides annually the level of its expenditure on local parish purposes. That requirement is added to the district councils own council tax and included on the council tax account for payment. Expenditure by the parish council is then met from this 'additional' precept.

The statutory requirements relating to parish councils are contained in the *Local Government Act 1972*, Section 150(b) of which stipulates that accounts must be kept. The only prescription is that these accounts must be on a receipts and payments basis, as opposed to an income and expenditure basis, although some of the larger parish councils will operate on an accruals basis. In addition, the 1972 Act requires that one of the parish council officers shall properly administer its financial affairs and the accounts are subject to district, or approved, audit in the normal Audit Commission way.

The district council will therefore keep a personal account with each of its parishes, year end balances being carried forward for adjustment in the following year.

Suspense and holding accounts

Suspense accounts

Suspense accounts are those accounts which receive entries where there is uncertainty about their final location. They differ from holding accounts where costs are charged prior to a positive allocation on a previously agreed basis.

The most usual instance of a suspense account transaction can be exemplified by the receipt, at a local authority cash office, of a cheque without any indication of the sender, or to which account the money is due to be credited. Pending enquiries, perhaps through the banking system, the cheque would be placed in a suspense account and interest earned until the payer had confirmed the reason for the payment. A suspense account entry would also be necessary where the drawer of the cheque was known but it was uncertain as to which debts the cheque should be applied. The early clearance of all suspense account items is recommended because otherwise balances will tend to build up and the passage of time may cause difficulties in tracing.

Holding accounts

Holding accounts are accounts in which the costs of an activity are collected and controlled prior to their reallocation to the users of the activity.

They are used extensively by local authorities and examples include: transport pools, printing, central depots, shared computer facilities, central support services (e.g. legal, finance, surveyors) and administrative buildings.

The apportionment or recharge of the holding account is based upon an estimate of the benefit received from the activity by the user. The method enables costs to be held that could not individually and immediately be shared out to users. The recharge can also be more accurately based upon the actual costs of specific tasks.

Holding accounts are prepared in accordance with the standard form, i.e. expenditure first, then income using the standard groupings. However it is sometimes more convenient to present holding accounts using a horizontal layout, especially where columns can be used to relate several holding accounts to each other.

Holding accounts recharge their cost to users on a wide variety of bases:

- transport pool, by hourly, daily or mileage vehicle charge
- central depots, by space utilised
- shared computer facilities, by individual pricing on jobs not common to all users, and by estimated proportion of usage for the balance
- central support services, by time spent on direct service department work (estimated or ascertained from time sheets)
- administrative buildings, by floor area occupied by the departments benefiting.

Any balance on a holding account at the year end is an amount either under or over-recovered and is carried forward to the next financial year.

Chapter 10 of this book reports more recent developments in the allocation or recharging of holding account costs and particularly the development of internal contracts, known as 'service level agreements'.

A practical example of the use of the holding accounts is given below.

A local authority operates three holding accounts for the following:

- pooled vehicles
- vehicle maintenance
- central depot.

The example below sets out the pooled vehicles, vehicle maintenance and central depot holding accounts for the year ended 31 March 1994, in columnar form.

Example

	£
Pooled vehicles	
Wages	313,200
Clothing and uniforms	7,224
Petrol	237,696
Insurance	13,200
Other expenses	1,440
Debt charges	48,000
Vehicle maintenance	
Wages	250,560
Salaries	36,000
Oil	28,800
Printing, stationery, advertising, etc.	3,456
Insurances	792
Other expenses	5,280
Central depot	
Wages	751,680
Rates	66,000
Printing, stationery, etc.	11,688
Insurance	1,056
Debt charges	60,000
Revenue contributions to capital outlay	1,320

Other information

1) The following balances on the holding accounts were brought forward as at 1 April 1993.

	£
Pooled vehicles	1,440 Cr
Vehicle maintenance	2,496 Dr
Central depot	3,840 Dr

The balance on each holding account is to be completely recharged as at 31 March 1994.

2) Eleven of the 12 insurance premiums due have been paid at 31 March 1994.

3) Half of the total costs on the vehicle maintenance account are to be recharged to the pooled vehicles account. The remaining balance is to be recharged to equal proportions to the highways and works committee and the parks committee.

4) Ten per cent and 40 per cent of the total costs on the central depot account are to be recharged to the vehicle maintenance account and pooled vehicles account respectively. The remaining balance is to be recharged in equal proportions to the highways and work committee and the housing committee.

5) An account for £984 for petrol for the pooled vehicles account was due but unpaid at 31 March 1994.

6) Twenty-five per cent and 75 per cent of the total costs of the pooled vehicles account are to be recharged to the general purposes committee and the highways and works committee respectively.

Example

Holding accounts for year ended 31 March 1994

	Pooled vehicles £	Vehicle maintenance £	Central depot £
Balance b/f 1 April 1993	—	2,496	3,860
Employees			
Salaries		36,000	
Wages	313,200	250,560	751,680
Premises related expenses			
Rates			66,000
Transport related expenses			
Petrol (237,696 + 984)	238,680		
Oil		28,800	
Supplies and services			
Closing	7,224		
Printing and stationery		3,456	11,688
Insurance	13,200	792	1,056
Add unpaid	1,200	72	96
Other expenses	1,440	5,280	
Capital financing costs			
Loans fund	48,000		60,000
Direct revenue financing			1,200
	622,944	327,456	895,680
Recharge from central depot	358,272	89,568	—
Recharge from vehicle maintenance	208,512	—	—
	1,189,728	417,024	895,680

	Pooled vehicles £	Vehicle maintenance £	Central depot £
Balance b/f 1 April 1993	1,440	—	—
Recharged to vehicle maintenance			89,568
Pooled vehicles		208,512	358,272
Highways and works committee	891,216	104,256	223,920
Housing committee			
Parks committee		104,256	223,920
General purposes committee	297,072		
	1,189,728	417,024	895,680

8 NHS structure and funding

This chapter considers the changing framework within which the NHS operates, and such developments as NHS Trusts and GP fundholding. The broad capital and revenue financial relationships with central government are then summarised. The chapter concludes with a comment on corporate governance in the NHS.

Introduction and brief history of the Health Service

The National Health Service (NHS) was founded in 1948 to provide health care to all citizens of the United Kingdom, regardless of their ability to pay. The principles of the NHS were outlined in the 1944 Beveridge report, *Social Insurance and Allied Services* and then developed into legislation through the *National Health Services Act 1946*.

The principle that 'medical treatment and care should be made available to rich and poor alike in accordance with medical need and by no other criteria' was reaffirmed in the *National Health Services Act 1977* which defines in broad terms the objectives of the NHS:

It is the Secretary of State's duty to continue the promotion of a comprehensive health service designed to secure improvement

- in the physical and mental health of the people, and
- in the prevention, diagnosis and treatment of illness,

and for that purpose to provide or secure the effective provision of services in accordance with this Act.

The services so provided shall be free of charge except in so far as the making and recovery of charges is expressly provided for by or under any enactment whenever passed.

The National Health Service 1948–74

The present organisation of the National Health Service has grown from three essentially separate areas of the Service which existed between 1948 and 1974. These could be summarised as follows:

- *Local authorities* were responsible for the provision of local health and school health services, which were collectively referred to as community health services. These services included such items as health centres, home nursing, vaccination and immunisation, ambulances and school clinics. The revenue cost was met out of local authorities' rate income, together with a central government contribution known as the Rate Support Grant.

- *Hospital authorities* were responsible for by far the largest element of the total National Health Service expenditure in providing for the whole range of institutionally-based hospital and specialist services. Finance for these services was provided in the form of an annually fixed allocation determined by the Department of Health and Social Security (DHSS).
- *Executive councils* administered and paid for the services of family practitioners, i.e. doctors, dentists, pharmacists and opticians, apart from the cost of the executive councils' own administration, for which the DHSS provided an annually fixed allocation. The cost of services provided by family practitioners was not subject to any predetermined ceiling.

The Health Service underwent major structural changes upon local government reorganisation in 1974 which unified the three branches, and placed them under the control of the new health authorities. This structure was modified further in 1980 in England and Wales. The 1980 changes were preceded by a Royal Commission which reported in 1979 and which had been given the following terms of reference:

> To consider, for the whole of the UK, in the interests both of the patients and of those who work in the NHS the best use and management of the financial and manpower resources of the NHS.' (Cmnd 7615)

The government's response to the Royal Commission was set out in a consultative paper *Patients First*. The paper deliberately emphasised that the needs of patients must be paramount. This emphasis was also made in the Royal Commission report, which had set out what it believed would be generally accepted objectives for the NHS, bearing in mind both the original philosophy of the service and the political differences that occur in its interpretation.

The National Health Service from April 1974

After 1 April 1974 a more integrated approach was adopted to the provision and financing of health care. The new health authorities were made responsible for the provision and integration of all community, hospital and family practitioner services within their areas, and the total cost of these services covered by an annual allocation determined by the Department of Health and Social Security with one significant exception. The family practitioner services were administered by a separate family practitioner committee, independent of the health authority, but having a small degree of common membership. The services themselves continue to operate under an 'open ended' budget. This meant that whereas the hospital and community services had to provide health care facilities within a pre-determined financial limit, the family practitioner services' expenditure was reimbursed directly without any constraint in financial terms being placed upon the general practitioners, dentists, pharmacists and opticians.

Because of the substantial sums of public funds involved, the direct allocations that health authorities received carried significant controls and limitations on their use. The duties and responsibilities of health authorities, which they exercised as agents of the Secretary of State, were decided by statute and this limited the purposes for which expenditure could be incurred. However, the principle of free access to health care facilities for the whole population continued to be the cornerstone of all legislation covering the National Health Service.

Health Service Act 1980

The present structure of the NHS was established by the *Health Service Act 1980* and became operative in 1982. In England the NHS was organised as a three-tier administrative structure. In Scotland, Wales and Northern Ireland there were only two tiers. In recent years, the NHS has undergone considerable structural development, most notably the establishment of the Policy Board and the (Management) Executive, together with the recommendations of the 1989 White Paper *Working for Patients* which affected the structure and constitution of health authorities.

April 1991 reforms

In January 1989, the Government published a White Paper *Working for Patients* which proposed wide ranging reforms of the NHS. These reforms were to secure the following key changes (and subsequently became the *National Health Service and Community Care Act 1990*).

- To make the Health Service more responsive to the needs of patients, as much power and responsibility as possible would be delegated to local level.
- To stimulate a better service to the patient, hospitals would be able to apply for new self-governing status as NHS Hospital Trusts.
- To enable hospitals which best meet the needs and wishes of patients to get the money to do so, the money required to treat patients would be able to cross administrative boundaries.
- To reduce waiting times and improve the quality of service, to help give the individual patients appointment times they can rely on, and to help cut the long hours worked by some junior doctors, 100 new consultant posts would be created over the next three years.
- To help the family doctor improve service to patients, large GP practices would be able to apply for their own budgets to obtain a defined range of services direct from hospitals.
- To improve the effectiveness of NHS management, regional, district and family practitioner management bodies would be reduced in size and reformed on business lines, with executive and non-executive directors.
- To ensure that all concerned with delivering services to the patient make the best use of the resources available to them, quality of service and value for money would be more rigorously audited.

The main elements of the reforms are outlined below:

- *Managing the service* – The NHS is to continue to be funded by government mainly from tax revenues and as such the Secretary of State for Health must be accountable to Parliament. However, wherever possible decisions on operational matters in the NHS must be taken locally by operational units, with ministers being responsible for policy and strategy.

- *Self-governing hospitals* – Major acute hospitals with more than 250 beds would be encouraged to become 'self-governing'. Thus hospitals would be formally vested in a new and separate legal body, to be known as an NHS Hospital Trust, run by a board of directors with a chairman appointed by the Secretary of State. These trusts would be empowered by statute to employ staff; to enter into contracts both to provide services and to buy in services and supplies from others; and to raise income within statutory limits. The hospitals would earn the revenue by selling services to district health authorities, general practitioners, private patients, insurance companies, etc. The aim was to stimulate more efficient and effective performance. The first 'wave' of self-governing hospitals were established in 1991.
- *Funding health authorities* – Changes were proposed to the method of centrally funding health authorities. These changes are described in Chapter 9.
- *GP fundholders* – Family doctors with over 11,000 patients would be offered budgets with which to buy hospital care and out-patient care from either NHS hospitals or the private sector and for drugs, staff and premises.
- *External audit* – On the financial side it was proposed that the Audit Commission takes on the statutory audit of health authorities and also 'value for money' studies in the NHS.
- *Community care and local authorities* – For many years, community care had been the subject of much criticism mainly due to the ineffective national and regional planning, as well as to wide variations in provision by local authorities and health authorities. The government issued a White Paper in October 1989 entitled *Caring for People*, which identified that local authorities should take the lead role in community care. The main elements of the White Paper were:
  - local authorities should be given the lead role in community care planning, but should conduct their planning exercises in close co-operation with district health authorities (DHAs) and family health service authorities (FHSAs);
  - users should no longer have to 'fit in' to existing services, but rather services need to be redesigned to meet user needs which have been uncovered by new multi-disciplinary assessment systems;
  - budgets should be devolved as close to the user as possible to allow flexible, local purchasing; a 'care management' system is seen as the preferred way to obtain user-sensitive provision;
  - local authorities to assume more of an enabling role through the allocation of funds, but a declining role in service provision; instead, services were to be increasingly provided by a mixed economy of care based largely upon the private and voluntary sectors;
  - the transfer to local social services authorities of the care element of social security income support currently paid to residents of private and voluntary residential and nursing homes; local authorities would have discretion on how to use this funding.

These proposals were enacted through the *NHS and Community Care Act 1990* with a view to implementation in April 1991. But soon after the passage of the Act, the government announced an implementation delay on the ground that local authorities were not sufficiently prepared for the changes. Some took the view that a more pertinent reason for the delay was concern about the local authority expenditure implications at a time of high sensitivity about poll tax levels.

Instead, it was decided that implementation would be spread over three years, commencing in April 1991. The timetable has been as follows:

–   April 1991: inspection units and complaints procedures to be established by local authorities; first availability of specific grants for mental illness and for drug and alcohol abuse;
–   April 1992: the first community care plans to be produced by local authorities, DHAs and FHSAs;
–   April 1993: new assessment procedures to be in place; social security income support to be transferred to social services authorities; realignment of commissioning and providing roles within social services departments;
–   onwards: development of care management and new service patterns based on the assessment of individual needs.

A consequence of these important structural changes was the creation of an 'internal market' in the NHS, with purchasers and providers negotiating contracts to provide the best types of health care within the overall cash limited sums available.

Broad financing arrangements

The NHS is funded partly out of employer's and employees' national insurance contributions, but mainly from general taxation. Some diagnostic services and treatments are free to patients requiring them. For other items such as spectacles, dentistry and drugs prescribed by GPs, most patients bear at least part of the cost, but there are important exemptions. Recent governments have introduced charges for certain previously free items such as eye tests, though NHS consultations with GPs and specialists, as well as NHS hospital treatment, remain free.

The National Health Service is therefore almost wholly dependent upon central government funding. Unlike local government, it has no independent source of revenue equivalent to business rates or the community charge, but instead its finances are determined by the Cabinet in the annual public expenditure allocation process. Health authorities can raise limited amounts of money by fund-raising activities.

Present organisation in the United Kingdom (Spring 1995)

The National Health Service in England is now organised into:

● eight regional health authorities (RHAs) in England primarily responsible for strategy;
● approximately 160 district health authorities (DHAs) responsible for purchasing services for their residents;

- approximately 600 'Directly Managed Units' responsible for providing services on contract to district health authorities.

Also from April 1991, 57 units became legal entities known as self-governing trusts. Their accountability is direct to the Secretary of State. Further waves of trusts have been established annually since then, and there are currently over 500 trusts.

Each statutory authority has ten members: five executive (General Manager and Finance Director being mandatory), and five non-executive plus a chairperson appointed by the Secretary of State.

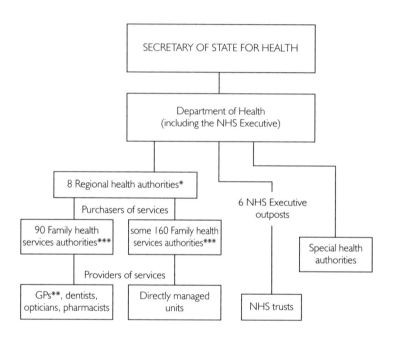

```
                  SECRETARY OF STATE FOR HEALTH

                       Department of Health
                    (including the NHS Executive)

   8 Regional health authorities*
                                              6 NHS Executive
        Purchasers of services                  outposts

  90 Family health      some 160 Family health
services authorities*** services authorities***
                                                       Special health
                                                         authorities
        Providers of services

  GPs**, dentists,      Directly managed
opticians, pharmacists       units              NHS trusts
```

*   All RHA's will have gone by April 1996
**   Some GPs are fundholders
***   DHAs and FHSAs will merge from April 1996 and become Commissions

The present structure in England

The broad position in the rest of the United Kingdom is:

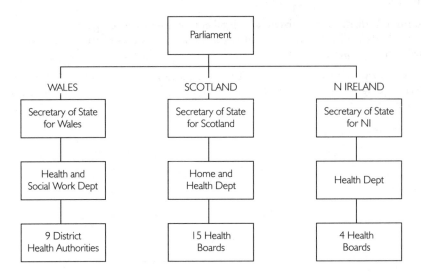

April 1996 planned reforms

This position, however, will be short-lived as radical reorganisation plans were announced in Parliament on 21 October 1993 by the Secretary of State for Health.

They include:

- the abolition of the 14 statutory RHAs and the reorganisation of the NHSE to include eight regional offices – each headed by a regional director – to replace both the RHAs and the existing NHSE outposts;
- the creation of a clear identity for the NHS Executive, within the Department of Health, as the 'headquarters of the NHS';
- the appointment of non-executive members to the NHS Policy Board to cover each of the eight new regions thereby providing a link between ministers and local DHA, FHSA and trust chairmen; and
- enabling DHAs and FHSAs to merge to create stronger local purchasers with such mergers being encouraged actively.

Timing

As a first step towards the new structure, the government merged the existing RHAs into eight new interim regional health authorities from 1 April 1994. The boundaries of the eight new RHAs would match those of the eight newly-created regional offices of the NHSE.

A consultation document on RHA mergers was published on 1 November 1993 and bodies consulted had until 15 January 1994 to respond.

Legislation will provide for the abolition of RHAs and to enable DHAs and FHSAs to merge, as from 1 April 1996.

Regional directors took up posts from 1 April 1994 as members of a restructured NHS Executive. Selected individuals are also acting as regional general managers of the transitional RHAs, retaining responsibility for residual RHA functions.

The regional offices of the NHSE also began operating from 1 April 1994, incorporating the functions of the existing NHSE outposts.

Functions

It is recognised that RHAs have played an important role in NHS management for many years and the decision to abolish them has not been taken lightly. However, the development of the NHS reforms has already brought about a shift of responsibility towards local purchasers and providers and it is considered that there is no longer a need for 14 separate statutory bodies at an intermediate level.

The new NHSE regional offices will take on those functions of the RHAs which remain the responsibility of central management. They will be responsible for developing the purchasing function and primary care within the health service and will also take over the task of monitoring NHS trusts from the existing NHSE outposts.

The functions of the regional offices in relation to purchasers and providers will be kept clear and distinct. The regional offices will provide a link between strategic and local management; they will not become involved in detailed operational matters which are the responsibility of local health authorities and trusts.

The regional offices will be much smaller than the present RHAs and will employ fewer staff. The total staffing budget for each office will be set when the allocation of functions across the new structure has been finalised and these limits will be adhered to rigorously. A similar overall limit will be set for the NHSE as a whole.

The functions of the eight NHSE regional offices will be:

- ensuring compliance with the regulatory framework of the internal market
- managing the performance of both purchasers and providers
- arbitration on disputes
- approving GP fundholder applications and budgets
- purchaser development; targeted contributions to central work on policy and resources
- working with the professions
- working with universities
- public health
- aspects of human resource management.

The finances of the National Health Service

In 1992/93, total spending on the NHS was in excess of £34.4 billion. At 1949 prices spending has doubled from £400 million to about £800 million.

As a percentage of gross domestic product, NHS spending in the United Kingdom since 1980/81 has broadly moved as follows:

	%	
1980/81	5.0	
1981/82	5.1,	then a gradual decline to ...
1989/90	4.75,	then a gradual increase to ...
1992/93	5.5	

Although taxation has always been the main source of NHS finance since its inception, there has been an overall reduction in the burden on general taxpayers, as other sources of finance have emerged. A summary of the position at ten-year intervals shows:

	Taxation %	Contributions %	NHS authorities %	Local health patients %
1949	100.0	–	–	–
1959	73.6	13.7	8.6	4.1
1969	78.8	10.4	7.3	3.6
1979	88.3	9.5	–	2.2
1989	80.8	16.1	–	2.1
1993	82.9	14.2	–	3.0

Allocating NHS finance

For the purposes of revenue distribution, the NHS is divided into two parts:

● the hospital and community health services (HCHS)
● family health services (FHS).

HCHS covers district health authorities, while the FHS includes general practitioners, dentists, opticians and pharmacists. GP fundholders are allocated their own budgets direct, with which to purchase health care on behalf of their patients. About 75 per cent of the total NHS budget is allocated to HCH services on a cash-limited basis, via the regional health authorities. RHA allocations are designed to meet specific regional needs and problems. Subsequent allocations are made on broadly similar considerations.

The Department of Health

Responsible to Parliament is the Secretary of State for Health, aided by Ministers for Health. These Ministers are served by the civil servants of the Department of Health and the NHS Executive.

The *National Health Service Act 1977* sets out the powers and duties of the Secretary of State. The principal duties are

to continue the promotion in England and Wales of a comprehensive health service designed to secure improvement

- in the physical and mental health of the people of those countries

- in the prevention, diagnosis and treatment of illness

and for that purpose to provide or secure the effective provision of services in accordance with this Act.

The services so provided shall be free except in so far as the making and recovery of charges is expressly provided for by or under any enactment, whenever passed.

It is the Secretary of State's duty to provide throughout England and Wales, to such extent as is considered necessary to meet all reasonable requirements:

- hospital accommodation
- medical, dental, nursing and ambulance services
- facilities for the care of expectant and nursing mothers and young children as is considered appropriate
- facilities for the prevention of illness, the care of persons suffering from illness, and after-care of persons who have suffered from illness, as is considered appropriate
- other services as are required for the diagnosis and treatment of illness.

The key functions of the Secretary of State and the Department of Health are centred on establishing national plans, priorities and policies for the NHS and monitoring how successfully such policies are implemented by the lower tiers of the NHS. Thus the Secretary of State is continually monitoring the efficiency and effectiveness of the lower tiers. Having established plans and priorities it is the Secretary of State's responsibility to obtain a share of the national resources to administer the NHS and distribute these resources throughout the country in order that the plans will be achieved. The mechanisms for distribution are discussed in Chapter 9. It is mandatory for health authorities to keep their drawings within the approved cash limit plus any additional income which can be generated locally. Monthly returns of key financial figures are made to the NHSE.

The Policy Board and the Management Executive

The Secretary of State announced that from 1989 two bodies would assist the Secretary in the national planning and management of the NHS: (i) the Policy Board and (ii) the NHS (Management) Executive. The Policy Board comprises the Secretary of State and appointed members from industry, and is responsible for determining the strategy, objectives and finances of the NHS in the light of government policy.

It sets objectives for the Management Executive which has responsibility for the operation and management of the NHS within the framework set by ministers and the Policy Board. It informs the Policy Board of resource needs, proposes distribution of funds to regions, and deals with pay and personnel issues. It is also responsible for setting health authorities' objectives and monitoring them through regional planning and review processes. The members of the Management Executive Board are appointed by the Secretary of State, headed by a chief executive and supported by officers responsible for specific functions such as finance, personnel and nursing. Its membership is drawn from the NHS, Civil Service and the private sector.

Regional health authorities (RHAs)

In England at second tier level there are currently 8 regional health authorities which cover geographical areas extending over several local authority boundaries.

Regional health authorities interpret the policies of the Department of Health and draw up policies which suit the particular needs of their regions in regional strategic plans. These plans are produced after consultation with the third tier of the NHS, the district health authorities. The plans attempt to assess the health care pattern for particular regions over the following ten-year period. The regional strategic plan must be submitted to the Department of Health for approval.

When approved, the plans will form the basis of health care policy over a period of time and subject to an annual review. Each regional health authority is responsible for allocating the funds, received from the Department of Health, to the district health authorities within the region. These funds will be allocated in a way which will allow the regional strategic plan to be achieved. It is each region's responsibility to then subsequently monitor the expenditure of its district health authorities.

Regions give advice to the districts on policy implementation and are directly responsible for managing some services, on a region wide basis, so that the benefits of economies of scale may accrue. In many cases, these regional services, e.g. ambulances, blood transfusion, Information technology are either provided by trusts, or by the private sector.

Structure and role of regional health authorities

The RHA as a governing body consists of ten members plus a chairman appointed by the Secretary of State for Health.

The RHA is responsible for strategic planning and controlling the health service for the patients living in its geographical area. It receives the revenue and capital cash limit for the region and is responsible for allocating it between itself and the DHAs in the manner it sees most appropriate. Broadly speaking it will operate the same rules for cash limits as are operated by the Department of Health, i.e. allocation according to population, with the same carry-over and virement rules for revenue and capital cash limits.

However, the RHA is free to vary these rules and may for instance give a DHA a very large capital allocation in one year to allow a large capital project to be completed with a consequential reduction in future years. The responsibility for all the DHAs and RHAs to keep within the regional cash limits lies with the RHA.

The RHA is also responsible for allocating the proceeds from the sale of any fixed assets used by DHAs in its region to the DHAs. The Department of Health has required that this be operated in such a way that DHAs who sell the assets they use benefit from the sale, but ultimately this distribution is the responsibility of the RHA.

The requirement of hospitals and community health service to pay capital charges to the RHA for the assets that they use has been introduced by the *NHS and Community Care Act 1990* and came into effect on 1 April 1991. As already stated, these charges are paid to the RHA who may allocate the proceeds to the DHAs for revenue expenditure as they see fit. For further details of capital charges, see Chapter 10.

If a DHA has a capital scheme costing over £5m this will be carried out by the RHA on behalf of the DHA and all accounting entries relating to such schemes will appear in the books of the RHA until the scheme is complete. The scheme is then transferred from the RHA to the DHA in the accounts of the appropriate directly managed unit.

District health authorities (DHAs)

There are about 160 district health authorities in England. These authorities are responsible for providing hospital and community health services, through directly managed units (DMUs), but with the introduction of the internal market and, especially, of NHS trusts, the DHA is moving to become the purchaser of health care services from other bodies. Thus the DHAs are the providers of health services in line with policies set at a national and regional level. It is at the district level that health needs are identified and fed back into the planning systems of the Department of Health and the region. It is the districts' responsibility to identify service deficiencies and to apply to the regions for funds to meet such deficiencies or to cut existing services or find other economies. The funds allocated by the regions to DHAs are based on such indicators of need as population, demography (i.e. population structure), and various health and cost indicators. DHAs and FHSAs will all have merged by April 1996 to become commissions.

Structure and function of DHAs

The DHA as a governing body consists of a chairman appointed by the Secretary of State for Health and ten other members.

The *NHS and Community Care Act 1990* provided that from 1 April 1991, the role of the DHA in planning the services to be provided was separated from their role of administering and managing the provision of hospital and community services.

This means that the DHAs now have two separate roles, as a purchaser of services and as a provider of services. As a purchaser of services the DHA receives a revenue allocation from the RHA and decides which services are required for the population living in their area. It then enters into contracts with the following bodies to purchase the services required:

- directly managed units
- NHS trust hospitals
- private sector hospitals and services.

These contracts, which are an important part of the internal market, do not have the legal status of normal contracts and if a dispute arises in connection with them, the Secretary of State or his/her representative acts as arbiter. Contracting is further considered in Chapter 9.

Some people living in a district will be patients of general practitioners who are budget-holders. In these cases it is the general practitioners and not the DHA who receive an allocation of funds and are responsible for purchasing the health care required by their patients (Chapter 9).

The DHA also receives a capital allocation from the RHA and is required to allocate this among the services they are responsible for, according to their plans for the service.

Although the amount of the revenue and capital allocation is decided by the RHA the actual cash is requisitioned directly from the Department of Health by the DHA.

Directly managed units (DMUs)

Under the *NHS and Community Care Act 1990*, all the hospital and community services previously run by the DHA are required to be organised into a number of directly managed units (DMUs). These are managed as separate entities which decide on which services they can provide, and the price of these services. They also keep separate accounts which show the surplus or deficit achieved by the activities of the DMU. The units are under the control of the DHA and their accounts are consolidated with those of the DHA.

Some hospitals and community services which were previously run by the DHA have now become NHS trusts and are thus self-governing and responsible directly to the NHSE outposts.

The major source of income of a DMU is the payment it receives from the DHA for the provision of services. This is paid by the DHA out of its revenue allocation from the RHA.

DMUs have limited powers to carry out income-generating schemes and are also empowered to provide services to non-NHS patients and receive money from this source. Units may also receive donations for both revenue and capital expenditure and this will be recorded in the first instance in the charitable (trust) fund's accounts, which is a separate set of accounts for recording donations (see Chapter 9). When it is transferred to the DMU it will be recorded in their accounts as income.

If fixed assets have been purchased from donations, they will be recorded in the accounts of the DMU in such a way that the DMU will not have to pay capital charges on these to the RHA. The reason for this is that it is considered appropriate that the DMU receiving such donations should be able to benefit from them rather than their benefit reverting to the RHA. Fixed assets are also purchased from the capital allocation of the DHA but generally the financing of these assets will appear in the accounts of the DHA and when they are purchased, these assets will be transferred to the books of the DMU.

Common services

There may be certain activities which were in the past carried out by the DHA, such as payroll or laundry services and which are now used by a number of DMUs and possibly the DHA in its purchaser role as well. These are called common services, and it is now necessary for separate accounts to be kept for these services. These accounts will be kept in precisely the same way as those for DMUs, and will be consolidated with those of the DHA. The only difference is that the revenue income will be the 'internal market' payments made by other sections for the use of their services.

The following paragraphs, from the 1993 year book of the National Association of Health Authorities and Trusts, provide additional information on key aspects of the present NHS organisation.

Family health services authorities (FHSAs)

FHSAs exist to manage the services provided by GPs, dentists, retail pharmacists and opticians. These family practitioners are independent contractors and not NHS employees. The terms and conditions under which they work are negotiated nationally between the health professions and the government. FHSAs are responsible for implementing the national contracts in their areas.

As a result of the NHS reforms, emanating from the *1990 NHS and Community Care Act*, the role of FHSAs has been strengthened and they are now much more actively involved than hitherto in planning the development of services in their areas.

For historical reasons, the boundaries of FHSAs differed from those of DHAs. There are 90 FHSAs in England serving populations which range from 130,000 to 1,600,000, but boundaries are now becoming aligned with those of DHAs.

Each authority comprises a chairman appointed by the Secretary of State, five lay non-executive members and four professional non-executives (a GP, dentist, pharmacist and community nurse) appointed by the RHA, and a general manager. The functions of FHSAs include:

- managing the contracts of family practitioners
- paying practitioners in accordance with their contracts
- providing information to the public
- dealing with complaints from the public
- allocating funds for GP practice developments.

Family practitioners retain considerable influence over the running of services. An important channel of influence for GPs is the local medical committee. This committee is elected by GPs in each area to express the views of GPs to FHSAs. The local medical committee operates alongside similar committees for other family practitioners. FHSAs and DHAs will all have merged by April 1996 to become commissions.

National Health Service trusts (NHS trusts)

NHS trusts were first established in 1991 under the NHS reforms. The function of trusts is to provide hospital and community services on behalf of the Secretary of State. Trusts are self-governing units, with their own boards of directors and with freedom to organise their own affairs, subject only to the legal framework within which they operate, and the contracts they have negotiated with purchasers.

The performance of trusts is monitored by the NHS Executive outposts. Each trust is required to prepare an annual business plan outlining, among other things, its proposals for service developments and capital investment. This is examined by the management executive outpost to ensure the trust meets its financial responsibilities.

The main financial duties of trusts are:

- to break even
- to earn a 6 per cent return on their capital
- to contain capital expenditure within the external financing limit set by the Secretary of State.

Outposts of the management executive monitor financial performance in trusts on a regular basis to ensure that they meet financial targets. Outposts also review the published annual reports and accounts of trusts to check that financial duties have been fulfilled.

The number of trusts is increasing as the NHS reforms continue to be implemented. There is an annual cycle of applications for trust status and it is anticipated that most if not all NHS services will be running as trusts by 1995. When this happens, there will be a complete separation of purchaser and provider roles. Further details of NHS trusts are contained in Chapter 9.

General practitioner (GP) fundholders

The introduction of general practice fundholding is one of the major developments in the NHS and reflects the general practitioner's position as one of the purchasers of health services.

The initiative was introduced in order to give the practitioner and hence his or her patient, the ability, within the finance available, to exercise a greater freedom of choice.

Subject to a minimum practice list size and subject to ability to manage funds practices may opt to become fundholders. In doing so the doctors within the practice are empowered to contract with the hospital or unit of their choice for certain treatments and services and to decide whether or not the money allocated is to be applied to drugs, hospital or community health services, or other forms of care.

The 'fund' is allocated to the practice by the RHA and comprises three parts: practice staff reimbursement, applicable hospital and community health services and drugs. Whilst the fund is allocated under the three headings in the first instance, the practitioner is able to transfer money from one heading to another and to carry forward savings from one year to another. Savings may then be spent on further services.

GP practices that are accepted as fundholders are responsible for purchasing a defined range of services for their patients. These services include:

- selective non-emergency in-patient and day case treatments
- out-patient services
- domiciliary visits
- direct access tests and investigations (pathology, radiology, audiology)
- direct access therapy (physio, occupational, speech, dietetics, chiropody)
- community health services, including, e.g. nursing and health visiting services
- drugs
- employment of practice staff.

Other services are purchased for patients of GP fundholders by their DHAs.

Originally, it was anticipated that only practices with 11,000 or more registered patients would become fundholders. This limit has since been reduced by the government and encouragement has been given to smaller practices to apply for fundholding status. FHSAs are gradually assuming responsibility on behalf of RHAs for administering fundholding and monitoring the use of resources by GP fundholders.

The resources allocated to fundholding practices are deducted from the allocation of the relevant district health authorities. It is the government's aim to move to a funding formula in which the money fundholders receive is based on the number of patients served, adjusted for age, sex and other factors. This will replace the current funding formula, which allocates resources according to the use made of services in the past and the hospital referral patterns of GPs.

Community health councils (CHCs)

Community health councils have existed since 1974 as patient 'watchdogs' to represent the public's interest in the NHS. They are statutory bodies, established by RHAs, and there is usually one CHC for each DHA. CHCs have no executive powers. Their main job is to advise DHAs and FHSAs on the views and concerns of patients and the public.

The members of CHCs are drawn from voluntary organisations, local authorities and the local community. These members are supported by a full-time secretary (or chief officer) and one or more assistant. A typical annual budget for a community health council, provided by the RHA, is around £40,000.

CHCs have interpreted their responsibilities in different ways. Some have chosen to concentrate on helping members of the public by giving advice and assistance with complaints procedures and providing information. Others have given priority to lobbying NHS authorities and trusts and mounting pressure group campaigns.

To support them in their role, Parliament has agreed that CHCs should have the following rights:

- to relevant information from NHS authorities
- to access to certain NHS premises
- to inclusion in consultation on substantial developments or variations in services
- to send observers to meetings of district health authorities and family health services authorities.

Each CHC has a duty to publish an annual report and this is discussed at meetings with the DHA and FHSA.

Central government funding and controls

Introduction

Regional health authorities receive the major part of their funds for both revenue and capital expenditure from central government via the Department of Health. Each RHA is given a capital and revenue cash limit for the provision of health services to the population living in their region. The amount of the cash limit is related to the size of the population in the area and is then allocated by the RHA between itself and the DHAs in its region.

If the RHA overspends the cash limits, this must be carried forward and deducted from the cash limit for the next year. If underspending occurs, up to 1 per cent of the revenue cash limit and 10 per cent of the capital cash limit can be carried forward to the next year. Any underspending greater than this is lost to the RHA. Flexibility is also possible between revenue and capital cash limits in one year up to a maximum transfer of 10 per cent on the capital and 1 per cent on the revenue cash limits.

RHAs may make local arrangements with individual health authorities for a limited amount of transfers between revenue and capital allocations and the carry forward of underspending on the cash limits.

Hospitals and community services which are under the control of the DHAs are required to pay capital charges to the RHA for the use of their fixed assets. This income to the RHA is then distributed to the DHAs for revenue expenditure. Income from the sale of fixed assets used by the DHAs is paid to the RHA. This is then distributed to the DHAs for capital expenditure in whatever way they think is most beneficial to the service.

Controls, by the central government directly through the Department of Health, or via the NHSE, are an important feature of the administration of the NHS. This chapter deals with the outlines of financial, audit and other controls. Chapters 9 and 10 deal with specific matters in more detail.

National fund allocations

National allocation

The funds made available nationally to the NHS are announced in the November budget statement. The total planned central government expenditure on health in 1994/95 for the UK was £37.1 billion.

Government expenditure on the NHS is under two main headings, hospitals and community health services (HCHS) and family health services (FHS), each of which is sub-divided into revenue and capital. Other expenditure headings are the Central Health and Miscellaneous Services (CHMS), providing services which can most effectively be administered centrally, and the administrative costs of the Department of Health.

In addition to government funding, other sources of finance are as follows:

- income from charges and other receipts (mainly land sales). These sources fund approximately 8 per cent of total NHS expenditure
- sums of money donated by individuals or organisations to be used either at the discretion of the authority for the welfare of patients or staff, or for a specific purpose in accordance with a bequest or trust. These non-exchequer funds are considered separately in Chapter 9.

One of the major debates surrounding HCHS finance, relates to the national revenue allocations and inflation. Depending on the inflation index used, differing conclusions can be drawn regarding the real purchasing power of health authorities.

In recent years, cost improvement programmes, or so called internally generated funds, also need to be considered, producing at least three commonly used measures of growth in NHS resources:

- real terms increase, using a measure of inflation in the economy as a whole
- real terms increase, using a health service specific price index
- both points above plus cost improvement programmes.

Each of these measures is compared with a target growth figure based on the estimated percentage real change in expenditure necessary to cope with changes in demography, advances in medicine and the funding implications of government policies.

Cash limits

Cash limits have covered the majority of government expenditure since 1976. Until 1981 however, expenditure plans were produced on a constant price basis, enabling the measurement of the movement in the real level of expenditure (volume). Volume planning was criticised as protecting public expenditure from inflation, and thus, in 1981, the move was made to cash planning. Plans are now expressed in cash terms based on a predicted level of inflation and these are translated directly into cash limits. Thus when inflation (pay or price increases) is above the forecast, there is no automatic assurance that the excess will be funded.

Revenue allocations to RHAs

Since the inception of the NHS four distinct periods can be identified:

- 1948-70 – allocations were based on existing services. The 1962 Hospital Plan was designed to achieve a more equal distribution of hospital beds, but generally the variations that existed before 1948 in services were perpetuated.
- 1971-76 – the 'Crossman Formula' calculated allocations based on population served, adjusted for age and sex, beds and caseload. The scale of the inter-regional differences necessitated a ten-year timetable for implementation.
- 1977-89 – the Resource Allocation Working Party (RAWP) was established in 1975 with the objective of allocating hospital and community service resources in a way which would eventually provide equal access to health care for people in equal need. RAWP reported in 1976 and the formula was introduced in 1977. The introduction of the formula resulted in the disparities between the better provided and the less well provided parts of the country being reduced.

Some elements of the formula received criticism however, and the NHS Management Board reviewed the operation of the formula, producing a final report in July 1988. The changes recommended in the report were never implemented and have now been superseded by the changed method of allocation following the implementation of *Working for Patients*.

- 1990 onwards – resident/capitation based funding – A major change in resource allocation methodology commenced in 1990/91 with the move to resident population based funding.

Each region's population is 'weighted' to reflect the demands placed on health services by the different age groups. These 'capitation rates' are based on the estimated expenditure per head for different age groups and certain geographical supplements are then built into allocations.

Cross-boundary flows (CBFs) are not taken into account in allocations – they are now the subject of contracts. It was originally the government's intention that full weighted capitation funding would be achieved at regional level by 1992/93 but in allocations for 1991/92 it was announced that this process would be at a slower rate in order that all regions receive a minimum level of growth. Subsequently, lower growth levels in the service for 1993 onwards, due to economic factors have led to a likelihood of this objective not being achieved until 1994/95 or even 1995/96.

A new funding formula, the York formula was introduced from April 1995. This takes into account the cost of living index as well as health needs.

Revenue allocations to districts and GP fundholders

Regions have some discretion in determining their own sub-regional allocation formula, but any mechanism must be clear, simple and stable and needs to be on 'broadly the same basis' as the national formula. In the first year (1991/92), each district's allocation reflected the actual costs of care for its own residents, (i.e. by an increase to reflect the cost of outward CBFs of residents and reductions to reflect the cost of patients treated who are residents of other districts). This placed districts in a position to purchase broadly the services currently received by its residents, and in most parts of the country was implemented successfully.

Regions have to decide on the speed in moving districts' allocations to the assessed weighted capitation allocation. In the longer term it is planned that capital charges will be incorporated within the general distribution of resources subject to weighted capitation.

FHS allocations

FHS expenditure remains largely non cash limited and at present is assumed to continue at the existing level (i.e. not be subject to a weighted capitation approach). However, GP fundholder expenditure on practice staff/premises and GP computing are subject to cash limits which will be accounted for by RHAs although expenditure will be administered by FHSAs. These allocations to the RHA are currently ring-fenced and cannot be transferred to HCHS. FHSA administration costs are also subject to cash limits. Although indicative amounts are provided to the RHA for both primary and secondary sectors, there is no ring-fencing and funds are allocated to these sectors according to the RHA's priorities. RHAs, are now giving consideration to how, over a longer timescale, a joint capitation approach between FHSA and HCHS expenditure could be developed to ensure the overall level of resources in each community is appropriate to its needs and as equitable as possible.

From April 1991 approved general practices became responsible for budgets for certain non-emergency health treatment and are now acting as purchasers of services. Allocations have been transferred from funds available to direct health authorities. From 1993/94 onwards, the GPFH initiative was enlarged, to take a somewhat greater proportion of the purchasing responsibility from the relevant DHA.

Capital allocations

A new definition of HCHS capital expenditure (see Chapter 10) was introduced on 1 April 1991. This reduced the threshold above which spending is classified as capital from £7,500 to £1,000. Thus more spending was to be counted as capital and £120m was transferred nationally from HCHS revenue to capital in 1991/92 to reflect this. This change was partially revised on 1 April 1993 back to £5,000, because of over complexity in the original system, with an equivalent reversal of cash limit back to revenue.

Capital expenditure by NHS trusts is financed through accumulated depreciation, surpluses and borrowing through the external financing limit (EFL) mechanism. For the remainder of the NHS, a separate capital allocation continues.

This is currently allocated between regions on a RAWP based formula. Regions allocate to districts in line with their strategic programmes. The capital allocation is split into differing programmes such as:

- major building schemes
- medical equipment costing more than £50,000
- ambulance services
- priority services such as:
  - mental handicap
  - mental illness.

A proportion is delegated to districts for items of medical equipment, vehicles, minor building alterations, fire precautions and staff housing. Medium-sized schemes may be delegated to districts, but overall financial management is retained at regional level. By 1995 it is likely that all or almost all capital will go via the trust EFL mechanism.

Joint finance

Joint financing was introduced in 1976 to promote collaboration between health and local authorities. Funds are allocated through RHAs to districts according to the incidence of mental handicap and mental illness and the size of the over-75 population. The purpose of the fund is to 'pump prime' initiatives which will introduce new services, extend existing services, or prevent the premature abandonment of services which already exist. Funding from this source is time limited and responsibility must transfer to either social services, the health authority or a voluntary organisation.

Funding approved is normally for a period of five or seven years but can in some cases be provided for up to ten years at 100 per cent with a tapering effect to a maximum of 13 years in total. This latter approach has become more commonplace given its relevance to the key 'Care in the Community' issue.

Constituent authorities – health, local, family health service authorities, voluntary bodies –

prepare and approve a programme of schemes through the Joint Consultative Committee (JCC). Each scheme requires the specific approval of the sponsoring body and the health authority set out in a memorandum of agreement. This document explains the benefits of the scheme proposed and details the funding arrangements as the initial joint finance diminishes.

The JCC is supported by the Joint Care Planning Team (JCPT) which uses joint officer groups to develop specific policy proposals.

The direct transfer of funds was introduced through the 'Community Care' initiatives in 1983 to promote the discharge of patients from hospitals to the community. This mechanism allows the permanent transfer of funds through savings achieved in health authority services.

Joint Finance is in facilitating the implementation of the 'Caring for People' part of the 1990 White Paper. 'Care in the Community' which flows from this White Paper is a major issue requiring effective collaboration between health authorities (DHAs, FHSAs and trusts), local authority social services departments and GP fundholders.

Corporate governance in the NHS

The NHSE has been very active in pursuing the principles of corporate governance and their application to the health service. A corporate governance task force has recently reported to the NHSE Chief Executive and its central recommendations are:

- there should be an NHS code of conduct
- a code of accountability for NHS boards should be adopted as the basis of the delegation of functions from Secretary of State to NHS authorities and trusts
- directors of NHS boards should declare private interests which are material and relevant to NHS business and these should be recorded in board minutes: directorships should be published in the annual report (see below)
- clearer definitions of the functions of chairmen and non-executive directors should be introduced and form the basis of the appointment and induction processes
- improved arrangements for the formal induction and development of newly appointed chairmen and non-executive directors should be introduced as soon as possible
- the NHS Management Executive should clarify the position on all financial constraints which apply to NHS authorities and trusts and should communicate them to the service in one clear and readily-understood summary
- the current directions on financial management should be urgently updated to take account of developments since they were last issued in 1991
- NHS boards should be required to establish formal committees on audit and on remuneration and terms of service of executive directors
- NHS boards should be reminded of their responsibility for high standards of financial stewardship through effective financial planning and strategic financial control and through maximising value for money, and should receive guidance on:
  - organising and presenting financial and performance information to NHS boards
  - audit and remuneration committees

   – financial control
   – finance training for board-level non-specialists

- standing orders of NHS boards should prescribe the terms on which committees and sub-committees may be delegated functions and should include, where adopted, the schedule of decisions reserved to the board
- NHS authorities should be obliged to publish an annual report (already mandatory for trusts) on their performance in purchasing health service and on their stewardship of public finances
- the total emoluments from NHS sources of chairmen, executive directors and non-executive directors should be published in annual reports.

A Code of Conduct for NHS Boards was issued by the NHS Executive in April 1994. This code records that there are three crucial public service values which must underpin the work of the health service – accountability, probity and openness and contains guidance on each of these values. A separate Code of Accountability for NHS Boards was issued at the same time.

9 NHS financial issues

This chapter examines five key aspects of the finances of the NHS. First it looks at the main financial and business planning framework and then at the contracting process, including the different types of contract between health bodies. Costing and pricing techniques are examined. The financial aspects of NHS trusts are considered and finally the structure and financial arrangements for charitable funds are dealt with.

Financial and business planning: national planning framework

Financial planning is an essential and integral part of NHS finance and forms a major part of the annual planning process.

The financial planning system (FPS) is based on a set of proformas setting out the minimum information required by the NHS Executive.

The proformas are completed by DMUs, DHAs and RHAs, each level assessing and summarising plans before onward submission. FHSAs return their plans direct to RHAs and NHS trusts direct to NHSE outposts. An overview of the FPS is shown below:

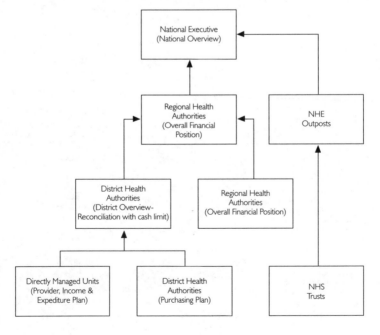

The regional consolidated plan is submitted to the NHSE and this forms the basis for monitoring progress during the year and also for comparison with the outturn after the year end. RHAs monitor DHAs and FHSAs.

Directly managed units

Careful business planning is essential for DMUs to ensure sufficient income is attracted, through the provision of services, to meet the total cost of the provider unit.

In compiling business plans DMUs will have regard to inflation, levels of activity and the requirement to balance expenditure to income.

Business plans should aim to minimise risk associated with income not secured by contracts and this will require working closely with purchasers in developing service contracts. Income from contracts with purchasing DHAs will be a major source of revenue for DMUs.

Other income will include that from GP fundholders, and non-NHS purchasers, which will require careful assessment and agreement where possible.

DMUs submit their income and expenditure plans together with an analysis of the sources of expected income to their managing DHA for assessment and consolidation into the overall district financial plan, before that is submitted to the regional health authority.

District health authorities

DHAs have a responsibility both as purchasing authorities in their own right and also as managers of provider units (DMUs). Districts have four key roles in the financial planning process:

- the preparation of purchasing plans
- assessing plans of provider units and balancing those with their own purchasing plans
- preparation of plans for other DHA activities including administration
- compiling a picture of the overall financial position of the district.

In preparing their own plans, DHAs will have regard to the overall availability of resources, and where demand exceeds resource availability, balancing measures will need to be taken.

Purchasing plans will need to be discussed with provider units before they are finalised.

DHAs are expected to demonstrate achievement of efficiency gains in their purchasing role, by comparing changes in activity with changes in real terms expenditure.

In assessing and agreeing the plans of their directly managed provider units, DHAs will carry out a number of steps including:

- checking that commitments have been provided for
- analysing the risk from non-contracted income expectations
- checking the adequacy of contingency plans
- looking for efficiency gains
- assessing the overall plan for realism.

Family health service authorities

FHSAs will prepare plans for submission to RHAs, the main elements being

- to manage within cash allocations
- to avoid overcommitting recurrent resources
- to manage in-year cost pressure within recurrent resources.

Financial processes will need to be in place to ensure that the plans contain balanced and realistically forecast income and expenditure.

Plans are submitted to the RHA for inclusion in the consolidated Regional plan.

NHS trust business plans

Each trust is required to prepare an annual business plan covering a three year period. The business planning cycle for trusts needs to align with that of health authorities because of the inter-relationship between trust finance and service strategies and those of purchasing authorities.

The NHSE outposts agree business plans and summaries for publication with trusts. They collect annual, quarterly and monthly monitoring information from trusts and agree corrective action as necessary.

The outposts appraise business plans against a number of financial criteria before they are submitted to the NHSE.

Preparation of a business case

Since solutions that involve capital spending will introduce new capital charges with a long-term effect on NHS finances and prices, the first consideration of managers should be whether a capital solution is necessary. Where capital spending is the optimum solution, attention needs to be given to options that offset increased capital charges by releasing savings from land sales or reducing running costs. This presents opportunities to improve estate utilisation and also, through rationalisation, to reduce backlog maintenance.

Because the impact of capital investment is by nature long-term, it usually involves risk. Consequently, throughout the business case process, NHS managers will need to identify risks and consider strategies for managing them. These include not only risks that could arise to jeopardise the completion of the project according to plan, but also those that could result in the benefits of the investment not being obtained.

The preparation of a business case is the process that supports submissions for the funding of new capital projects. Underlying the presentation of a business case is the sound framework for option appraisal that has been required in the NHS for some time.

The business case process is divided into three phases, involving setting strategic direction and producing outline and full business cases. The three phases are depicted in the diagram below. The investment which the business case supports must meet a definable health need.

A business case must convincingly demonstrate that the project is economically sound, is financially viable and will be well managed. In addition a business case for any investment should show that the proposal has clearly identified benefits for patients and is supported by purchasers.

Preparing and presenting a robust business case can be costly: it may involve a great deal of management time to assess changing needs and conduct detailed analyses to identify a solution that considers costs, benefits and potential risks. It is therefore important to understand the process and plan for it carefully. It should clearly present value answers to the key questions:

- What services should be provided now and in the future?
- How will these service requirements be met in the most efficient and effective way?
- Why is capital spending proposed?
- Why does this proposal offer good value for money?
- How will the project be managed if the proposal is accepted?

Since April 1991, revenue accounts have been subject to capital charges for the use of assets.

In November 1992, the Chancellor of the Exchequer launched the Private Finance Initiative (PFI) which promotes and encourages the use of private sector expertise and capital and was intended to transfer risk to the private sector. The cost-effectiveness of many NHS projects has already increased as a result of implementing a range of PFI projects and NHS managers are encouraged to put forward realistic proposals for PFI funding.

The contracting process

The separation of responsibility for purchasing and providing health care is an essential prerequisite for the contracting process. The two roles may be summarised as follows:

- The purchasing role – districts have a primary responsibility to ensure that, within available resources, services are secured to meet the health needs of their resident populations. RHAs and GPFHs will also be purchasers of specific services. The Department of Health also acts as a purchaser in respect of overseas patients treated under reciprocal agreements and supra regional services, e.g. heart and lung transplants.
- The provider role – health care units deliver contracted services within quality and quantity specifications to one or a number of purchasers, in return for agreed charges. The provider units are, in the main, either trusts, or to a much smaller extent, directly managed units.

Purchasers and providers thus enter into contracts, setting out the range and quality of services which a provider will deliver and the price which the purchaser will pay.

As a background to preparing contracts, the purchaser will be concerned with an assessment of the districts needs and the translation of those needs into service specifications and proposals. The provider units will be primarily concerned with service provision proposals and how they fit into development plans. Discussion and negotiation between the two roles, before a patient care contract is prepared, will be mainly concerned with ensuring that income and expenditure commitments are acceptable within the financial and strategic plans of contracting bodies.

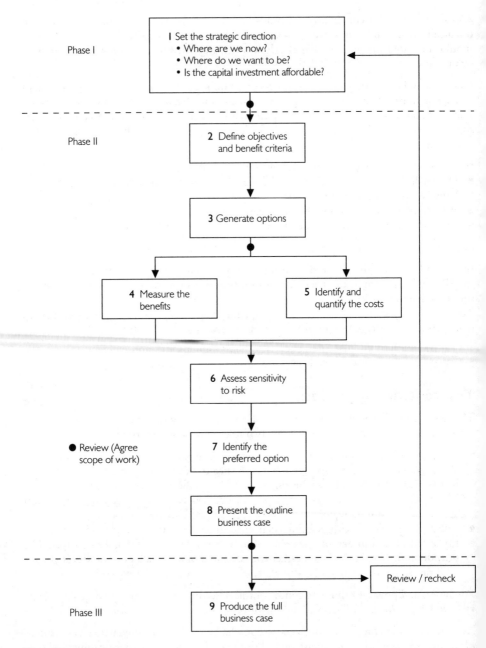

The business case process

The particular elements relating to finance that are covered in this chapter are:

- types of contract
- costing and pricing

- invoicing, authorisation and settlement
- budgetary and financial control (including contract monitoring).

A separate section is devoted to regionally led contracting including education and training and the Service Increment for Teaching and Research (SIFTR). It should be noted that the remainder of this chapter is concerned with contracting for patient care services. There will be a wide range of contracts between health units for the provision of other services (for example laundry, financial services).

Types of patient care contract

There are three types of contract:

- *Block contracts* – the provider is paid an annual sum in instalments, in return for access by the purchaser's residents to a defined range of services with limited volume specifications. Payment is due on the 15th of every month.
- *Cost and volume contracts* – the provider receives a sum in return for treating a specified number of cases. There may also be a variable price per case component between a threshold and ceiling. Payment is due within 30 days of the invoice.
- *Cost per case contracts* – the purchaser agrees the price to be paid for the treatment of individual patients. Payment is due within 30 days of the invoice.

A proportion of patient referrals will not be predictable and hence not be covered by contracts. This proportion is normally small. These cases are known as extra contractual referrals (ECRs) and will be of two types: emergency and non-emergency (elective). Purchasers are obliged to pay for the emergency treatments but for the non-emergency cases the provider is required to obtain approval from the purchaser before treatment commences.

So far, the majority of contracts have been block, using indicative volumes for costing, pricing and monitoring purposes, but increasingly purchasers and providers are experimenting with more sophisticated cost and volume and cost per case contracts.

Payment arrangements

Invoicing

All services, whether under contract or extra contractual, have to be invoiced:

- Referrals under contract – in-patients
  - patient is admitted, and allocated to a contract. This is done by means of the post-code, which determines the district of residence, or in the case of GPFHs, the GPs list;
  - after discharge, patients notes have clinical codes attached to them to identify the type of treatment provided;
  - within one month of discharge an invoice must be sent to the purchaser for payment.
- Referrals under contract – all others
  Details as agreed within the contract must be fed into the finance department within a month of the event occurring, in order to prepare an invoice.
- Extra contractual referrals
  As above, except that for non-emergency (elective) ECR, the purchaser must provide an authorisation to pay.

Authorisation

It is the purchaser's responsibility to authorise requests for payment from providers. The exact nature of the authorisation will depend on the type of contract, although in all instances the principles of internal check and the separation of duties at key parts of the payments process should be applied.

Settlement

It is important that NHS purchasers settle payments to NHS providers promptly as failure to do so will present cash flow problems. A framework of rules has been developed, incorporating the following:

- monthly payments, payable in the second half of the month should be made for block contracts and for the fixed part of cost and volume contracts
- for contracts where the total sum payable over a year varies with activity, parties should agree payment terms for the activity related element
- for ECRs, payment should be made within one month of the date at which the invoice was sent (which itself should be within one month of the end of the month in which the episode of care ended). Where an episode of care is likely to extend over a long period, invoices may be submitted monthly
- mechanisms for preventing delayed payment have been established, e.g. time limits specified for solving uncertainty about payments.

Financial control

This section is considered from the perspectives of the provider (whether DMU or NHS trust) and district (as purchaser and manager of DMUs) respectively.

Provider unit control

- *Budget setting* – Each provider will set budgets for income and expenditure.
  Income: the volume of work expected to be undertaken multiplied by the price for each item of service.

  Expenditure: a plan of what the hospital expects to spend in the following year in each functional or clinical area of the hospital.

  The volume of work should be that agreed within contracts plus the estimated number of extra contractual referrals. It is essential that the unit contains its expenditure within total anticipated income.
- *Budgetary control*
  Expenditure: actual expenditure incurred is compared and measured against the budget, both for the month concerned and cumulatively. Expenditure control and variance analysis is undertaken for each functional and/or clinical area. When variations are revealed, enquiries are made to ascertain the reasons for the variation and corrective measures determined.

  Income: actual income due is compared to the income budget and corrective action taken in respect of variations.

  Two types of variance may arise:
  - price variances: the volume of work anticipated is being achieved, but the prices have been set incorrectly: income is either higher or lower than budgeted;

– volume variances: the volume of work anticipated is not being achieved or is being over-achieved.

Contract monitoring will be undertaken by monthly contract reports which contain variance analysis.

District control
Health authorities have to manage at two levels:

- Cash: receipts and payments during the period 1 April to 31 March.
- Income and expenditure: expenditure incurred, and income received, relating to the financial year.

The Department of Health requires health authorities not to exceed the cash limit. At a local level financial performance is reported on an income and expenditure basis as this reflects the actual level of resources consumed.

Costing and pricing

Introduction and principles
In outlining the NHS contracting process, costing and pricing were listed as key financial elements of the internal market.

The process of costing is aimed at identifying and expressing the financial impact of a particular activity or the production of a particular unit of output. Within the NHS, costing has mainly been used for monitoring and comparison purposes, and has generally been based on historical information from prior year accounts. However, the new contractual arrangements between purchasers and providers of healthcare, and the importance of more clearly defining the NHS product, has increased the need for improved systems to establish prospective costs to enable prices to be set.

The link between prices, essential in any contractual arrangement, and cost is fundamental, especially as the basic approach to pricing set out in Department of Health guidance is that:

- prices should be based on costs
- prices should generally be arrived at on a full cost basis (marginal costing is only allowed where there is spare capacity for a short-term period)
- there should be no planned cross subsidisation.

In order for the internal market to operate it is essential that prices reflect cost differences between providers, i.e. prices should be based on the costs of the provider concerned rather than, for example, regional or national average costs for specific services.

Each provider needs to match income to expected expenditure (and the financial target for NHS trusts) through the contracting process. It will therefore be necessary to make assumptions about the service levels the hospital will be providing (which, in turn, will be based on assumptions about the volume of work which will be won through contracts) and to plan to ensure that all costs are recovered through the prices set for those contracts and any extra contractual work which is expected to be carried out.

In order to be effective in supporting the internal market, it is essential that any costing approach adopted should operate consistently, in terms of the overall principles on which it is based, within and between individual units. If this is not the case management decisions within both purchaser and provider organisations may be based on incorrect information.

It is desirable that the costing approach takes account of other uses of costing information (besides contract pricing) so that managers are not faced with the task of running different management information systems for different people.

Reconciliation of costing information with the devolved management budget or control total of planned income and expenditure is essential in order to validate the costing information in total, to ensure that overall financial control is maintained and to plan to ensure that all costs are recovered.

As the contracting system develops and matures requirements will change. Budget holders will become more informed about individual contractors' use of resources, service providers will become more sophisticated in pricing contracts and purchasers will become more demanding in specifying and monitoring contracts. The costing and pricing arrangements must be capable of changing and developing to meet these requirements and to move, over time, from what may initially be limited and relatively simple approaches, to a position where high quality information systems are available to facilitate the pricing of contracts.

Costing techniques

A number of different approaches to 'product' costing are currently in use in commercial organisations. All of them could have applications in costing hospital services, although only some of them are appropriate to support contract pricing.

Direct costing is not a full cost approach and is therefore inappropriate for setting contract prices.

Total absorption costing overcomes this weakness because indirect and overhead costs are 'absorbed' into product costs using allocation or apportionment techniques. Prices can then be set on the basis of full costs. However there are two factors in this approach which need to be recognised when setting prices; the procedures for overhead absorption into 'product' costs may be arbitrary and total cost per unit will only be correct at the 'sales' volume assumed at the time of calculating overhead absorption rates, i.e. if actual volumes are greater or less than the assumed volume, fixed costs will be over or under recovered respectively.

The marginal cost approach focuses on those costs which are variable with the volume of output produced. Other costs are treated as fixed or 'period' costs. Marginal costing is appropriate for setting prices for the sale of spare capacity where the costs of increasing output may be limited to the cost of additional materials used because labour costs are already paid or committed for the period in question.

Standard costing can be integrated with either a total absorption or a marginal costing approach. Essentially it is a control mechanism. As its name implies, the approach establishes technical and costs standards for each process in order to establish not only what a product will cost, but also what it ought to cost. Comprehensive standard costing systems are not appropriate for the NHS contracting environment. However, establishing some simple standard costs in certain areas may be helpful in building up a procedure cost, for example. This type of standard costs are already being used by resource management sites.

Activity based costing is not so much a new approach to costing as a means of refining the procedures for overhead cost absorption. The approach taken is to examine the activities undertaken in each department in order to identify the true 'cost drivers' and then use these as the means of absorbing indirect costs into product costs. In the commercial and manufacturing sectors, for example, overhead costs have traditionally been attributed to 'products' on the basis of the direct labour hours or direct materials cost for the product concerned. The activity based costing approach identified suitable activity measures for each overhead department and then uses these to attribute the costs for that department to products.

In summary the techniques appropriate for costing most contracts in the NHS are total absorption costing using activity based costing for absorption of overheads. Marginal costing will be important to support decisions about the sale of spare capacity and simple standard costs may be helpful in building up individual procedure costs.

Cost allocation framework

The framework has a number of elements, including the identification of costs and income, making assumptions about the level of service to be provided and the number and type of contracts expected and finally attributing costs and income to contracts. This approach is not intended to be prescriptive. Each provider unit will need to develop its own framework.

In order to attribute costs to individual contracts assumptions about service levels are required. A planned level of capacity and volume of service for individual sites of departments needs to be established, in order that, at the price set, the budgeted level of service will recover all costs.

Attributing costs to services and contracts requires that costs are classified and analysed in order to identify the direct, indirect, overhead and capital charge elements and the fixed, semi-variable and variable components. This is a complicated task. Classification and analysis will need to vary from one unit to another in order to reflect local circumstances, and the sophistication of existing information systems. The analysis of costs into their fixed, semi-fixed and variable components will depend on the individual circumstances in which the information is being used.

Establishing total costs

Total costs will be the sum of the following elements:

- direct patient treatment costs
- indirect and overhead costs
- costs of services received from the DHA or RHA
- capital costs – depreciation and interest for directly managed units and depreciation plus the financial rate of return for a NHS trust
- other costs, e.g. teaching or research costs which relate to the delivery of clinical services
- offsetting SIFT revenue, donations, revenue from income generation schemes, use of trust funds to meet revenue service costs, income earned from other units, e.g. for pathology services and miscellaneous income, e.g. shops.

This gives a total of net costs which must be recovered through income from contracts and extra contractual referrals.

In establishing total costs, individual providers will need to satisfy themselves that they can produce a reasonable estimate of all these costs and revenues. Although historic information may provide a starting point, this will need to be rolled forward, taking account of planned workload changes and likely pay and price increases, in order to provide prospective costs as the basis for contract prices.

Levels of service

The assumed level of service is the total level of service expected to be provided in the forthcoming year on which total costs are to be recovered at the prices set.

It is a key element in estimating prospective costs and attributing these to contracts. If the level is set too low, prices will be unnecessarily high; if too high, costs may not be fully recovered. It will therefore be necessary to make assumptions about patient activity levels at specialty level and probably procedure level in certain areas. It will also be necessary to make assumptions about activity levels in all hospital departments, e.g. pathology and radiology requests, as a basis for allocating these costs to specialties.

If the costing and pricing process is starting from historic specialty cost information, it will be important to understand how these costs behave if the assumed level of service in any particular area is significantly different from historic levels. This requires an analysis of costs into their fixed, semi-fixed and variable components.

The assumed level of service will be greater than the volume of service covered by contracts in place at the start of the year, whether these be with DHAs or GP practice fundholders. The difference will be accounted for by contracts entered into during the course of the year and by extra contractual referrals in the year.

Quality assumptions should also be reflected in the assumed level of service, e.g. length of stay.

Cost attribution

Costs may be attributed to activity at a number of different levels, e.g. patient, procedure, diagnostic related groups (DRG) or specialty. Requirements will be determined by detailed contract specifications.

In most cases, specialty based contracts will be the norm, though procedure based contracts may be appropriate in certain areas.

Specifying contracts at DRG level would present costing difficulties that would need to be handled sensitively. For example:

- although the provider may be able to classify its output in this way, particularly when resource management systems become more developed, it may not be an appropriate way for all purchasers to specify needs – GP fundholders, for example, may be unfamiliar with these categories
- given the large number of DRGs, individual providers may have only a small number of patients in many groups, this may produce unreliable average costs which differ significantly from year to year and from those of other providers
- DRGs do not cover outpatients or long-stay patients.

Cost classification and analysis

Having established the total cost and the assumed level of service the next step is to classify and analyse costs in order to facilitate the attribution of costs to contracts. Cost may be classified or analysed as illustrated above. Items of income, e.g. SIFTR could be classified or analysed in a similar way. These two approaches may be used separately, but a more flexible approach would be to integrate them, so that for example, direct costs could be analysed into their fixed, semi-fixed and variable components.

The first task is to classify costs as to whether they are 'direct' treatment costs, e.g. medical and nursing staff costs or drugs; 'indirect' treatment costs, e.g. catering, laundry and linen; overhead costs, e.g. management and administration and estate management costs or capital charges.

The sophistication of available information systems will determine the level or costing detail that can be achieved, e.g. specialty or patient. Having made that decision direct costs will be attributed directly, indirect cost can be allocated using units of activity appropriate to the department concerned and overhead costs can be apportioned on some relatively simple basis, e.g. patient days. Capital costs should where possible be identified to the relevant 'facility' (e.g. ward or theatre) or department using the assets. In this way they can be either attributed directly to the specialty concerned (if, for example, a ward is used exclusively by one specialty) or allocated to specialties along with the other costs of the department concerned, e.g. laundry.

If unplanned spare capacity arises within a particular year, it may be 'sold' at a price which represents marginal or variable cost. In this situation it is therefore necessary to understand the fixed, semi-fixed and variable components of costs. Fixed costs would be excluded when setting prices, while all variable costs would be included. Each item of semi-fixed cost would need to be considered separately as to how it would be affected by the proposed contract. Each time the opportunity to sell spare capacity arises the analysis of costs into their fixed, semi-fixed and variable components will be influenced by the size and duration of the proposed contract.

Following the allocation or apportionment of all costs and relevant income to specialties, costs will need to be attributed to individual contracts on the basis of assumed levels of service so that the budgeted level of service will recover all costs at the prices set.

It is therefore necessary, to divide the total assumed level of service between the individual contracts (with either DHAs or GPs) which the provider expects to enter into, and the extra contractual work which it expects to do in the year. This will provide a framework for attributing costs and income to individual contracts.

National Steering Group on Costing (NSGC)

The NHSE had some concern during 1991/92 and 1992/93 about the wide variations in prices charged for seemingly like services across the country. A National Steering Group on Costing (NSGC) was therefore established to examine costing for contracting.

The NSGC has endorsed the cost allocation principles first explained in EL(90)173, 'Cost Allocation Principles'. The guidelines allowed a large degree of discretion in the detailed methods that a provider can adopt in their cost allocation and apportionment methods, provided that the methods conform to the basic pricing policy which can be stated as:

Price must be based on full (net) costs so that, for a provider's annual assumed volume of service, income from contracts (and ECRs) will recover the quantum of cost with no planned cross subsidisation between contracts.

The NSGC has now recommended a minimum standard that all providers should reach in analysing costs in their fixed, semi-fixed and variable elements and classifying them into direct, indirect and overhead. Providers are strongly encouraged to develop methods of attributing cost directly to specialty where possible and to use the minimum standard method of apportionment between specialties when required.

The NSGC has re-stated the need for the sharing of information between provider and purchaser, thereby better informing the contracting process.

Cost allocation: General Principles and Approach for 1993/94 published by the NHSE in April 1993 contained full details of this approach and during the financial year 1993/94 use of sub-specialty costs bands was tested at several pilot sites around the country.

Revised arrangements for the 1994/95 contracting round were published by the NHSE in August 1993 (FDL(93)59).

Unit costing

Health authorities produce a wide range of patient and workload statistics and unit costs are developed from these.

Financial Return HFR21 (see Chapter 10) lists the following services and units of work measurement.

A	Patient treatment services	Unit of work measurement (see below)
A1		
	A and E departments	h
	Community dental services	b
	Community medical services	c
	Community nursing and midwifery services	c
	Day-care facilities	b
	Out-patient clinics	b
	Wards	a
A2		
	Artificial limb and wheelchair services	d
	Audiology	b
	Chiropody	e
	Dietetics	e
	Electrocardiography	f
	Electroencephalography	g
	Health education/promotion	s
	Industrial therapy	b
	Lithotripsy	b
	Medical illustration and photography	*
	Medical physics	*
	Miscellaneous patient treatment services	*
	Nuclear medicine	f
	Occupational therapy	e
	Operating theatres	h
	Optical services	e
	Pathology:	
	(i) Chemical pathology	g
	(ii) Cytogenetics	g
	(iii) Haematology	g
	(iv) Histopathology	g
	(v) Immunology	g
	(vi) Microbiology	g

(vii) Spare	–
(viii) Spare	–
Patient transport service (non emergency)	i
Pharmacy	j
Physiotherapy	k
Psychology	k
Radiology	f–100
Radiotherapy departments	l
Speech therapy	e

Total A

B	Unit/Estate support services	Unit of work measurement (see below)

B1

Building maintenance	p
Catering	n
Community dental services	*
Domestic	m
Energy/water and sewerage	*
Engineering maintenance	p
Laundry/linen	o
Portering/transport	o

Total B1

B2

General manager	q
Unit Office Support	q
Employee services	r
Procurement of goods and services	q
Medical records	o

Total B2

B3	Training education	*
B4	Miscellaneous	*

Total A + B

Add: Purchase of tertiary referrals

Grand total (S/C 200 + S/C 210)

Key to units of work measurement:

a	patient day
b	attendance
c	1,000 resident population served by this community service
d	item issued
e	face-to-face contact
f	weighted request
g	request
h	operating tour
i	patient journey
j	£1,000 expenditure on drugs
k	first contact

l	exposure
m	100 sq metres cleaned
n	1,000 occupied bed days plus 40 per cent of day care attendances
o	1,000 weighted occupied bed days
p	building volume (100 cubic metres)
q	proportion of payroll costs
r	1 person employed (WTE)
s	1,000 resident population served.

*   There is no unit of work measurement

Performance indicators

Performance indicators have been collected on a national basis since the early 1980s. Health authorities are required to submit statistical returns to the Department of Health and also to publish performance indicators as part of their annual report. The Department has published annually in July, statistics relating to the performance of individual hospitals and trusts.

The Department of Health uses the statistics to manage, plan and review the activities and performance of health authorities.

The use of unit costs as a performance indicator is widespread in all public sector organisations. It is the basic indicator and health authorities calculate unit costs for nearly all their activities. Some examples are

- cost per in-patient day
- cost per out-patient attendance
- cleaning costs per square metre
- nursing costs per in-patient day
- pharmacy costs per in-patient.

Health authority managers use unit costs as a basis for planning, controlling and reviewing the various activities and services they manage. Within health authorities unit costs are produced for individual wards, operating theatres and specialisms such as occupational theory – managers are therefore able to monitor and compare the performance of wards and specialisms.

Intermediate performance indicators are also used as a basis for planning, controlling and reviewing activities. They support the unit cost indicators. Some examples are as follows:

- bed occupancy rates
- average waiting times for hospital treatment (split between specialisms or illness)
- operating theatre usage rate
- percentage of day cases
- average length of stay.

National Health Service trusts

Introduction
NHS trusts, which are established by statutory instrument, are hospitals and other units which have their own Boards of Directors. The Board consists of a non-executive chairman (appointed by the Secretary of State), up to five non-executive directors (of which two are

appointed by the RHA) and an equal number of executive directors, up to a maximum of five (including the Chief Executive and Director of Finance). In contrast to DMUs, they are operationally independent of district health authorities and they have the freedom to:

- acquire, own and dispose of assets to ensure the most effective use is made of them
- make cases for capital developments direct to the NHS Management Executive
- borrow money, within annually agreed limits, primarily for new building and equipment and for upgrading existing buildings
- create management structures
- employ staff, determine staffing structures, and set terms and conditions of employment
- advertise their services, within the guidelines set down by professional codes of practice on such advertising.

Trusts are accountable to the Secretary of State (via the NHSE).

In several significant respects, the financial regime of NHS trusts differs from that of DMUs. These differences are covered in this chapter.

In particular:

- trusts receive no direct funding from the Department and must earn all their income
- trusts can borrow funds, within annually approved limits, for purposes such as acquiring or replacing assets
- trusts usually retain depreciation and any surpluses after meeting financial obligations and can use this money to repay loans, to invest or for capital spending
- trusts must make a 6 per cent return on their assets and break even taking one year with another
- trust accounts are commercial in style, following Companies Acts requirements where appropriate.

As with DHAs, trusts must ensure that they have sufficient cash available on a daily basis to meet their commitments.

Revenue and pricing

Like other health service units, trusts earn most of their revenue from contracts to provide health services. These contracts are made with health authorities, GP fundholders and private patients or their insurance companies.

Trusts may also receive funds:

- from extra-contractual referrals
- for supporting medical and dental education and research
- for the education and training of other health care professionals
- from income generating activities.

Trusts price their services on the basis of covering their costs, including depreciation on their assets, and achieving a 6 per cent rate of return on the current value of their net assets.

Trusts are expected to attribute their costs using principles common to the NHS as a whole. They are not allowed to plan to cross-subsidise services between contracts and are expected to use marginal costing only when they have unplanned spare capacity arising during the year.

When setting prices for NHS contracts, trusts should not plan to achieve more than a 6 per cent rate of return on their assets, since higher rates would reduce the volume of patient care which health authorities could afford to purchase. Contracts with the private sector are not subject to this restriction and these contracts should be priced at the level the market will bear, subject to the need to make a minimum of 6 per cent return on assets. If a higher return than 6 per cent is made this may be used to reduce the prices which would otherwise be charged to NHS purchasers.

Originating capital debt

Each trust owns its assets – land, buildings, and equipment. The value of the net assets (assets less liabilities) transferred to a trust when it is set up (except any assets donated to the NHS since 1948) is matched by an originating capital debt which is owed by the trust to the consolidated fund.

The originating capital debt is made up of two elements:

● interest bearing debt (IBD) which has defined interest and repayment terms
● public dividend capital (PDC) which is a form of long-term government finance on which the trust pays dividends to the government.

The balance between IBD and PDC is set individually for each trust by the Secretary of State, with the consent of the Treasury.

Asset valuation

Trust assets are valued on the same basis as those of the directly managed sector. Generally:

● Land and buildings held for operational use are valued by the District Valuer at their open market value for existing use. If land and buildings become surplus to requirements they are valued at open market value for alternative use.
● Other tangible fixed assets, e.g. medical equipment or furniture, are valued at their current cost.

Intangible assets, such as intellectual property, are valued individually.

Current assets, for instance stocks and debtors, are valued in accordance with normal accountancy principles.

All trusts need to maintain asset registers to record and value fixed assets, which should include any donated assets.

Borrowing and debt repayment

There are two sources of finance to enable a trust to maintain and expand its facilities and to obtain working capital:

● funds generated by the trust itself from depreciation and retained surpluses, or from sales of land, buildings and equipment
● external borrowing from either the Secretary of State or the private sector.

Trusts are able to borrow from the Secretary of State or commercial sources. The Secretary of State can guarantee a trust's loan from the private sector which would reduce borrowing costs. In seeking such a guarantee the trust would have to demonstrate distinct advantages over borrowing from the Secretary of State.

A trust needs to demonstrate its ability to pay interest on, and repay, loans before they are made. Trusts may not borrow money before they need it. It is unacceptable for them to borrow at low rates from the government and put the money on deposit at a higher rate to generate income. However, trusts are free to use interest-earning bank accounts for day-to-day transactions.

There are two sources for short term borrowing for periods up to a year:

- conventional bank overdrafts, which are most often suitable where they are likely to be significant fluctuations in the timing or amount of borrowing needed
- temporary borrowing from the Secretary of State to meet more significant and defined short term needs.

Borrowing is normally in the form of interest bearing loans at either fixed or variable interest rates depending on the trust's financial position. An element of PDC finance may be considered in particular circumstances, for example where expenditure is spread over a period of years and where a building or other facility does not become operational immediately, and in the light of the trust's overall financial position as shown in its annual business plan.

Each trust has to repay its interest bearing debt, including the interest bearing portion of its originating capital debt, over a defined period which is related to the lives of its assets but in general does not exceed 20 years. The repayment methods are:

- equal instalments of principal
- equal repayments
- maturity loans, with interest rolled up during the life of the loan.

The trust may apply to repay any interest bearing debt early, including any originating capital debt. Original interest bearing debt is repaid over 25 years and any new debt, over a period up to 20 years. The trust needs, within these periods, to balance its borrowing portfolio.

Business planning process

Each trust is required to prepare an annual business plan covering three forward years. The business planning cycle for trusts needs to align with that of health authorities because of the inter-relationship between trust finance and service strategies and those of purchasing authorities.

Each trust is expected to send its business plan to the NHSE by early March each year, i.e. at broadly the same time as regional health authority short term plans are submitted to the NHSE. The first year of the accompanying financial proforma forms the basis for the in-year financial monitoring of the trust.

In preparing plans trusts need:

- to develop considered and explicit assumptions of the level of revenue purchasing power of their major purchasers over the period of the plan
- to make clear assumptions about the likely impact of inflation over the period of the plan
- to set out clear and well justified plans for capital developments and the funding arrangements for such developments
- to provide sensitivity analyses based on different assumptions.

In addition, trusts need to ensure that their business planning enables them to satisfy a range of financial criteria, including, achievement of financial targets and duties, satisfactory appraisal of capital investment proposals, and consistency with the trust's own strategy.

External financing limits

An external financing limit (EFL) is, in effect, a cash limit on net external financing for a trust. External finance is the difference between agreed capital spending by a trust and internally generated resources. Put simply, an EFL comprises:

- new loans taken out by the trusts; less
- repayments of loans during the year; plus or minus
- net changes in deposits and other holdings of liquid assets.

A national total for trust EFLs is determined through the annual PES process. The NHSE sets an individual EFL for each trust within the national total, taking account of its business plan. A trust can be given an EFL which is positive, zero, or negative, and is expected to keep within its EFL each year, although there is limited flexibility.

Financial duties

Each trust has two financial duties in addition to staying within its EFL:

- to achieve its financial target. This is a real pre-interest return of 6 per cent on the value of net assets – essentially an average of the opening and closing assets shown in the accounts
- to break even on income and expenditure account, after payment of interest and PDC dividends, taking one year with another.

There is also a general requirement for trusts to ensure that their activities are carried out in such a way as to achieve best value for money.

Surpluses

While trusts have a duty at least to break even they are expected to make a revenue surplus after allowing for interest payments and dividends on PDC. Any net surplus can be used for capital expenditure, to repay loans, or for investment. Temporary cash surpluses can be held in government securities or in other approved public or private sector investments.

Where a trust has a cash surplus considerably greater than its reasonable need for funds – for instance, from the sale of land or buildings at a price reflecting development gain – the Secretary of State may require the trust to pay the government all or part of its reserves.

Annual accounts

A trust's annual accounts will be presented as an integrated document comprising three statements (income and expenditure account, balance sheet and cash flow statement) supported by three sections, accounting policies, notes to the income and expenditure account and notes to the balance sheet.

The annual accounts must be approved by the trust prior to presentation at a public meeting. In normal circumstances the deadline for such a meeting should be the end of September following the end of the relevant financial year.

Accounts

Each trust must keep proper accounts and present them annually in a specified format. The format of the accounts is based on the requirements of the Companies Acts, but with variations to reflect the special circumstances of trusts. The accounts must show 'a true and fair view' of the trust's financial affairs and, generally speaking, the relevant Statements of Standard Accounting Practice are followed.

The accounts are submitted to the Secretary of State and are the corporate responsibility of the Trust Board. However, the trust's chief executive, advised by the director of finance, is responsible for ensuring, on behalf of the Board, that all accounting and financing matters are in order. This includes ensuring that:

- all public funds are properly managed and safeguarded
- standing financial instructions are complied with
- the accounts of the trust are properly presented.

The director of finance is responsible for ensuring that financial systems and controls meet the requirements of good financial management. The chief executive, advised by the director of finance, is responsible for answering, on behalf of the Trust Board, any questions on the accounts of an individual trust, and for informing the NHSE if, at any time, the long-term financial viability of the trust is at risk.

The accounts of each trust are audited by the Audit Commission. The National Audit Office (NAO) is responsible for auditing the consolidated accounts of NHS trusts and laying them before Parliament. The NAO has right of access to papers and other records relating to each trust's financial, accounting and auditing matters. Both the Audit Commission and NAO may conduct value for money studies in trusts.

The accounts should be faced by a page in the following format:

Foreword to the accounts

NYZ NHS Trust

These accounts for the year ended 31 March 19XX have been prepared by the XYZ NHS trust under Section 98(2) of the *National Health Service Act 1977* (as amended by Section 24(2), Schedule 2 of the *National Health Service and Community Care Act 1990*) in the form which the Secretary of State has, with the approval of the Treasury, directed.

Example ———————————————————————————————

Income and expenditure account for the year ended 31 March 19XX

	Note	£'000	(Previous year) 19XX-XX £'000
Income from activities			
Continuing operations	2	X	X
Other operating income	3	X	X
Operating expenses			
Continuing operations	4,5	(X)	(X)
Operating surplus (Deficit)			
Continuing operations		X	X
Profit (loss) on disposal of fixed assets	6	X	X

Surplus (Deficit) before interest		X	X
Interest receivable	7	X	X
Interest payable	8	(X)	(X)
Surplus (Deficit) for the financial year		X	X
Public Dividend Capital dividends payable		(X)	(X)
Retained surplus (Deficit) for the year		X	X
Financial target performance	9	X.X%	X..X%

Balance sheet as at 31 March 19XX

				(Previous year) 19XX-XX
	Note	£'000	£'000	£'000
Fixed assets				
Intangible assets	10	X		X
Tangible assets	11	X		X
			X	X
Current assets				
Stocks and work in progress	12	X		X
Debtors	13	X		X
Short-term investments	14	X		X
Cash at bank and in hand		X		X
			X	X
Creditors: Amounts falling due within one year	15		(X)	(X)
Net current assets (liabilities)			X	X
Debtors: Amounts falling due after more than one year	13		X	X
Total assets less current liabilities			X	X
Creditors: Amounts falling due after more than one year	15,16		(X)	(X)
Total assets employed			X	X
Financed by:				
Capital and reserves				
Public dividend capital			X	X
Revaluation reserve			X	X
Donation reserve			X	X
Other reserves			X	X

Income and expenditure reserve   X   X
                                        ─   ─
                                        X   X

Signed on behalf of the board on (day, month, year)

Chairman

Chief executive

Cash flow Statement for the year ended 31 March 19XX

	£'000	£'000	(Previous year) £'000
OPERATING ACTIVITIES			
Net cash inflow from operating activities		X	X
RETURNS ON INVESTMENTS AND SERVICING OF FINANCE			
Interest received	X		X
Interest paid	(X)		(X)
Interest element of finance lease rental payments	(X)		(X)
Dividends paid	(X)		(X)
Net cash outflow from returns on investments and servicing of finance		(X)	(X)
INVESTING ACTIVITIES			
Payments to acquire fixed assets	(X)		(X)
Receipts from sale of fixed assets	X		X
Payments to acquire investments	(X)		(X)
Receipts from sale of investments	X		X
Net cash inflow/(outflow) from investing activities		X	X
Net cash inflow/(outflow) before financing		X	X
FINANCING			
New public dividend capital received	X		X
New long-term loans – Government	X		X
New long-term loans – Others	X		X
New short-term loans – Government	X		X

New short-term loans – Others	X	X
Grants received	(X)	(X)
Repayment of loans – Government	(X)	(X)
Repayment of loans – Others	(X)	(X)
Capital element of finance lease rental payments	(X)	(X)
Net cash inflow/(outflow) from financing	X	X
Increase (decrease) in cash and cash equivalents	X	X

Statement of total recognised gains and losses for the year ended 31 March 19XX

		19XX-XX
	£'000	£'000
Surplus (deficit) for the financial year before dividend payments	X	X
Unrealised surplus (deficit) on fixed asset revaluations/ indexations	X	X
Increases in the donation reserve due to receipt of donated assets	X	X
Reduction in the donation reserve due to the depreciation/disposal of donated assets	(X)	(X)
Additions/(reductions) in 'other reserves'	X/(X)	X/(X)
Total recognised gains and losses for the financial year	X	X
(Prior period adjustment)	X/(X)	
Total gains and losses recognised in the financial year	X	X

NHS trusts

A series of supporting notes gives more detail on a number of aspects of NHS trusts' financial performance:

Note 1   –   Accounting policies

Notes to the income and expenditure account

Note 2   –   Income from activities

Note 3   –   Other operating income

Note 4   –   Operating expenses

Note 5   –   Staff details
Note 6   –   Profit and loss on disposal of fixed assets
Note 7   –   Interest receivable
Note 8   –   Interest payable
Note 9   –   Financial target performance

Notes to the balance sheet
Note 10 –   Intangible fixed assets
Note 11 –   Tangible fixed assets
Note 12 –   Stocks and work in progress
Note 13 –   Debtors
Note 14 –   Short term investments
Note 15 –   Creditors
Note 16 –   Long term loans
Note 17 –   Movement on reserves
Note 18 –   Cash flow
Note 19 –   Capital commitments on reserves

Other notes to the financial statements
Note 20 –   Post balance sheet events
Note 21 –   Contingent liabilities
Note 22 –   Pensions
Note 23 –   Clinical negligence
Note 24 –   Reconstruction of movements in government funds

Financial returns
TFR2 Speciality and programme costs
TFR3 Analysis of expenditure by type
TFR4 Ambulance Service expenditure
TFR9 Analysis of non-NHS income

Charitable (trust) funds

Definition
'Trust funds' (not to be confused with NHS trusts), or 'endowment funds' are charitable, as distinct from government or exchequer funds. They derive from donations by individuals or organisations or from legacies. Charitable funds for non-teaching hospitals were amalgamated to form the Hospital Endowments Fund in 1948 but this was redistributed in 1974 so that most districts (and RHAs) now have a district (or regional) general fund. Trust fund accounting is kept entirely separate from the remaining statutory accounts of the authority.

Powers
Health authorities have always had power to accept, hold and administer property on charitable trust. In 1980 they were given power to engage in fund raising activities. Considerable sums are also held on trust by other bodies for the benefit of particular health authorities or services, Leagues of Friends being one of the more common examples. An external trust should be registered as a charity and should not purport to represent the authority.

Property and investments

Trust funds held by a DHA or a Trust are usually within one of the two following categories.

General purpose funds

Funds which are held without any externally imposed restriction other than the general obligation to use such funds for purposes relating to hospital services or research and which may be used at any hospital administered by or for which trustees have a responsibility.

Special purpose funds

Funds which are held for purposes specified by the donor or legatee. Such funds should only be applied for the specific purposes named in the trust instrument (i.e. the letter enclosed with the donation, the will, etc.). Specific conditions may indicate the hospital or ward on which the money must be used or the particular branch of the service which should benefit (e.g. kidney transplants, heart disease, etc.).

The assets held on trust in the NHS have a value in excess of £600m. This includes both investments and property. In some cases the property has not been valued for many years and is probably worth much more. A very large proportion of the assets, particularly the property, is held by a comparatively small number of authorities, mainly teaching (undergraduate and postgraduate) hospitals. For most undergraduate teaching hospitals the trust funds are held by special trustees not the DHA.

Investments are managed by a variety of means. Funds are normally pooled so that only one single portfolio needs to be maintained. Unless wider powers have been granted by the Charity Commissioners new monies added to an investment pool must be invested equally in wider (equity) and narrower (gilts) ranges as laid down in the *Trustee Investments Act 1961*. It is normal to appoint an investment adviser or manager who will be a member of one of the regulatory bodies approved by the Securities Investment Board.

Income and expenditure

Income arises from gifts and legacies but also from property and investments or from fund raising. As the funds are charitable there is no tax liability.

Expenditure must be for the benefit of a charitable purpose provided by the authority and be in accordance with the purposes of the fund from which it is met and the charity's governing document. A very small number of funds are held on permanent endowment (described as capital in perpetuity in NHS accounts) so that only the income can be spent. For the rest of their funds authorities have a policy on whether and to what extent capital should be expended. The only other restriction on how funds are spent is any prohibition set by the Secretary of State. The one standing restriction is not to use charitable funds to increase staff rates of pay.

Where the purposes of a gift (or a legacy) are specified by the donor it should be held in a 'special purposes' fund in order to be able to demonstrate that it has been spent accordingly. When it ceases to be possible to use this money for the purposes for which it was given the Charity Commissioners may be asked to make a 'Cy Pres' scheme to vary the purpose. This could apply if a hospital is closed or if a special purpose no longer exists.

Management

Whilst the whole authority, as a corporate body, is the trustee of charitable funds it is normal to delegate the management to a small group of members to act on its behalf.

Charitable funds accounts

Separate accounts are maintained for charitable funds, comprising a balance sheet and income and expenditure account together with supporting notes. These are likely to be amended to comply with the Statement of Recommended Practice on Charities.

Proper books must be kept and the final accounts must be certified for authenticity by the appropriate treasurer. Trust fund balance sheets must comply with the *Trustee Investments Act 1961*. In addition the basis of the valuation of property must be identified, e.g. original cost, professional valuation or insured value.

The accounts should show the main purposes for which trust funds, whether special or general, have been spent. Four usual categories are:

- amenities for patients
- amenities for staff
- research
- other projects, including capital works and equipment.

Investments

Donations, legacies, dividends and interest received in any one year are unlikely to equal the demands made on trust funds in that year. Some years may see very large legacies and it may be considered desirable to spread the benefits over several years. Alternatively, it may be necessary to restrict the use of funds for several years in order to accumulate sufficient funds for a major project. For these reasons, trust funds generally have considerable surplus funds and these are either invested in fixed interest securities, shares or property to provide additional income.

The *Trustee Investment Act 1961* which applies to all NHS trusts, classifies investments as falling into three categories.

- *Part I* – Narrower range investments not requiring professional advice, for example National Savings Certificate, Defence Bonds, balances in a Trustee Savings Bank or the National Savings Bank;
- *Part II* – Narrower range investments requiring professional advice, for example government and local government stocks and bonds, fixed interest debenture stocks of certain UK companies, mortgages on UK land and so on;
- *Part III* – Wider range investments, all of which require professional advice, for example ordinary and preference shares of UK companies having over £1 million issued share capital and having paid a dividend on all their shares for the past five years. This category also includes other approved forms of equity holding, in particular unit trusts.

At least 50 per cent of the funds invested must be in the narrower range. For accounting purposes, investments are shown as either 'narrow range' (combining Parts I and II) or 'wider range'. A health authority may have additional investment powers, awarded under a court order, or perhaps inherited under an ancient charter. Investments held under such powers are known as 'special range' investments and are shown in the balance sheet as a third category, after the narrower range and wider range figures.

Investments are carried in the balance sheet at book value, although market value is also disclosed.

Where investments have been revalued, the basis of valuation and all relevant details, such as the name and qualification of the valuer, must be disclosed.

Trust fund accounts

The accounts are prepared in the standard form laid down by the Department of Health and consist of the following:

- an income and expenditure account
- a balance sheet
- notes to the accounts, including the 'capital reserve – other funds and capital reserve – capital in perpetuity'. (The total accumulated income from all sources which remains unspent at the end of the year is recorded on the balance sheet under capital reserves. If the income was received with the condition that it be invested and only the interest spent, then it is recorded under 'capital reserves – capital in perpetuity'. This is referred to later in the chapter. All the other unspent income is recorded in the 'capital reserve – other funds' on the balance sheet.)

Income and expenditure account
The surplus or deficit for the year is calculated as the closing balance on the income and expenditure account. The account is prepared on an accruals basis.

Example

Income and expenditure account: Health Authority Trust Fund for year ended 31 March 19X5

	£
Income	
Subscriptions and donations	X
Legacies	X
Dividends and interest	X
Net income from freehold and leasehold property	X
Income from fund raising	X
Other income	X
Net expenditure transferred to capital reserve – other funds*	X
Total income	X
Expenditure	
Administration expenses	X
Patients' welfare and amenities	X
Staff welfare and amenities	X
Research	X
Contribution to hospital capital expenditure	X
Fund raising expenditure	X
Other expenditure	X
Net income transferred to capital reserve – other funds*	X
Total expenditure	X

* Only one of these two entries will appear in the accounts, depending on whether there is more expenditure than income in the year or vice-versa.

Balance sheet
The balance on the 'capital reserve – other fund account' represents the total amount of the fund: the total amount which the trustees may spend on the services to patients and staff. At any one time most of this is held in the form of investments, but these may be sold to provide services to the extent of the 'other fund balance' if the trustees so wish.

If there has been an excess of income over expenditure in the current year then this amount will be added to the other fund balance in the balance sheet at the year end. If there has been an excess of expenditure over income on the other hand, then this will be subtracted, since the total amount of the fund has been reduced as a consequence of this year's activities.

Example _____

Balance sheet: Health Authority Trust Fund
as at 31 March 19X5

	£
Assets	
Property	X
Investments	
Narrower range (market value £X)	X
Wider range (market value £X)	X
Special range (including Charity Commission investment fund)	
(market value £X)	X
Stock in hand	X
Debtors	X
Cash in hand	X
Total assets	X
Reserves	
Capital reserves: funds held in perpetuity	X
General purposes	X
Special purposes	X
Capital reserves: other funds	
General purposes	X
Special purposes	X
Liabilities	
Sundry creditors	X
Cash overdrawn at bank	X
Total reserves and liabilities	X

The final accounts are supported by detailed notes to the accounts and these notes cover:

1	Accounting policies adopted (i.e. those approved by the Secretary of State)
2	Capital reserves: details of funds held in perpetuity
3	Capital reserves: other funds
4	Property valuations
5	Cash flow statement

Profit or loss on the sale of investments

If investments or property are sold for more than their book value then a profit is made. Since this occurs only occasionally and is not part of a regular annual income, it is not recorded in the income and expenditure account but is added directly to the 'other fund' account balance in the balance sheet. If there is a loss on the sale of investment or property, then the loss is deducted from the 'other fund' account balance.

Any profits or losses arising from the revaluation of property will be treated in the same way as those arising from the sale. Investments are shown at cost, but the market value at the year end will be disclosed by way of a note to the accounts. Property may be revalued on an ad hoc basis and the details of the revaluation will appear in the accounts.

NHS charity review – Charities Act 1992

The *Charities Act 1992* amends the *Charities Act 1960* and introduces new legislation to maintain an up-to-date public register of charities. The NHS charity review had identified that existing records held by the Charity Commissioners are out of date and the aims of the review are four fold:

- to obtain up-to-date information about NHS charities;
- to encourage those acting as trustees to use the small charities legislation contained in Sections 74 and 75 of the *Charities Act 1993*;
- to determine precisely how and what information should be entered on to the computerised register;
- to establish a registration timetable and procedure.

In addition to compulsory registration of charities, with appropriate penalties for non-compliance, a copy of the audited accounts of individual charities contained within trust funds will need to be submitted within a specified period to the Charity Commissioners each year.

Miscellaneous provisions allow the umbrella registration of very small individual charities, or those with very small income. Guidance and advice will continue to be given by the Charity Commissioners and the first set of annual accounts which need to be submitted to the Commissioners are understood to be those for 1994/95.

10 NHS accounting issues

In this chapter, the broad financial environment and accounting framework within which the NHS operates are examined. This section is followed by the key, recently introduced, area of charges for the use of capital assets and the capital expenditure regime within the Health Service. Finally, the annual accounts and returns requirements are discussed.

The NHS accounting environment: introduction and overview

Substantial changes to the financial and organisational framework of the NHS were made in the *NHS and Community Care Act 1990* and were operational from 1 April 1991.

The key changes which affected finance managers include:

- the separation of responsibility for purchasing and providing services, with the primary responsibility of district health authorities (DHAs) being to assess health needs and purchase health care for their residents
- a change in funding arrangements to resident based funding for DHAs from 1 April 1991 and then to weighted capitation; DHA allocations cover their residents. The home district of a patient is expected to pay for the health care provided either within agreed contracts or under extra-contractual referral arrangements. However, if a patient is registered with a general practitioner who is a fundholder (GPFH), the fundholder will be expected to pay for some types of health care
- the opportunity for providers of health care services to become NHS trusts
- the majority of income for provider units will be obtained through a system of contracting. Where contracts are not in place, invoices will be issued to the patient's district of residence or relevant GPFH to recover the cost of treatment
- expenditure of DHAs as purchasers of health care will be identified separately from that of directly managed provider units (DMUs) and common services
- costing, pricing and invoicing will be devolved closer to the point of delivery of services
- the cost of using capital assets will be charged to units of management and common services.

Financial environment

For the finance function, these changes represent a significant increase in the complexity of the financial environment. They also introduce elements of risk through uncertainty in the flows of income. In future, in their *purchaser* role, DHAs will need to:

- provide funds for their DMUs to meet the costs of treating their residents, whether under contracts or as extra-contractual referrals
- make payments within cash limits for both contracted services and extra-contractual referrals to providers outside the district, including NHS trusts and other districts' DMUs.

Provider units need to:

- have sufficient income from contracts and extra-contractual referrals to meet their operating expenditure
- have arrangements in place to invoice purchasers for the treatment of their patients
- ensure income is collected.

In their management role for DMUs, DHAs need to ensure that DMUs have these arrangements in place.

Monitoring and control

Maintaining financial viability within DHAs will require changes to monitoring and control mechanisms. In addition, the format of the annual accounts has been revised. The revised form reflects both purchaser and provider activities and incorporates commercial accounting standards (adapted to reflect differences in the public sector).

Monitoring and control systems and procedures within a DHA need to be reviewed. Information produced for monitoring and control should be sufficient for local management needs and to satisfy the reporting requirements of regional health authorities (RHAs) and the NHS Executive.

The district director of finance will be responsible for ensuring that financial systems and procedures are established which can maintain control and ensure that financial duties are met. The most significant of these is managing within the cash limit.

Accounting framework

The new financial environment requires the development of an accounting framework which covers a substantial proportion of the financial control and accountability issues facing DHAs. These include:

- funding flows
- cash management
- financial accounts
- financial control.

If the director of finance does not implement systems and procedures covering the above, the likely risks will be:

- loss of financial control
- qualified accounts
- failure to meet financial duties, including keeping within the cash limit.

The accounting framework

These changes were reflected, in detail, in the NHS Executive's Financial Management Training Initiative publication *The Accounting Framework* which was issued in 1991, and is revised annually in detail. The framework is based on four modules, each covering the four main aspects of financial control and accountability mentioned on page 243 *Introduction and overview* and also contains a practical example of the components of the accounting framework, based on a hypothetical health authority and containing the requisite journal entries and ledger accounts.

This publication is one of the two main volumes issued by the NHSE that will be of great practical value to students. The other document 'Health Authority Manual for Accounts' is covered in Chapter 10, and study of both publications is important. There are other, very detailed, NHSE books, including a separate manual for NHS trusts.

The following paragraphs pick out some of the more relevant (to students, as opposed to practitioners) sections of *The Accounting Framework* publication, which is based upon a district health authority.

Funding flows

Principles

a) At regional level

- regional health authorities will continue to receive funding allocations from the Department of Health
- this funding will be supplemented by capital charges payments made by DMUs within the region
- the region will allocate its money between:
  - RHA administration;
  - Family health services;
  - purchaser allocations to DHAs and GP fundholders;
  - costs of contracts between the RHA and provider units
- the RHA may provide common services (e.g. ambulance services, supplies, computing services) which are recharged to DHAs and other users.

b) At district level:

- DHAs main source of funding will be their allocations from their RHAs
- the level of funding for 1991/92 will be sufficient for a DHA to purchase broadly the current level of services for its residents wherever these are provided
- DHA allocations will be reduced where GPFHs have patients resident in the district. These funds will be used for budgets for GPFHs
- capital charges are payable to the RHA by DHAs in respect of the assets used by their DMUs and common services
- income will be received for services provided to residents of other DHAs and to patients of GPFHs
- payments will be made to other providers for services provided to district residents
- a major source of expenditure will continue to be the operating expenditure of the DHA where there are DMUs.

A table of funding flows from The Accounting Framework

Cash management

a) DHAs

Cash management is the process of ensuring that sufficient cash is available on a daily basis to meet commitments and that the authority operates within its cash limit. Funding for the payment of staff and for goods and services is obtained from the Department of Health by requisition into the health authority's bank account or transfer by Paymaster General's Order. Each authority is required to establish a PGO account which enables payment to be made between authorities without cash being drawn from the Exchequer. Cash requirements are forecast to the Department of Health through a series of weekly and monthly returns (the FIS returns).

The three main areas of 'risk' in relation to cash flows are:

- extra-contractual referrals payable to external providers by the purchaser
- extra-contractual referrals chargeable to other purchasers for services provided by DMUs
- potential timing mismatch between income received through DMU activities (e.g. through late payment) and the need to meet purchaser commitments on a scheduled and timely basis.

Cash management is the process whereby:

- the impact of the change on cash flow is established
- a strategy is developed to manage the risk
- cash flow performance is monitored and projections updated
- corrective action is taken when performance differs from plans.

b) NHS trusts

NHS trusts must ensure that they have sufficient cash available on a daily basis to meet their commitments. Cash is generated from contracts with and extra contractual referrals from purchasers as well as private patient income and other income generation initiatives.

To assist in cash management, NHS trusts are permitted to invest surplus cash and are allowed to borrow money within annually agreed limits. This is further discussed in Chapter 5.

The cash management chapter of *The Accounting Framework* summary gives the following guidance for a district health authority:

Key elements
Outflows:

- operating costs of DMUs and the common services function
- expenditure of the purchasing function and DHA administration
- contract payments for the purchasing function
- payment of invoices for extra-contractual referrals.

Inflows:

- cash drawn under revenue allocation for purchasing
- receipt of contract income from other purchasers
- receipt of extra-contractual referral income from other purchasers.

Administrative issues
Successful cash flow management requires appropriate administrative support including:

- appropriate information systems and procedures to link patients to contracts and interface with the invoicing system (minimum data sets)
- effective debtor management and cash collection, including resolution of queries with purchasers
- appropriate information systems and procedures for the identification of extra-contractual referral commitments and the verification and authorisation of payments by the purchasing function, including resolution of queries within providers
- good liaison within the unit or purchasing function for the resolution of queries
- banking arrangements in place and staff clear on the working arrangements for each account.

Monitoring systems
Systems need to be in place to ensure that the original cash forecasts are regularly monitored and updated so that corrective action can be taken.

Financial viability
If income and expenditure plans are not achieved, additional pressures will be placed on cash management which may result in the DHA not staying within its cash limit. The use

of cash forecasts can therefore highlight potential problems sooner than income and expenditure plans.

Financial accounts

This chapter is concerned with the new format of annual financial accounts and returns for the year ending 31 March 1992 and subsequent years. Details of these arrangements are contained later in this chapter.

Financial controls

The NHS reforms continue to place the responsibility for the overall financial performance of a health authority on the DHA. The director of finance is responsible for ensuring that adequate systems of financial control are in place. The one change to this accountability is where an NHS trust has been formed within the district. Responsibility for the financial performance of the trust rests with the trust's board and director of finance.

The role of the director of finance encompasses not only the establishment and maintenance of financial control systems and procedures but also reporting to the health authority on breaches of financial controls, including failure of the DMUs common services or purchasing function to attain financial viability. The overall framework for financial control is as follows.

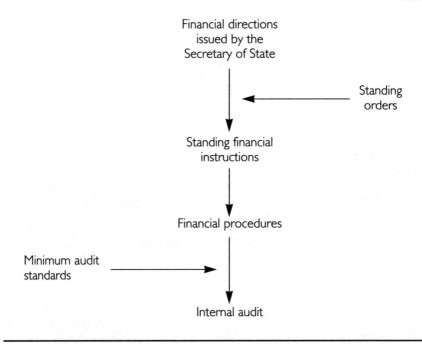

Source: The Accounting Framework, *Department of Health, 1991*

All health authorities continue to be required to maintain sound financial management of all their activities and services, including the purchasing function, DMUs and common services.

In summary, health authorities (including both executive and non-executive members) are required to:

- approve annual financial budgets
- monitor actual financial performance against those budgets
- lay down financial controls to safeguard the authority's resources
- ensure that the cash limit for the financial year is kept.

Each health authority will determine the financial responsibilities of individual executive members and health authority officers. The general manager (who is an executive member of the authority) has overall executive responsibility for all the authority's activities, is responsible to the authority for ensuring the authority remains within its cash limit and must ensure the authority is provided with financial information. The director of finance (who is also an executive member of the authority) will provide this information and financial advice to the authority and is responsible for designing, implementing and supervising the financial control and accounting systems.

DHAs need to be satisfied in particular with the financial procedures relating to DMUs. These procedures will specify the limits to delegated financial authority, including limits for the authorisation of contracts.

There are a number of different elements contributing to the framework for financial control. These include:

- financial directions
- standing orders
- standing financial instructions
- financial control procedures
- internal audit.

Each of these elements is now briefly explained.

Financial directions

Financial directions are issued by the Secretary of State for Health and set down in broad terms, the responsibilities and requirements for financial control in health authorities. These are minimum statutory requirements and should be the basis upon which authorities develop their own financial control policies, including standing financial instructions.

Standing orders

Standing orders are drawn up by the health authority and regulate the authority's business and its meetings. They normally exclude reference to the control of the authority's tendering and contracting procedures which are contained in the standing financial instructions.

Standing financial instructions

Standing financial instructions (SFIs) are drawn up by the health authority and describe in detail the way in which the financial directions are put into practice in the authority. The SFIs must be adopted by the health authority, subsequent to which the director of finance is delegated the task of drawing up and implementing detailed financial control procedures. Model SFIs have been produced by the Healthcare Financial Management Association (HFMA), on behalf of the NHS Management Executive, as a guide to health authorities, and a content summary is shown below:

> Introduction
> Terminology
> Responsibilities and delegation
> Audit
> > Audit committee
> > Director of finance
> > Role of internal audit
> > External audit
> Allocations, business planning, budgets, budgetary control, and monitoring
> > Allocations
> > Preparation and approval of business plans and budgets
> > Budgetary delegation
> > Budgetary control and reporting
> > Capital expenditure
> > Monitoring returns
> Annual accounts and reports
> > Bank and PGO accounts
> > General
> > Bank and PGO accounts
> > Banking procedures
> > Tendering and review
> Income, fees and charges and security of cash, cheques and other negotiable instruments
> > Income systems
> > Fees and charges
> > Debt recovery
> > Security of cash, cheques and other negotiable instruments
> Contracting for provision of services
> Terms of service and payment of directors and employees
> > Remuneration and terms of service
> > Funded establishment
> > Staff appointments
> > Processing of payroll
> > Contract of employment
> Non-pay expenditure
> > Delegation of authority
> > Choice, requisitioning, ordering, receipt of payment for goods and services
> > Grants to other bodies
> External borrowing and investments

External borrowing
Investments
Capital investment, private financing, fixed asset registers and security of assets
Capital investment
Private finance
Asset registers
Security of assets
Stores and receipt of goods
Bankruptcies, liquidations and receiverships
Disposals and condemnations, losses and special payment
Disposals and condemnations
Losses and special payments
Information technology
Patients' property
Funds held on trust
Introduction
Existing trusts
New trusts
Sources of new funds
Investment management
Disposition management
Banking services
Asset management
Reporting
Accounting and audit
Administration costs
Taxation and excise duty

Financial control procedures

Financial control procedures describe the operation of each financial system, clearly identifying procedures, checks, controls, responsibilities and limits to authority. Procedures should be fully documented and relevant staff trained to follow them. These procedures must also be consistent with and support the SFIs.

Internal audit

Internal audit is required to be maintained by a health authority, meeting the mandatory standards as set out in the NHS Internal Audit Manual. The primary role of internal audit is set out in the example below:

Internal audit will review, appraise and report upon:

- the extent of compliance with, and the financial effect of, relevant established policies, plans and procedures
- the adequacy and application of financial and other related management controls
- the suitability of financial and other related management data
- the extent to which the trust's assets and interests are accounted for and safeguarded from loss of any kind, arising from:

a) fraud and other offences;
b) waste, extravagance, inefficient administration;
c) poor value for money or other causes.

Capital expenditure and capital charges

Introduction and objectives

Since its inception in 1948 the NHS has received separate revenue and capital allocations. Once capital expenditure had been incurred, no further revenue charges arose. On 1 April 1991, however the capital charges scheme came into operation, introducing charges for the use of capital assets. Local government is currently going through a similar process (see Chapter 5).

The objectives were:

- to increase the awareness of health service managers of the costs of capital
- to provide incentives to use capital efficiently
- to ensure that capital charges are fully reflected in the pricing of hospital services, in order to promote fair competition within the NHS and also between the NHS and the private sector.

Capital charges enable contracts with NHS provider units to use prices which reflect the consumption of capital.

Scope and definition

Capital charges are payable on all assets which are owned by the NHS, except for assets acquired by gift (although not forming part of the capital charge, these are depreciated and charged as an expense).

The definition of expenditure on a capital asset is 'expenditure on a tangible product resource with an expected life in excess of one year. The items will usually require repair and maintenance'.

In practice, capital expenditure comprises expenditure over £5,000 (increased from £1,000 on 1 April 1993) on:

- acquisition of land and premises
- individual works schemes for the initial provision, extension, improvement, adaptation, upgrading, renewal, replacement or demolition of parts of the estate
- items of equipment, including vehicles
- costs of staff engaged on capital schemes.

Valuation of assets and asset lives

The operation of capital charging is dependent upon:

- an initial valuation of existing assets
- an estimate of the length of life of assets.

Valuation of assets

- Land and buildings are valued by district valuers every three years at their current value. Land and buildings held for operational use are valued at their open market value for existing use; those surplus to requirement are valued at open market value for alternative use. Values are indexed between the three year valuation.
- Other assets are valued at current cost, which is normally depreciated replacement cost.
- The district valuer is expected to revalue assets when a DMU has been granted trust status, prior to the transfer of assets to the trust.
- NHS estates are to be valued every five years, the next revaluation being due on 1 April 1995.

Asset lives

Different types of assets have different life expectations, and are therefore depreciated over varying lengths of time. Authorities are required to work to nationally determined standard life expectancies, e.g:

Engineering installations	5, 10 or 15 years
Vehicles	7 years
Mainframe IT installations	8 years
Furniture	10 years
Main structures	up to 80 years maximum
Land	Permanent: not depreciated

At the inception of the system, assessment was made of the remaining life of all assets. Assessment of building structures was undertaken by the district valuer who determined the remaining life based on the physical state of the buildings.

Assets are revalued on a current cost basis. The valuation of assets included on an authority's balance sheet will therefore show:

- value of assets at current cost replacement value, less
- depreciation to date,

and all assets are to be entered in a fixed asset register which will, as a minimum, record the following details:

- asset identification and description
- asset location
- date of acquisition
- method of acquisition
- initial capital expenditure
- gross replacement cost (for equipment)
- depreciated replacement cost (for buildings)
- assessed or standard life

Capital charges calculations – depreciation and interest

Capital charges consist of two elements – depreciation and interest, and a distinction is made between DMUs and NHS trusts.

Depreciation

The depreciation calculation for a financial year was based on the average value of assets during the year but since April 1993 annual indexation has applied. There are two methods for calculating depreciation, one for assets subject to periodic revaluation and assessment of remaining life, i.e. buildings and one for assets with a standard life, i.e. equipment. Both methods are straight line.

Interest
Interest charges are based on the opening value of assets. In order to synchronise the calculation of depreciation and interest, the opening values used are the quarterly ones arrived at for the purposes of the depreciation calculation. The interest rate currently applicable to capital charges is 6 per cent in real terms.

DMUs versus NHS trusts
Although the arrangements have been designed to ensure that there is common treatment of capital costs in the pricing of hospital services, there are important distinctions between DMUs and NHS trusts in respect of capital charge payments.

These distinctions are as follows:

	DMU	NHS Trust
Depreciation	Payable to RHA and subsequently 're-allocated' to purchasers.	Depreciation is retained within the Trust. This together with accumulated surpluses will be one source of funding subject to its External Financing Limit for subsequent capital acquisitions.
Interest	Payable to RHA and subsequently allocated to purchasers.	Trusts do not make interest payments but are required to earn a target rate of return (6 per cent) on the current value of their net assets.

Impact on resource allocation and pricing for contracts

Both elements of the capital charge are paid by DMUs to the RHA and form part of the allocation process. In the longer term it is intended that this will, as with revenue resources, be in accordance with a resident population based formula.

The funding flows for capital charges for DMUs are shown below. In respect of NHS trusts, the arrangements for depreciation and interest outlined above ensure prices are calculated on a common basis. In order to provide additional finance to DHAs to purchase services from NHS trusts (which is then partly financing trust capital) the Department of Health transfers resources from capital to revenue which are added to the weighted capitation allocation.

The following diagram shows DMUs funding flows for capital charges. It illustrates how capital charges generated by DMUs, are 'recycled' to augment the annual revenue allocation from the Health Department to an RHA.

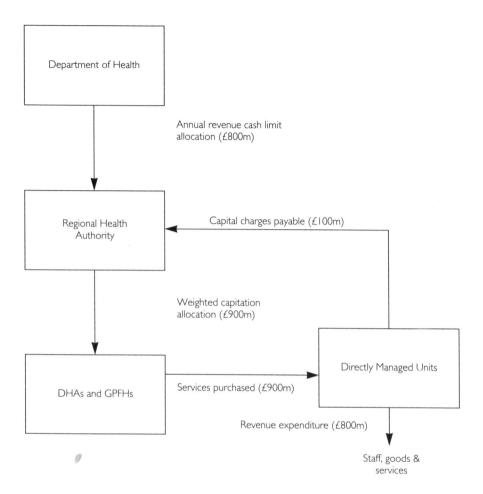

Accounting for capital charges

The main principles are as follows:

- All assets (and groups of related assets) with a replacement value exceeding £5,000 and a useful life of more than one year are defined as capital items (this includes land and buildings, equipment, fixtures and fittings).
- Who will pay capital charges? Directly managed hospitals will pay capital charges to RHAs for all their capital assets.
- Exemption from capital charges – gifts and certain regional and district headquarters expenses (those which relate to the purchaser function) are to be exempt from capital charges.
- Capital charges do not apply to NHS trusts – self-governing hospitals will not pay capital charges but will need to depreciate their assets and will have to achieve a specified revenue return on the value of their assets.
- Land bears an interest charge but is not depreciated for.

- Maintaining a fixed assets register – a register needs to be kept and updated for recording and valuing the authority's assets and calculating capital charges.
- Including the cost of capital on budget statements – charges for capital should be shown on revenue budget statements.

Why were capital charges introduced?

Under conventional bookkeeping principles, private sector companies depreciate their fixed assets. This is because although fixed assets are held for continued use, they will deteriorate with use and with time. Therefore, it would be wrong to continue reporting them in the accounts at their original cost.

It is, therefore, customary to provide for this loss in value by reducing the balance sheet value year by year over the life of the asset. These reductions are known as 'depreciation provisions'.

Historically, the NHS has not accounted for fixed assets (i.e. not produced a balance sheet as part of its accounts which includes the value of its fixed assets). Therefore, authorities have had little idea of the extent and value of fixed assets held.

Moreover, until now there has been no incentive for health authorities to consider the financial consequences of their demand for more capital expenditure since there was no penalty for asking for more money for fixed assets.

The White Paper *Working for Patients* recognised this weakness in NHS accounting principles and from 1 April 1991 authorities have had to account for their assets.

DHA-managed hospitals will therefore have to think carefully when they buy assets because the more assets they have, the higher capital charges they will have to pay.

The capital charge that DHA hospitals pay is a depreciation charge based on the current value of authorities' capital assets and an interest charge of a percentage of the current value of assets. The interest charge percentage is set by the Department of Health and is currently 6 per cent.

DHA-managed hospitals pay capital charges on capital assets such as:

- land and buildings
- fixtures and fittings
- equipment (e.g. electro-medical, computing and catering).

Note that charges are not just paid on new assets; they are paid also on assets which hospitals owned before 1 April 1991.

Health authorities depreciate using 'replacement cost' rather than 'historic cost'. Replacement cost is known as 'current cost'. Set out below are examples of calculating depreciation on an historic cost basis and a replacement cost basis.

Depreciation based on historic cost

- Company X bought a van in 1988 for £7,000.
- In 1988, it is estimated that the van will last seven years.
- Company X estimates they will scrap the van for nothing in 1995.
- Therefore company X will lose £7,000 in seven years.
- It will cost Company X £1,000 (on average) each year because of depreciation.

This method of calculating depreciation is often called the 'straight line method'.

Depreciation (for 1991) based on replacement cost (current cost)
- Health authority Y bought a van in 1988 for £7,000.
- It is estimated that the van will last for seven years and then be disposed of for nothing.
- In 1991, the price of vans has increased by 10 per cent (i.e. the replacement cost of the van is £7,000 + 10 per cent = £7,700).
- Current cost depreciation for the year 1991/92 = £7,700 ÷ 7 = £1,100.
- Therefore, it will cost health authority Y £1,100 in real terms in 1991/92 because of depreciation.

From 1 April 1991 the NHS has used replacement costs to depreciate its assets. In order to calculate depreciation based on replacement cost, it is necessary to increase the replacement cost by an index relating to the price of that type of asset to arrive at the current replacement cost. This is then depreciated. The Department of Health will provide hospitals with an index to take account of the increasing value of fixed assets over time. Finance departments will need to use this index when calculating replacement cost depreciation charges. The assets' current replacement value and depreciation will be calculated quarterly.

NHS trusts do not pay capital charges but they are subjected to similar controls because they will need to depreciate their assets. Their overall rate of return must take into account 'money lost' due to depreciation.

Any contract prices quoted by a self-governing hospital must take into account depreciation for the use that is made of capital assets. NHS trusts do not pay their depreciation expense in cash. They have to pay an annual interest charge to the Department of Health and other lenders in respect of capital and pay interest on monies borrowed. When NHS trusts were established, they became indebted to the Department of Health to take account of the value of the NHS trust's fixed assets.

A simple example to explain these principles would show:

A NHS trust hospital has bought a new operating microscope at a cost of £25,000. Its lifetime has been set at eight years.

It is only used for cataract operations (200 per year). Staff, consumables and overheads for these operations in one year total £65,000.

A contract price for each cataract operation may be based on the following simple calculation:

		£
Staff and non pay expenditure	(£65,000 ÷ 200)	325.00
Cost of capital:		
a) depreciation	(£25,000 ÷ 8 years) ÷ 200	15.63
b) rate of return	(£25,000 × 6%) ÷ 200	7.50
Total costs		348.13

The principle is that each operation is not only charged for its share of the staff and consumables used but also for a share of the capital it uses. Note that the consultant should be charged on his budget not only for staff and consumables but for also the cost of capital. In the above example the quarterly cost of capital is as follows:

	£
Depreciation (£25,000 ÷ 8 years) ÷ 4	781.25
Rate of return (£25,000 × 6%) ÷ 4	375.00
Cost of capital per quarter	1,156.25

DHA managed units will also incur an interest charge on the value of their assets. The interest rate is set by the government, at 6 per cent. The cost of capital represents the capital charge paid to the RHA (i.e. £1,156.25 paid to the RHA per quarter). The capital charge of £23.13 (depreciation £15.63 + interest £7.50) will also be included in the contract price for each cataract operation.

Bookkeeping entries: general principles

Capital charges accounting entries
The following accounts are required in general ledgers to accommodate the capital charge entries:

a) In the books of trusts, DMUs, district health authorities, family health services authorities and regional health authorities:

- tangible assets – land value
- tangible assets – building value
- tangible assets – equipment replacement cost
- tangible assets – equipment accumulated depreciation
- assets under construction
- capital account
- capital creditors account
- revaluation reserve
- donation reserve.

b) In addition to the above, the books of a DMU also require:

- non cash settlement account to/from DHA
- capital charges expenditure account.

c) In addition to (a), the books of a DHA also require:

- non cash settlement account to/from DMU
- inter-authority account to/from RHA
- capital acquisitions and disposals control account (note: this is a suspense account)
- capital charges control account.

d) In addition to (a), the books of the RHA also require:

- inter-authority account to/from DHA

- capital acquisitions and disposals control account
- capital charges payments receivable account

The following entries are required to account for the components of capital charges.

Note: In the journals below Dr is debit and Cr is credit.

Depreciation

The calculation of depreciation gives rise to four entries; one pair depreciates the asset on the balance sheet and the other pair results in a charge to the income and expenditure account.

Balance sheet entries

Dr	Capital account	Depreciation
Cr	Tangible assets	for period
	Either: Equipment accumulated depreciation	
	Or: Land and buildings valuation	

Revenue entries

Dr	Capital charges (on the revenue account)	Depreciation for period
Cr	*Either:* Current account with RHA	
	Or: Non cash settlement account with DHA (this will depend on arrangements for the accounting entity to pay capital charges to the RHA)	

Interest

For health authorities, the interest element of capital charges is accounted for using the same entries as in the second journal above.

The following accounting treatments should generally be used in the particular circumstances to which they relate:

1 Purchase of an asset

This is the basic entry in the accounts for the acquisition of assets. An asset may be acquired by a purchase or a transfer from another authority.

Dr	Tangible assets:	
	Either: Equipment replacement cost	Value of
	Or: Land or buildings valuation	the asset
Cr	Capital account	

Additions to assets under construction are accounted for in the same way.

2 Revaluation of assets

When assets are revalued the balances in the accounts have to be adjusted to the new value. The valuation adjustment equals the difference between the old depreciation value and the new valuation. The entries for the revaluation of property are shown below. There would be a similar adjustment to revalue the replacement cost and accumulated depreciation for other assets.

Dr	Tangible assets:	
	Land and buildings valuation	Revaluation
Cr	Revaluation reserve	Adjustment

3 Indexation of assets
The following enters into the accounts the indexation applied to uplift the value of the asset:

Dr	Tangible assets:	Indexation
	Either: Equipment replacement cost	
	Or: Land and buildings valuation	
Cr	Revaluation reserve	

4 Indexation of accumulated depreciation
The indexation applied to the accumulated depreciation on equipment, called backlog depreciation, has to be entered in the books to give the correct current accumulated depreciation:

Dr	Capital account/Revaluation reserve	Indexation of
Cr	Tangible assets:	depreciation
	Equipment accumulated depreciation	

5   Disposal of an asset
When an equipment asset is disposed of or permanently taken out of use the net book value is written off to the capital account.

Dr	Capital account/Revaluation reserve	Net book value
Dr	Tangible assets:	Accumulated
	Equipment accumulated depreciation	Depreciation
Cr	Tangible assets:	
	Equipment replacement cost	Replacement cost

A similar journal arises on disposals of land or buildings, though in these cases the net book value equals the valuation; there is no separate accumulated depreciation.

6 Disposal adjustment
A capital charge arises from the adjustment on disposal of equipment assets (see also section 7.2). The adjustment on disposal is the difference between the net book value and the proceeds from sale. If the disposal results in a profit the entries are:

Dr	*Either:* Current account with RHA	Profit on
	Or: Non cash settlement	disposal
	account with DHA	
Cr	Capital charges	

The entries are reversed if there is a loss on disposal.

7 End of asset's depreciation life
When an equipment asset reaches the end of its standard depreciation life it is fully depreciated, giving a nil net book value. If it continues to be used no adjustment is made in the books and its cost and full depreciation continue to be carried (though the net of these two is nil), until it is no longer available for use.

Fully depreciated assets should continue to be recorded in the asset register. The replacement cost and accumulated depreciation continue to be indexed but as the same index is applied the net book value remains nil.

No further capital charges arise.

Final accounts and returns

This section sets out the principal requirements for final accounts, supporting statements and financial returns.

Annual accounts and financial returns

The purpose of the accounts is to satisfy the 'primary requirements of public accountability for the use of NHS financial resources', including performance against the parliamentary vote. The annual accounts are used as the basis for the summarised accounts which the NHS Executive is required to prepare and submit to the Comptroller and Auditor General who examines these accounts, certifies them and lays copies of them, together with his report, before Parliament.

The accounts must be accompanied by a statement of accounting practice and must be certified by the director of finance and acknowledged by the chairman prior to audit. The required date for completion of the annual accounts is the 30 June after the financial year to which they relate.

As a general rule DHAs and NHS trusts are expected to prepare annual accounts in accordance with accounting standards issued or adopted by the Accounting Standards Board (ASB). The annual accounts of both DHAs and NHS trusts are integrated documents comprising three main statements supported by a series of notes to the accounts.

The three main statements are:

- income and expenditure account
- balance sheet
- cash flow statement.

A series of supporting notes augment these summary statements. In addition to the annual accounts, DHAs and NHS trusts are required to complete a set of financial returns to provide various analyses of expenditure which are not obtainable from the annual accounts.

Accounting standards

General

The prescription of accounting requirements for NHS trusts is a matter for government. However, since trust accounts are prepared on commercial lines to give a true and fair view, trusts are generally expected to prepare annual accounts in accordance with accounting standards issued or adopted by the Accounting Standards Board (ASB) i.e. statements of standard accounting practice (SSAPs) and financial reporting standards (FRSs), and also to follow relevant Urgent Issues Task Force (UITF) abstracts. Trusts are therefore expected to be familiar with these requirements. Trusts are also expected to be aware of possible future changes contained in ASB exposure drafts (FREDs). It should be remembered, however, that accounting standards and UITF abstracts need not be applied to immaterial items.

The government considers certain principles under ASB pronouncements to be inappropriate to trusts, or considers other to be more appropriate, in which case alternative treatments are laid down in this manual. This chapter lists the current accounting standards and UITF abstracts, together with a note as to their applicability to individual NHS trust accounts, and provides details of any accounting practices for trusts which differ from standard accounting practice.

Trusts should consult with their auditors where they consider the recommended ASB or manual for accounts treatment would be inappropriate.

Where an accounting transaction or other event is neither covered by ASB promulgations nor by this manual, the trust should follow UK generally accepted practice (UK GAAP), which is discussed in accounting publications.

Standard practice and its application to trusts

The current accounting standards and UITF extracts and their applicability to trusts are shown in the following.

SSAP	Title	Comment
1	Accounting for associated companies	Not applicable
2	Disclosure of accounting policies	Relevant
3	Earning per share	Not applicable
4	Accounting for government grants	Relevant
5	Accounting for VAT	Relevant
8	Treatment of taxation under the imputation system	Not applicable
9	Stocks and long term contracts	Relevant
12	Accounting for depreciation	Relevant
13	Accounting for research & development	Relevant
15	Accounting for deferred tax	Not applicable
17	Accounting for post balance sheet events	Relevant
18	Accounting for contingencies	Relevant
19	Accounting for investment properties	Relevant
20	Foreign currency translation	Relevant
21	Accounting for leases and hire purchase contracts	Relevant
22	Accounting for goodwill	Not applicable
24	Accounting for pension costs	Relevant
25	Segmental reporting	Not applicable

FRS	Title	Comment
1	Cash flow statements	Relevant
2	Accounting for subsidiary undertakings	Not applicable
3	Reporting financial performance	Relevant
4	Capital instruments	Relevant
5	Reporting the substance of transactions	Relevant
6	Acquisitions and mergers	Not applicable
7	Fair values in acquisition accounting	Not applicable

UITF	Title	Comment
3	Treatment of goodwill on disposal of a business	Not applicable
4	Presentation of long-term debtors in current assets	Relevant
5	Transfers from current assets to fixed assets	Relevant
6	Accounting for post-retirement benefits other than pensions	Relevant

7	True and fair view override disclosures	Relevant
8	Repurchase of own debt	Relevant
9	Consolidation of foreign subsidiaries in high inflation countries	Not relevant

Balance sheets

This is a statement of the assets and liabilities at the beginning and end of the financial year, and it appears in the following format:

Total fixed assets (see note 5.1)
Net book value   X

Current assets
Stocks and work in progress (see note 5.2)   X
Debtors (see note 5.3)   X
Cash at bank and in hand   X
                                                                                          ——

Subtotal   X
Creditors: amounts falling due within one year
(see note 5.4)   X
Net current assets/(liabilities)   X
Creditors: amounts falling due after more than
one year (see note 5.5)   X   X
                                                                                                      ——

Total net assets   X

Financed by:

Capital account (see note 5.7)   X
Donation reserve (see note 5.7)   X
Balance due to/(from)
Department   X
                                                                                                      ——
Total   X
                                                                                                      ——

Cash flow statement

The cash flow statement restates the information that is given in the balance sheet and income and expenditure account, to give particular emphasis to the source and application of funds as follows:

Net cash inflow/(outflow) from operating activities
(see note 6.1)
Transfer of cash

Investing activities:

Payments to acquire tangible fixed assets
Receipts from the sale of tangible fixed assets
Net cash inflow/(outflow) before financing

Financing:

Capital funding
Donations
Net cash inflow/(outflow) from financing
Increase/(decrease) in cash and cash equivalents
(see note 6.3)

Additional statements

In addition to the income and expenditure account, balance sheet and cash flow statement, a series of supporting notes give more detail on a number of aspects of authorities' financial performance.

Notes to the income and expenditure account

Note 2.1   Source of Health care purchased
           Own DMUs
           Other DMUs
           NHS Trusts
           Other providers
Note 2.2   Authority administration, purchasing, other services, CHCs
Note 2.3   Authority members' remuneration
Note 2.4   Staff costs
Note 2.5   Note on expenditure of staff benefits and salary ranges

Accounts of DMUs and common services

Note 3.1   Net revenue operating surplus or deficit of DMUs
Note 3.2   Income from patient services (analysed by source)
Note 3.3   Other operating income
Note 3.4   Operating expenses (analysed subjectively i.e. by type of expense)
Note 4   Net revenue operating surplus or deficit of common services

The principle of maximum devolution of services to operational level has resulted in the emergence of a range of activities that are managed centrally to provide support services to units. These include ambulance and patient transport services managed at regional or district level

Notes to the balance sheet

Note 5.1   Fixed assets – analysis showing additions, disposals and revaluations
Note 5.2   Stocks and work in progress
Note 5.3   Debtors
Note 5.4   Creditors – amounts falling within one year
Note 5.5   Creditors – amounts falling due after more than one year
Note 5.6   Patients money – Statement of custodianship of funds held on behalf of

Note 5.8
patients in care of the Authority
Contingent liabilities; items not included in the accounts but for which uncertainty exists (e.g. claims for medical negligence, third party claims and bad debts)

Note 5.9   Post balance sheet events; a narrative giving details of the event with an estimate of the financial effect

Note 5.10   Capital commitments; contract commitments or recorded decisions which will lead to capital spending in future years

Note 5.11   Balances with the Department of Health, Health Authorities, Family Health Services Authorities and NHS Trusts

Note 6.1   Net cash inflow/outflow

Note 6.2   Analysis of changes in financing during the year

Note 6.3   Analysis of cash and cash equivalents

Financial returns

In addition a number of detailed financial returns are required by the Department.

Annual accounts in practice

NHS Manual of Accounts
The NHS Executive's *NHS Manual for Accounts* lays down the format of the accounting statements produced by the various tiers of the Health Service.

The accounting statements
Each RHA and DHA is required to produce an income and expenditure account, a balance sheet and a cash flow statement. These annual financial statements are supplemented by very detailed notes and financial returns as indicated on page 264 and above.

The latest edition of the *NHS Manual for Accounts* sets out the requirements for final accounts in great detail and to reproduce those requirements in this book would result in several additional volumes. What this section therefore does, is to summarise the contents of the *NHS Manual for Accounts* and then give examples of the three main accounting statements.

In local government parlance, the manual is equivalent to a combination of CIPFAs *1993 Accounting Code of Practice*, (which sets out the format of annual accounts to be published) and CIPFAs separate publications, 'The Standard Form of Published Accounts' and the 'Standard Classification of Income and Expenditure', which provide the detail behind the Code of Practice. The NHS requirements are, however, far more prescriptive, although CIPFAs Code of Practice requirements are intended to be a minimum. Thus, there is absolute standardisation of the format of the accounts of each health authority – an important ingredient to ensure central consistency and uniformity – when the NHS Executive summarises all the returns for audit and its subsequent report to Parliament.

11 Financial reporting and accountability

The external audit arrangements of local authorities and health bodies are considered first in this chapter. The wider public reporting and accountability requirements of local government are then considered.

Accountability

Typical dictionary definitions of accountability are 'liable to account' or 'responsible'. Public sector organisations, particularly local government, have for many years been required to produce evidence of accountability. Requirements have increased significantly since the birth of the Audit Commission and the Citizens' Charter.

Accountability in a local authority requires the production and publication of many pieces of specific, or financial information, to a large number of people. Looking just at financial information, a typical local authority produces:

- an annual report
- a statement of accounts
- an annual revenue budget and capital programme
- an information leaflet to accompany the local taxation demands
- nationally published statistics and unit costs.

That information is available to electors, council tax and business ratepayers, users of council services, the local and national press, elected members of the council, trade unions, other local authorities and, of course, government departments. There is a duty for counties and districts to consult the public on their expenditure proposals, including capital expenditure, before they fix their precept or tax rates.

External audit and the Audit Commission

The external audit of local authorities was substantially changed by the *Local Government Finance Act 1982*.

Section 2 established a body known as the Audit Commission for Local Authorities in England and Wales. This is a body corporate whose members are appointed by the Secretary of State. The Commission appoints a chief officer, known as the Controller of Audit, and subordinates.

The main task of the Commission is to appoint the external auditors of local authorities. The auditor may either be an officer of the Commission or an outside accountant or firm of accountants, although the auditor must be a member of the ICAEW, ICAS, ACCA, CIPFA, or ICAI. Before the 1982 Act, the responsibility for appointing the external auditor rested with the local authority itself.

Section 15 requires that:

1   An auditor shall by examination of the accounts and otherwise satisfy himself:
    a) that the accounts are prepared in accordance with regulations ... and comply with the requirements of all other statutory provisions applicable to the accounts
    b) that proper practices have been observed in the compilation of the accounts
    c) that the body whose accounts are being audited has made proper arrangements for securing economy, efficiency and effectiveness in its use of resources.
2   The auditor shall comply with the code of audit practice as for the time being in force.
3   The auditor shall consider whether, in the public interest, he should make a report on any matter coming to his notice ...

A unique feature of local government auditing (which had been in existence long before the 1982 Act) is the power given to the public to inspect the accounts and all supporting documents; and to make copies. Further, local government electors are given the opportunity to question the auditor of their local authority; the elector can also make objections to the accounts (Section 17, 1982 Act).

The auditor is given the power to apply to the courts for a declaration that a given item of account is contrary to law and the court has the power to recover the amount so declared (Section 19). The auditor has the responsibility to certify that certain sums are due from individuals. These relate to:

● sums which have not been brought into account;
● losses which have been incurred or deficiencies caused by wilful misconduct.

The individuals must either pay the sums due or appeal to the courts. Audit fees are determined by the Commission.

The Commission has other significant powers and responsibilities. It has the power to order an extraordinary audit of a local authority. It is also given the responsibility for undertaking or promoting studies 'designed to enable it to make recommendations for improving economy, efficiency, and effectiveness' (Section 26).

In setting up the Commission, one aim was to make the audit of local authorities independent of the authorities themselves.

Sometimes the government was seen to support the auditor and this was seen by councillors as interference with the auditor's independence. Views became more polarised when the council was of a different political 'colour' from the government.

The balance has been achieved by not making the officers or members of the Commission civil servants. So that, although the Secretary of State appoints the members of the Commission, he or she does not have direct control over their day-to-day functioning.

There is an argument for saying that the audit certificates on the accounts of local authorities, and the accounts themselves, have less significance to the general public than do their equivalents in PLCs. This is because of the powers given to members of the public to examine all accounts and supporting documents, as well as those given to electors to question their authority's auditors.

The requirement for the external auditor to carry out the three Es audits (economy, efficiency, effectiveness) should strengthen the role of the internal auditor in the same area. This is because, more so than with the narrow financial audit, annual (or bi-annual) visits of external auditors could not (and are not expected to) cover all the areas of spending. Consequently, there will be greater reliance on the continuous work of the internal audit department.

The Audit Commission did not replace the District Audit Service; the staff of the District Audit Service were transferred to the Audit Commission on 1 April 1983. It has a wider role than the District Audit Service and looks at the efficiency of the various public sector organisations as well as the stewardship of public funds:

- it appoints auditors to audit accounts of all local authorities and health authorities in England and Wales and other bodies
- it undertakes studies on economy, efficiency and effectiveness
- it encourages authorities to learn from one another and thus to apply good management practice which was effective elsewhere
- it prepares and keeps under review the code of local government audit practice.

England and Wales are divided into seven regions each headed by a regional director. Within each region, district auditors are appointed as auditors to all authorities, other than those for which the audits are carried out by private firms.

The district auditor and his team are responsible for completing the statutory external audit of local authority financial statements produced as at 31 March each year.

Powers of the external auditor

The auditors have a legal power to obtain the information necessary to enable them to carry out their duties. They have a statutory responsibility to disclose matters involving illegality or losses caused by deliberate inadvertent misconduct. They are ultimately answerable to the courts in exercising these powers.

Duties of the external auditor

The auditor's duties are contained in the *Local Government Finance Act 1982*. The auditor appointed by the Audit Commission, either a district auditor employed by the Audit Commission or an approved auditor, has the duty to:

- by examination of the accounts and otherwise, be satisfied that the accounts are prepared in accordance with regulations made under Section 23 of the *Local Government Finance Act 1982* – these include the *Accounts and Audit Regulations 1983*, the *Code of Practice on Local Authority Annual Reports* and the latest CIPFA *Code of Practice on Local Authority Accounting*

- be satisfied that proper practices have been observed in the compilation of the accounts (this means that accepted accounting principles and concepts should have been applied)
- by examination of the accounts and otherwise, be satisfied that the body whose accounts are being audited has made proper arrangements for securing economy, efficiency and effectiveness in its use of resources
- comply with the *Code of Local Government Audit Practice* for England and Wales – the statutory code came into effect in 1983 and was revised in 1988 and again in November 1990
- consider whether, in the public interest, he/she should make a report on any matter coming to his/her notice in the course of the audit in order that it may be considered by the body concerned or brought to the attention of the public.

Recent developments relating to unlawful income and expenditure

The *Local Government Finance Act 1988* introduced a duty whereby the 'responsible financial officer' appointed under Section 151 of the *Local Government Act 1972* must make a report if it appears to him/her that the authority, a committee or officer of the authority, or a joint committee on which the authority is represented:

- has made or is about to make a decision which involves or would involve the authority incurring expenditure which is unlawful
- has taken or is about to take a course of action which, if pursued to its conclusion, would be unlawful and likely to cause a loss or deficiency on the part of the authority
- is about to enter an item of account the entry of which is unlawful.

The chief finance officer is also given the duty to make a report if it appears that the expenditure of the authority incurred (including expenditure it proposes to incur) in a financial year is likely to exceed the resources (including sums borrowed) available to it to meet that expenditure.

The chief finance officer has a duty to send a copy of the report to the local authority's external auditor and the councillors of that local authority.

The Act introduces a prohibition period of 21 days which runs from the day copies of the report are sent out. In that time the councillors, must consider the report and decide whether it agrees or disagrees with the chief finance officer's views contained in the report and what action (if any) it proposes to take in consequence of it.

The external auditor of the authority has to be notified of the time, date and place of the proposed meeting.

During the prohibition period, the course of conduct which led to the report being made shall not be pursued, and the authority cannot enter into any new agreement which may involve the incurring of expenditure (at any time) by the authority.

The *Local Government Act 1988* gives the power to the external auditor of a local authority to issue a prohibition order addressed to the authority or officer concerned and a statement of his/her reasons for issuing the order. An authority can appeal against the order to the High Court.

A prohibition order can be revoked at any time by the external auditor or by the High Court on appeal. So long as a prohibition order has effect, it shall not be lawful for the authority concerned to make or implement the decision, to take or continue to take the course of action or, as the case may be, to enter the item of account to which the order relates.

The *Local Government Act 1988* also gives the power to the external auditor of a local authority to make an application for judicial review with respect to:

- any decision of that authority
- any failure of that authority to act

which (in either case) it is reasonable to believe would have an effect on the account of that body.

An important case directly relevant to the duties which external auditors owe to councils was considered by the Court of Appeal on 1 December 1994. The case, *West Wiltshire District Council v Garland and others* decided that district auditors employed by the Audit Commission to audit the accounts of local authorities under the provisions of Part III of the *Local Government Finance Act 1982* owed a statutory duty to a local authority whose accounts were being audited and a breach of that duty gave to the local authority a right of action against the auditors. Further, those auditors owed a common law duty of care to local authorities, breach of which gave rise to a right to bring an action in negligence.

The Court further held that district auditors, in addition to their statutory duty, owed a common law duty of care to the council.

The Code of Local Government Audit Practice

Section 14 of the *Local Government Finance Act 1982* requires the Audit Commission for local authorities in England and Wales to prepare and keep under review a code of audit practice prescribing the way in which auditors are to carry out their functions under the Act. The code must embody what appears to the Commission to be the best professional practice with respect to the standards, procedures and techniques to be adopted by auditors, and cannot come into force until approved by a resolution of each House of Parliament. The latest code dates from 1991.

The main provisions of the code are in five parts. The first sets out the duties of an auditor appointed by the Commission; the second relates to the conduct of the audit; the third sets out the auditor's reporting responsibilities; the fourth describes the particular responsibilities with regard to the audit of local authorities bodies; the fifth describes the auditor's specific responsibilities with regard to the audit of health service bodies.

The first code was issued in 1983. The general duties of an auditor under the headings of 'independence', 'professional care' and 'responsibilities to the public' are set out. The second main section is about conducting the audit. This says that in carrying out legality and regularity audits, the auditor must comply with the operational standards promulgated for the private sector and those promulgated by CIPFA. But the code also explicitly deals with questions of fraud, corruption and value for money. An appendix is also provided giving forms of audit certificates. The most important aspects of these is that the certificates say that the statements of accounts 'present fairly' the financial position.

A theme that runs through this code is the more exacting requirements of local government audit compared with company audit. For example, under the code it is difficult for an auditor, without approval and subject to a de minimis limit, to provide management consultancy to the same authority – in order to protect audit independence.

Value for money

In addition to the auditor's traditional responsibility towards the probity of an authority's accounts the Act imposes a responsibility in the field of the value for money of an authority's transactions. The Act requires the auditor to satisfy himself by examination of the accounts and otherwise that the authority has made proper arrangements for securing economy, efficiency and effectiveness in its use of resources.

Economy is concerned with the terms under which the authority acquires human and material resources. An economical operation acquires these resources in the appropriate quality and quantity at the lowest cost.

Efficiency may be defined as the relationship between goods or services produced and resources used to produce them. An efficient operation produces the maximum output for any given set of resource inputs; or, it has minimum inputs for any given quantity and quality of service provided.

Effectiveness relates to how well a programme or activity is achieving its established goals or other intended effects.

The Commission publishes reports of national studies which promote good management practice for specific services and functions. This it has done for a wide variety of individual local government services and in the spring of 1995, the Commission published, naturally, a comprehensive series of performance indicators for selected services in each type of local authority. This publication is further referred to at the end of this chapter.

In publicising these indicators and unit costs for consideration and further examination both by itself and by individual authorities, the Commission is clearly seeking to maximise value for money in local government by recognising that economy, efficiency and effectiveness all impact upon the costs and delivery of individual services. Thus, it would not be difficult for a district council to produce the lowest housing maintenance costs per unit, if the quality and frequency of its repairs were of a very basic standard. Economy of expenditure which fails to achieve political targets or local needs is, additionally, not delivering value for money.

It is *not* the external auditor's function to question policy. It is, however, his responsibility both to consider the effects of policy and to examine the arrangements by which policy decisions are reached. To this end, he should consider, for example:

- whether policy objectives have been determined, and policy decisions taken, with appropriate authority and advice;
- whether the authority considered costed alternative options;
- whether established policy aims and objectives have been clearly set out;
- whether the costs of alternative levels of service have been considered, and are reviewed as costs and circumstances change.

Internal audit requirements

Internal audit is an independent appraisal function established within an organisation for the review of the internal control systems as a service to the organisation. It objectively examines, evaluates and reports on the adequacy of internal control as a contribution to the proper use of resources.

In local government, the *Accounts and Audit Regulations 1983*, provide *inter alia* that the responsible financial officer of the local authority, shall 'maintain an adequate and effective internal audit of the accounts' of the authority. Internal audit is, therefore, compulsory as part of the legal framework of public sector bodies regulated by the *Local Government Finance Act 1982*.

Most local authorities maintain their internal audit section within the chief financial officer's department but, in some authorities, the necessary independence of internal audit is felt to be better achieved by making the section responsible directly to the chief executive. Internal audit is thus primarily responsible for detailed systems, control and checking work, liaising with the external auditor on tasks or projects as necessary, and particularly to support the external auditor on value for money work.

CIPFA draft standard of professional practice on auditing

In November 1994 CIPFA issued this draft standard to reaffirm the professional standards with which CIPFA members are required to comply in order to ensure the integrity of audits for which they are responsible. As such, it is concerned with professional competencies, and with working methods, practice and procedures.

This statement is intended to set down the standards for CIPFA members and students to observe when undertaking audits. It should be observed by all members, whether acting as internal or external auditors, and whatever form of financial audit is being carried out. Apparent failure to comply with this statement may result in investigatory, disciplinary or regulatory action.

In due course, the document will appear as one of CIPFA's Standards of Professional Practice, which serve to define the professional obligations of individual members.

Reporting financial statements

Annual statement of accounts

A requirement of the *Local Government Finance Act 1982* is that all accounts shall be made up early to 31 March and audited by an auditor or auditors appointed by the Audit Commission. Section 15 of this Act lays down the general duties of the external auditor to examine the accounts and be satisfied:

- that the accounts are prepared in accordance with regulations made under Section 23 of the 1982 Act and comply with the requirements of all other statutory provisions applicable to the accounts;
- that 'proper accounting practices' have been observed in the compilation of the accounts; and
- that the body whose accounts are being audited has made proper arrangements for securing economy, efficiency and effectiveness in its use of resources.

Regulation 7 of the *Accounts and Audit Regulations 1983* lays down that the annual statement of accounts shall include the following:

- summarised statements of the income and expenditure of each fund or undertaking;
- a summarised statement of capital expenditure in respect of different services and showing the sources of finance of the year's total capital expenditure
- a consolidated balance sheet
- any balance sheet relating to a fund, the balances in respect of which are not shown in the consolidated balance sheet
- a statement of source and application of funds
- particulars of the main principles adopted in the compilation of the accounts which shall include:
  - the basis on which debtors and creditors outstanding at the end of the relevant year are included
  - the nature of substantial reserves, provisions, contingent liabilities and deferred charges included
  - the basis on which provision is made for the redemption of debt
  - the basis on which capital works or expenses are recorded
  - the basis of valuation of real property and investments
  - the basis of depreciation provisions
  - the extent to which central administrative expenses are allocated over services.

Code of Practice on Local Authority Annual Reports 1981

The purpose of a local authority's annual report and accounts is to provide interested parties with clear information about the authority's activities. The *Local Government Planning and Land Act 1980* empowers the Secretary of State for the Environment to issue a code or codes of recommended practice as to the publication of information by local authorities about the discharge of their functions. The Secretary of State can either prepare the codes or can request some other body to do so.

The *Code of Practice on Local Authority Annual Reports* issued in 1981 is based largely on suggestions put forward by the Chartered Institute of Public Finance and Accountancy (CIPFA), and the Secretary of Local Authority Chief Executives (SOLACE), in conjunction with the Local Authority Associations.

The code recommends to local government a basis for the information to be published in its annual report to ensure consistency of practice and a minimum standard of content. It is acknowledged within the code that authorities have complete discretion as to the layout of their report, but the intention of the code is that every local authority in England and Wales should publish an annual report as specified in the code.

The code therefore has been used by local authorities as a basis for the production of their annual reports since 1 April 1981, and in practice a wide variety of publications is produced.

The code recommends that the annual report of a local authority should contain the following information:

- details of revenue expenditure and income for the year ended 31 March, including a comparison with budgeted expenditure and income and comparison with the previous year, and a consolidated balance sheet
- a summary of capital expenditure by service and a statement showing the sources of finance for the total capital expenditure during the year and future commitments
- general statistics for major services, including measures of cost;
- a set of key service indicators which measure performance and aid comparison with other authorities
- a year-end manpower statement.

Code of Practice on local authority accounting

Under Section 23 of the *Local Government Finance Act 1982*, the Secretary of State for the Environment is empowered to make regulations which:

> make provision with respect to the keeping, form, preparation and certification of accounts and statements of accounts, and the publication of information relating to accounts and the publication of statements of account.

The *Accounts and Audit Regulations 1983* introduced interim regulations pending general developments in accounting and audit practices. In 1986 the minister for local government announced that plans to revise these regulations had been shelved and invited local authority associations, in conjunction with the accountancy bodies and the Audit Commission, to formulate their own proposals for securing further improvements in local authority accounting practice.

The *Accounting Code of Practice* that was produced and which came into effect from the financial year commencing on 1 April 1987 was formulated in the context of the reporting requirements of the *Code of Practice on Annual Reports*.

The *1987 Accounting Code* applied formally in England and Wales to principal local authorities, joint committees, joint boards of principal authorities, police and fire authorities and residual bodies.

The code set out the individual financial statements which comprise the statement of accounts and the minimum information which should be contained in each statement. The code also detailed the accounting concepts and principles that must be followed in the preparation of the individual financial statements.

The 1987 Code was updated by CIPFA's Local Authority Accounting Panel in 1991 and the 1991 Code was again updated by CIPFA in September 1993 and April 1995.

Local Government Act 1992

Since the *1980 Local Government Planning and Land Act* the government has been committed to improving the performance of local authorities. Competition with the private sector is being used in an attempt to change the culture of local government. In addition the Citizen's Charter, published in 1991, is designed to promote public accountability.

These ideas have been reflected in law by the *Local Government Act 1992*, the chief provisions of which are:

- local authorities must publish information on the standards of service and cost achieved. The Audit Commission lays the basis of this information (see section on performance indicators)
- local authorities must go on public record in response to the recommendations of auditors as to the action they intend to take
- the Audit Commission can publish details of late filing of accounts and failure to give performance indicators
- the Secretary of State is empowered to regulate behaviour deemed contrary to compulsory competitive tendering legislation
- the establishment of a government commission to review the structure of local government and propose structural, boundary and electoral changes.

In June 1994, the Audit Commission announced that it was proposing to publish composite indicators – and possibly a single measure – to compare how well councils are performing overall. It is proposed that initial indicators could be published in the spring of 1995. Some figures may be published as league tables and others in bands of performance.

The Commission had two objectives for the publication of these indicators. To stimulate public debate about the performance of councils and to make councils aware of their relative performance and help them to identify areas where they do not reach standards which they and the public think appropriate. To help choose relevant indicators, the Audit Commission asked national opinion polls to interview 1,500 people and draw up a short-list of the ten most popular indicators for each service.

CIPFA's weekly journal 'Public Finance' reported in its 9 December 1994 edition that the Commission was 'close to dropping plans for national league tables of council performance after an overwhelmingly hostile response from councils', but the first comprehensive tables covering about 20 key statistics appeared in March 1995. Doubtless the Commission will refine and expand these published figures over the years.

The Citizen's Charter

The Citizen's Charter, was described as 'a bold programme to improve public services in the 1990s'. As outlined in a White Paper published in July 1991, it addresses not only services still in the public sector, such as state schools, the police, the Post Office and public transport, but also privatised utilities like electricity. Its intention appears to be to compensate for the fact that many of these services have a captive customer base, and therefore are not motivated to please their customers, by imposing targets and objectives relating to customer care.

The more specific proposals announced under the Charter umbrella include:

- limits on the permissible waiting times for certain NHS treatments
- better liaison between schools and parents, and publication of 'league tables' comparing schools' exam results
- improved procedures for tenants on council estates to get repairs done
- compensation for British Rail passengers when services fall below a prescribed standard of punctuality, with plans for progressive privatisation of the rail service
- promotion of competition in the delivery of letters
- incentives for contractors to complete motorway repairs within the agreed timescales.

General proposals include:

- publication of league tables and other information allowing the public to compare the performance of education authorities, health authorities and councils
- better information to be given to the public about service level targets compared with actual performance
- employees of public services to wear name badges and give their names when writing or speaking on the phone
- lay experts to be appointed to the inspectorates responsible for ensuring quality of services such as schools
- appointments of regulators for some services which do not yet have them, such as post and railways
- easier complaints procedures with adjudication at local level.

Individual charters for government departments, agencies and public sector bodies were planned to follow the White Paper.

The Charter had a mixed reception. Most applauded the notion of inculcating a more customer-friendly attitude among public 'servants' who all too often have behaved like anything but servants. The main criticism was that the Charter was thin in the area of implementation; in particular, it was doubted that funding would be forthcoming to help hard-pressed services such as the NHS meet their new performance targets. There was scepticism as to whether the organisations concerned would compete for the accolade of the 'Chartermark' as hotly as the White Paper seemed to anticipate.

Following the 1992 election William Waldegrave was given the job of implementing the Charter initiative, assisted by an advisory panel of industrialists. A few months later, as Britain prepared for its presidency of the European Commission, it became clear that John Major would seek to introduce a European Citizen's Charter. It was expected that this initiative would not only add an element of accountability to the Brussels bureaucracy, but would also seek to privatise some aspects of its work.

Many local authorities are producing their own versions of the Citizen's Charter for the whole authority or for individual services. These often point out rights to information, standards of service performance measurement and complaints procedures.

Local councils will have to publish 20 new performance indicators for 1994/95, taking the total number of indicators to be published in the second year of the Charter to 43.

Glossary of terms

This glossary is split into four separate sections and is designed to incorporate terms found within this book and in the wider accounting and public sector worlds.

The sections are as follows:

- general accounting terms
- terms which relate particularly to the National Health Service
- terms which relate to local government accounting
- terms which relate to the wider world of local government finance.

General accounting terms

Account

A structured record, kept in a ledger or on a computer file, of all the financial transactions relating to one individual customer, supplier, asset, or liability.

Accounting, accountancy

The recording, analysis, and presentation of financial data relating to the transactions of an organisation in a form which conforms to the practices and conventions of the accountancy profession. All activities relating to the financial aspects of an organisation, with regard to historical data, control of current financial matters and financial planning for the future.

Accounting concepts and conventions

The name given to a series of accepted principles and practices relating to the recording and analysis of financial data, which should be followed in the preparation of all financial statements.

Accruals, or matching, principle

Costs and revenues should be accounted for in the period in which they occur, regardless of when cash changes hands. Any payments in advance for an expense should be excluded from the expenses charged against a particular accounting period.

Business entity

Any business is deemed to have an identity which is distinct and separate from that of its owner(s). Financial matters relating to the owner's personal affairs must be kept separate from the business finances at all times.

Consistency convention
Once an accountancy policy has been established by an organisation it should be used consistently unless there is good reason for a change. For example, the method of depreciation chosen by a firm should not be changed frequently but should be used consistently.

Cost concept
Assets acquired by an organisation should initially be valued at cost, regardless of the apparent market value of the item. If an organisation believes it has bought an asset at a bargain price, it should still appear in the books at cost and not at the value which the organisation places on it.

Going concern principle
Books of account should always be prepared on the assumption that the organisation is going to continue trading. The affairs of the organisation should not appear differently if changes in size, ownership, structure, type of business or style of trading, are planned for the near future.

Materiality principle
Items which are to be used over a period of time, but which cost only a small amount, will be charged to the period in which they are bought and will not be treated as fixed assets. It would not be appropriate, for example, to treat pencils, rubbers and rulers as fixed assets and therefore to depreciate them over a number of accounting periods. The purchase of this kind of item will simply be charged as an expense in the stationery account.

Prudence convention
When a choice has to be made regarding asset values, liability values or estimated expenses, the accountant will always choose that value which shows the organisation in the least favourable light. This convention of caution, conservatism and prudence ensures that the true and fair views which the accounts should present do not overstate the well-being of the firm and thus mislead investors or others dealing with it. For example, stock should always be valued at cost or net realisable value, whichever is the lower, thus ensuring that it does not appear at an unrealistically high value in the balance sheet.

Realisation concept
Profit is deemed to occur when a sale takes place and not when cash changes hands. Thus if a transaction is on credit the sale is accounted for as having occurred when the goods change hands, and a debt is then formed between buyer and seller which, when settled at a later date, does not produce any profit.

Accrued expenses

Costs relating to a period which have not yet been taken into account because they have not yet been invoiced by the supplier or paid (CIMA definition). These will include such items as electricity and telephone, which are generally invoiced in arrears.

Assets

An asset is an item with a reasonable financial value which is owned by an organisation.

Current assets
Current assets are items which are owned by the organisation but which are constantly changing in nature and/or amount. Most organisations classify their current assets as stock, debtors, prepayments, balance at bank, and cash in hand.

Fixed assets
Fixed assets are those items which an organisation expects to retain for a period of years to enable it to develop its business (e.g. land, plant, vehicles).

Balance sheet

The document which shows the current financial state of an organisation. It includes all assets and liabilities of an organisation at a given point in time. The account is balanced because capital, the third category of item shown on the balance sheet, is defined as *assets less liabilities*. Thus by displaying assets on one side, opposite capital and liabilities, the accounting equation (capital = assets *less* liabilities) makes the two sides of the balance sheet equal.

The balance sheet is an important document when interpreting the financial affairs of an organisation, especially with respect to liquidity, capital structure and gearing.

The two figures will rarely coincide because of delays in the presentation of cheques, the transmission of data between bank and client, and various other reasons.

Regular reconciliation of the figures is an important aspect of cash control in any organisation.

Budgeting

The preparation of financial plans, based upon the organisation's objectives, for a future period (usually a year). The constituent budgets may relate to costs, revenues, working capital movements, capital expenditure and cash flows.

Capital

Capital = total assets *less* total liabilities

When a firm starts up, its capital is the amount of funds invested in its activities by its owner or owners. As profits are earned and retained in the firm ('ploughed back') the capital grows in accordance with the above accounting equation. It may be said to be the amount which the firm owes to its owners, since in the event of closure, after assets are realised and liabilities discharged, the balance which is the capital reverts to the owners of the firm.

Share capital
The amount of shareholders' funds, being the original amount contributed by shareholders plus retained profits, representing the commitment of funds to the firm by the shareholders.

Despite being an external liability for the firm, the term capital is still applied to such loans because of the long-term nature of the commitment.

Capital expenditure

Expenditure on fixed assets or on the improvement of fixed assets in such a way as to increase their value. Expenditure is capitalised if its cost is included in the balance sheet and then subjected to depreciation procedures, rather than being simply charged to the manufacturing, trading or profit and loss accounts for the period as revenue expenditure.

See also revenue expenditure

Cash book

The cash book consists of a combination of the records of cash in hand and the current bank account of an organisation. All receipts and payments related to cash or bank balances are recorded in the book, which forms part of the overall double-entry bookkeeping system. It is a particularly important document in relation to the control of cash, and the reconciliation of records kept by the organisation with those held by the bank. This reconciliation of the cash book balance with the bank statement is called a bank reconciliation statement.

Cash budget

A budget showing the pattern, from period to period, of:

- cash flow into the organisation (receipts)
- cash flow out of the organisation (payment)
- the resultant effect upon bank balances or overdrafts

Contribution

The difference between sales value and the variable cost of those sales, expressed either in absolute terms or as a contribution per unit (CIMA definition).

Cost centre

A location, function or items of equipment in respect of which costs may be ascertained and related to cost units for control purposes (CIMA definition).

Credit sales

Sales in which the goods or services are delivered but payment is delayed until a later date. The seller of the goods or services becomes a creditor of the person or organisation to whom they are sold until payment is made.

Current liabilities

Liabilities which an organisation would normally expect to settle within a relatively short period (normally one year) e.g. creditors, dividends and tax due for payment; also that part of long-term loans due for repayment within one year.

Debtor

A person or organisation who owes money to another person or organisation. The amount of the debt is shown as a current asset in the balance sheet of the person or organisation to whom it is owed.

Depreciation

The term given to the reduction in book value of a fixed asset which is charged as an expense to the profit and loss account. It is not a transfer of funds but a non-cash book transfer which enables the cost of fixed assets to be spread evenly through their useful life. When the accumulated depreciation charged against an asset is deducted from the original cost, the remainder is known as the book value.

The accumulated depreciation to date is shown as a deduction from the appropriate class of fixed assets in the balance sheet.

Discounting methods

A series of techniques for the appraisal of capital investment projects which evaluates costs and revenues taking into account the time value of money. Because money can earn interest over time, cash received sooner is worth more than cash received later. By taking into account the interest which earlier receipt could earn, or *discounting*, future costs and receipts may be expressed in *present value* terms, thus making easier comparison of competing projects. Such *discounted cash flow* techniques include the calculation of a percentage rate of return for a capital investment which takes into account the timing of all payments and receipts relating to the project. The percentage measure is known as the *internal rate of return*.

Financial accounting

Reporting how the organisation has performed in the recent past, principally for the benefit of 'outsiders' via the organisation's financial statements. The work of financial accountants.

Final accounts

The term referring to the accounts produced by an organisation at the end of an accounting period in order to calculate profit or loss and then to update the balance sheet. The final accounts include a manufacturing account and trading account, a profit and loss account and, when appropriate, an end of period balance sheet. The equivalent accounts for a club or society or a public sector organisation are also sometimes referred to as final accounts.

Funds flow (or source and application of funds) statement

One of an organisation's financial statement which shows the way in which funds have been generated and used by the organisation, and how any resulting surplus of liquid assets has been applied or any deficiency financed. It provides a link between the balance sheet at the beginning of the period, the profit and loss account for the period, and the balance sheet at the end of the period, and forms part of the audited accounts of the company.

Historic cost accounting

Method of accounting that does not make allowance for the effects of inflation. A system of accounting in which all values (in revenue and capital accounts) are based on the costs actually incurred or as revalued from time to time.

Management accounting

The provision of financial information to the various levels of management within the organisation for the purposes of planning, decision making, and monitoring and controlling performance. The work of management accountants.

Management by exception

Control and management of costs and revenues by concentrating on those instances where significant variances occur.

Net book value or written down cost

The cost of an asset less its accumulated depreciation to date.

Net present value

A term relating to discounting techniques for project appraisal. The net present value of revenue is its value taking into account all costs, with both costs and revenues having been discounted to take account of the time value of money. If the net present value of a project is positive at a given rate of discount, this indicates that the project is producing a percentage rate of a return higher than the discount rate.

Overheads

A term given to those costs which are neither direct material, direct labour nor direct expense costs. They are operating expenses of the business and their cost behaviour may be either as fixed costs or variable costs. In terms of management control they are often the target for special attention since they may, if not carefully managed, account for a disproportionately high amount of the organisation's costs.

Payback period

A method of evaluating investment projects which assesses the time which it takes for cash inflows to pay back the initial cash outflows on an investment. Organisations often prefer projects with a short payback period, and the technique may be used as a method of sifting out those projects which take a particularly long time to pay back, remaining projects being ranked by other means. As a sole method of project appraisal, its biggest disadvantage is that it ignores all returns beyond the payback date.

Prepayments

Expenses paid for in advance of the accounting period to which they refer. Some expenses, such as rates and insurance, are generally payable in advance. Because of the accounting principle of matching revenue and cost for a period, advance payments are not counted against profit in the expenses figure used in the profit and loss account. Instead the amount paid in advance appears in the balance sheet as a current asset, as the organisation is owed a service by the person or organisation to whom the prepayment was made.

Profit and loss account

Part of the final accounts of an organisation drawn up at the end of each accounting period. The profit and loss account starts with the gross profit and deducts business in order to establish the net profit. A version of the profit and loss account is sometimes called an *operating statement*. The equivalent account is the case of a club or society is known as an *income and expenditure account*.

Profitability

The extent to which an organisation makes satisfactory earnings from its operations. Net profit, and in some cases gross profit, is compared with other figures in order to assess the performance of the organisation.

Ratio analysis

A technique used in the interpretation of accounts which makes comparisons between figures in a given set of accounts, or between the same figure in various sets of accounts, in order to judge the financial performance of the organisation. The main groupings of ratios are *activity ratios, liquidity ratios* and *profitability ratios*.

Revenue expenditure

Day-to-day expenses of an organisation which are charged to the revenue accounts (manufacturing, trading and profit and loss accounts) for the period in which they occur. In contrast capital expenditure is the expenditure on fixed assets which are expected to be used within the organisation for some considerable time in the future.

Semi-variable costs

Costs which include both fixed costs and variable cost components, i.e. costs which vary as the level of activity varies but not in strict proportion (e.g. a telephone bill rises as more calls are made but does not double if calls double, owing to the rental element remaining unchanged).

Standard accountancy practice

An agreed set of principles and conventions which enables accountants to communicate effectively with one another, and to give a true and fair view of the financial affairs of an organisation. Details of the accepted practice are contained in a series of *Statements of Standard Accountancy Practice* (SSAP) which provide concise guidelines on formats, principles and conventions. See also *Accounting concepts and conventions*.

Trading account

An account which forms part of the group of financial statements called the *final accounts*; it summarises transactions for an accounting period. The trading account is used for the calculation of gross profit by deducting cost of goods sold from sales. The equation of the trading account is:

Sales *less* cost of goods sold = gross profit

Cost of goods sold is found by applying a stock adjustment to purchases:

Opening stock *add* purchases *less* closing stock = cost of goods sold

The trading account follows the manufacturing account and precedes the profit and loss account in the final accounts.

Variable costs

Costs which vary in proportion to the level of activity (sales level of production level). For example, raw material costs would generally double if production or sales doubled and thus would be regarded as variable.

Variance

The difference between planned, budgeted or standard cost and actual cost (and similarly in respect of revenues) (CIMA definition). Variances are generally referred to as favourable or adverse, depending upon whether they increase or decrease profit.

Variance analysis

The analysis of variances arising in a standard costing system into their constituent parts (CIMA definition).

Working capital or net current assets

The capital available for conducting the day-to-day operations of the business. Usually defined as current assets less current liabilities (based on CIMA definition). Sometimes called net working capital.

Zero-based budgeting

Process for building up a budget from scratch ignoring all historical perspectives.

Terms which relate to the NHS

The following terms are those specific to the NHS as set out in the NHSE Financial Management Training Initiative 'Basic Skills Training'.

Allocation

Share of cash limit that the district health authority must work within.

Block contract

The purchaser of health care pays an annual lump sum to the provider for a given level, type and quality of service, e.g. a general service to a district. The nature of the service must be clearly defined.

Business plans

Plans of action used by the Health Service in the 'post White Paper environment' containing three year rolling programmes which act as a control mechanism to ensure objectives are properly inter-related and realistic.

Capital charges

Costs of using capital (the estate, plus plant, equipment and vehicles). Charges are incurred by hospitals based on the capital they possess.

Capital expenditure

'Capital expenditure' relates to money spent on land, buildings and individual or groups of related items of equipment which are valued at more than £1,000 (increased to £5,000 on 1 April 1993) and have a useful life of more than one year. Routine maintenance of buildings is classified as revenue expenditure.

Capital funding

The sum of money allocated to RHAs and DHAs for the purpose of buying capital assets.

Capital items

Items to be charged to capital expenditure. In the post White Paper environment, this meant an asset or group of assets costing over £1,000 with a useful lifespan of more than one year (increased to £5,000 on 1 April 1993).

Capitation funding

Method of funding health authorities based on the health and age distribution of the resident population within an authority and the relative cost of providing services.

Case mix

The various group of treatments received by patients within a specialty (branch of medicine).

Clinical directors

A clinician who is responsible for the budgets of his own specialty or group of specialties.

Cost and volume contract

The purchaser pays an annual lump sum but there is an agreement that if additional services are required over and above the volume initially paid for, an additional charge is levied.

Cost per case contract

The purchaser negotiates an agreement with the provider on a patient by patient basis with no prior commitment by either party.

Cross accounting vouchers (CAVs)

Non-cash transfers of money between different health authorities (usually within the same region), and often referred to as 'Inter-Authority Transfers'.

Cross boundary flows

The movement of patients across administrative boundaries for treatment.

DRGs

This stands for diagnostic related groups and is the name given to a system of classifying acute, non-psychiatric in-patients according to their diagnostic characteristics and what treatment requirements they will need.

Family practitioner committees

Responsible for spending the primary care allocation outside health authorities (e.g. spending on general practitioners, local dentists and opticians).

Health service price index

A listing issued by the Department of Health which shows the monthly movement in prices of typical goods and services purchased by the NHS (i.e. NHS version of the Retail Price Index).

Interest bearing debt

The current value of assets held by a hospital which is issued to calculate the interest element of capital charges payable to the regional health authority for district managed units and the interest repayments from NHS trusts to RHAs.

Internal market

This reflects the situation where districts and practice fundholding GPs act as purchasers of health care services from providers clients. A district may purchase a service for a client from an NHS trust or district managed unit in another part of the country as well as its local units.

Joint finance

Finance made available for projects relevant to both health authorities and local authorities.

NHS management executive

Senior management team at the Department of Health which implements the policies approved by the NHS policy board.

NHS policy board

Responsible for the overall NHS budget and strategic decisions facing the health service.

NHS trusts

Hospitals which do not come under the control of district health authorities but report direct to a Department of Health outpost (also referred to as self-governing hospitals).

Overseas visitors

These are people not ordinarily resident in the United Kingdom who are charged for the provision of NHS treatment. Many patients who are overseas visitors will be exempt from payment through reciprocal arrangements with their country of origin and other clauses.

Providers of health care

Units of management responsible, under the White Paper, for providing health care within a geographical area. These include directly managed hospitals (hospitals within districts which do not seek self-governing status), NHS trusts (self-governing hospitals), private sector hospitals. The providers are those bodies with whom purchasers contract to provide health care services.

Purchasers of health care

Organisations and individuals who are responsible for buying health care from the providers in the light of the need of the population in a district or GP practice area. These include district health authorities and general practitioners. Local authorities are the purchasers of health care in the community for the physically and mentally handicapped and elderly.

Referral patterns

When GPs ask for patients to be admitted to hospital they are referred to a medical consultant. Referral patterns show how recently and where certain types of patients are referred.

Special fund

Donations and legacies left to health authorities for specific purposes.

Special health authorities

Health authorities which provide specific, specialist health care services.

Specialty costing

Form of costing which apportions and allocates hospital costs to a particular branch of medicine (e.g. paediatrics, orthopaedics, mental illness).

Specialty cost returns

Part of the financial returns which show patient care hospital costs allocated into particular branches of medicine.

Standing financial instructions

Financial rules and regulations for health authorities.

Strategic plan

Ten year programme showing the need for health services of an authority ranked in priority order.

Superannuation

This term refers to pensions in the NHS. The NHS Superannuation Scheme (NHSSS) is the health service pension scheme to which all staff who work full-time and are aged over 16 and part-time staff who work more than half the contracted hours of full-time staff are eligible to join.

Trust funds

All property received, held and administered by health authorities, or by any other bodies, for any purpose related to the NHS which does not originate from the Exchequer or is not an Exchequer responsibility.

Unit management

A division of management responsible for providing specific services within a health authority. Each unit is managed by a General Manager (UGM) who in turn reports to the District General Manager (DGM) of the DHA.

Terms which relate to local government accounting

The glossary below lists some of the more usual terms that specifically relate to the annual report and accounts of a local authority.

Agency services

These are services provided by one authority on behalf of another. The responsible authority repays the authority actually providing the services for the costs incurred.

Balances (revenue account)

The accumulated surplus of income over expenditure. Balances can be used to reduce the precept on the collection funds.

Billing authorities

The local authority responsible for collecting the council tax.

Capital charges

Annual (mortgage) repayments of principal and interest on sums borrowed to finance capital expenditure. Advances are made for agreed periods.

Capital discharged

The accumulated payments, made out of revenue and other sources, to pay for capital expenditure.

Capital programme

The authority's plan of capital projects and spending over future years. Included in this category are the purchase of land and buildings, the erection of new buildings and works, design fees and the acquisition of vehicles and major items of equipment.

Capital receipts

Income from the sale of land and buildings which can only be used to finance new capital expenditure or repay outstanding debt on assets financed from loan.

Collection fund

A fund administered by each charging authority. The revenue support grant, business rate income and the community charge are paid into the fund whilst the net revenue spending of the county, district and parishes are met from the fund.

Contingency provision

An amount set aside for pay and price increases occurring after the November price base at which the following financial year's budget has been prepared.

Council tax

The local tax payable by most adults resident in the local authority's area.

Credit approval

Issued by government, a credit approval conveys permission to a local authority to borrow or enter into a credit arrangement. Approvals may take two forms, a basic approval issued annually to cover the general financing of capital spending and supplementary approvals for earmarked projects.

Deferred charges

Represent the debt outstanding on capital expenditure for which no tangible asset is held in the accounts, e.g. capital grants or where the original asset has been disposed of.

Loans account

The account through which all loans are raised to meet capital expenditure are pooled. The account 'borrows' from other internal cash balances wherever possible. Loans are raised externally where these balances are insufficient, or external terms are advantageous. Interest charged on advances is the average of the cost of all borrowing.

Precept

The county council precepts on the collector of funds for its net expenditure requirements. Balances can be used to reduce the precept.

Provisions

Amounts set aside in the accounts for liabilities which are anticipated in the future, but cannot be accurately quantified.

Renewal accounts

Accounts set up from annual revenue contributions to meet the cost of replacing equipment with the objective of equalising the cost over a number of years. The major purposes are for computer and equipment renewals.

Revenue account

An account that records an authority's day-to-day expenditure and income on such items as salaries and wages, running costs of services, and the financing costs of capital expenditure.

Revenue budget

The estimate of annual income and expenditure requirements, which sets out the financial implications of a local authority's policies and the basis of the annual local taxation requirements.

Revenue financing

The amount of capital expenditure to be financed directly from the annual revenue budget, that is, from current income.

Revenue support grant

A general government grant in support of local authority expenditure. It does not vary with actual spending levels. See also Standard Spending Assessment.

Specific grants

Central government grants towards specific services, usually on a fixed-percentage basis for particular services (e.g. police, probation, magistrates' courts) or projects (e.g. education support grant).

Standard spending assessment

The amount of net expenditure (after allowing for specific grants) which the government consider appropriate for each local authority to incur in providing a common level of service. This figure is compared with an authority's actual spending plans on the community charge bill. The standard spending assessment is the key factor in determining the amount of revenue support grant paid to each collection fund.

Total net expenditure

The total net spending requirement of the authority after deducting specific grants. An alternative term is net revenue expenditure.

Transport supplementary grant

A government grant specifically directed towards capital expenditure on approved highway schemes of more than local importance. The rate of grant is currently 50 per cent of accepted expenditure.

Uniform business rate

The rate in the pound charged on non-domestic properties. It is the same for all businesses in England and is set annually by government, on whose behalf it is collected by charging authorities. It is paid by the government into collection funds of charging authorities as a common amount per chargepayer.

Terms which relate to the wider world of local government finance

The glossary below contains some of the more relevant terms from the *Encyclopaedia of Local Government Finance*, produced by the Association of District Councils.

Aggregate external finance

The total amount of money which authorities receive directly from the government, which includes RSG, redistributed NDR income and a number of specific and transitional grants, is called the Aggregate External Finance (AEF), Authorities do, however, receive amounts of money from the government which fall outside the AEF, e.g. government contribution towards the cost of rent allowances, council tax benefit, mandatory student awards, etc.

Annual capital guideline

An annual capital guideline (ACG) is issued by the government to all local authorities. This equates to the amount of capital expenditure which the government thinks appropriate for an authority to undertake during the financial year consistent with national expenditure plans. Annual capital guidelines are announced for each of five groups of services, namely:

- housing (by the Department of the Environment)
- transport (by the Department of Transport)
- education (by the Department for Education)
- personal social services (by the Department of Health)
- other services (by the Department of the Environment).

In making its calculations, the government will make an estimate for the reserves of money which it thinks the authority will have available from capital receipts, e.g. 25 per cent of capital receipts from the sale of council houses under 'right to buy' are subsequently available to the authority to spend on capital projects. The receipts taken into account (RTIA) are deducted from ACG to give a permission to borrow known as the basic credit approval (BCA).

Put simply: BCA = ACG – RTIA

Audit Commission

The Audit Commission is an independent body established under the provisions of the *Local Government Finance Act 1982* and the *NHS and Community Care Act 1990*. Its duties are to appoint auditors or inspectors to all local authorities and health authorities in England and Wales and to help them bring about improvements in economy, efficiency and effectiveness directly through the audit process and through value for money studies.

Local authority audits may include analysis of value-for-money (VFM), as well as investigation into the property of accounts. The investigation of propriety will include matters of negligence, misconduct and legality. If the auditor believes that an authority has acted illegally with regard to its accounts, he/she may investigate court action which could result in the person(s) responsible being required to repay all or part of the expenditure.

The address for the Audit Commission is: 1 Vincent Square, London, SW1P 2PN (Telephone 0171 828 1212).

Basic credit approval

The basic credit approval (BCA) is the government's annual statement of what a local authority can borrow to finance new capital schemes. The BCA effectively restricts an authority's scope for borrowing or for entering into other forms of credit approval which are intended to reflect the authority's need to spend and its ability to finance such expenditure from usable capital receipts.

BCAs must be used in the year to which they relate and any unused BCA is not transferable from one year to the next. See annual capital guideline above.

Budget head

This refers to an individual budget within a cost centre (e.g. for equipment, salaries, etc.), against which costs are charged.

Budget requirement

The budget requirement is the net revenue expenditure calculated in advance each year by every billing authority and precepting authority. It is important for two reasons; as a step in the calculation of council tax and as a basis for local authority capping.

It is calculated as the estimated gross revenue expenditure minus the estimated revenue income, allowing for movement in reserves.

In calculating estimated revenue expenditure, authorities will not include any payment to the collection fund to cover a previous years' deficit and certain community charge payments and refunds for previous years.

In calculating estimated revenue income, authorities will not include income from RSG, NDR, certain other government grants, council tax, any surplus from the collection fund for previous years and certain community charge income in respect of previous years.

The budget requirement thus calculated will be the amount of revenue expenditure to be met by RSG, redistributed NDR, council tax and certain other central government grants.

It should be noted that the budget requirement for council tax purposes includes parish precepts, whereas the budget requirements for capping purposes does not.

Capital expenditure

Whereas revenue expenditure covers daily running costs and is financed from current income, capital expenditure is expenditure on something which will produce an asset capable of providing benefits to the community for several years to come. Such expenditure can be financed from a number of sources, including borrowing, capital receipts arising from the sale of other assets, capital grants from the government, by leasing land or buildings owned by the local authority, via agreements with the private sector, or by a contribution from the authority's current account. Examples of capital expenditure might include building a new leisure centre, modernising buildings, or purchasing computer equipment.

Various rules and regulations govern the manner in which local authorities undertake capital expenditure. For example, the Government places limits on the amount of money which local authorities can borrow to finance capital projects. Every year, each authority is given an annual capital guideline (ACG). The ACG is essentially the government's measure of the amount of capital expenditure which it thinks the authority should be allowed to undertake. In arriving at the ACG the government estimates what receipts the council already has in reserve from the sale of assets (e.g. the sale of council houses under 'right to buy'). The amount which remains after the receipts taken into account figure is a permission to borrow figure known as the basic credit approval (BCA).

Whilst the local authority may also use capital receipts arising from the sale or lease of assets, the usable part of such receipts is restricted by the government to 25 per cent for houses and flats sold under 'right to buy' and 50 per cent for land or buildings. For a temporary period between 13 November 1992 to 31 December 1993, the government decreed that the usable part of capital receipts would be 100 per cent.

Capping

Government powers to cap the budget of individual local authorities who are considered to be overspending, are continued under council tax. Both billing authorities and major preceptors (e.g. shire counties, metropolitan county police authorities, etc.) can be capped.

Each year, the Secretary of State for the Environment will set criteria to determine whether:

- an authority's budget requirement is 'excessive'; or
- the increase in the authority's budget requirement is 'excessive' compared with that for the previous financial year.

The basic principle is that it is the authority's budget which is determined as 'excessive' and capped, not its council tax levels.

All authorities are potentially subject to capping once they have agreed their demands or precepts for the financial year ahead.

Cash limited budget

A cash limited budget is a budget that is prepared with a strict upper limit to the amount of money that may be spent. Within the overall cash limit, it is possible for council committees to have considered freedom in spending the money, and virement rules may be relaxed.

Collection fund

This is the fund kept and maintained by each billing authority, *into which* are to be paid the amounts of council tax and non-domestic rates (NDR) which it collects, and *out of which* are to be paid precepts issued by major precepting authorities (e.g. counties), its own demands on the fund (including those of parishes) and payments into the national NDR pool.

Competitive tendering

Local authorities are required by law to allow private sector firms to bid alongside the authority's own operation (sometimes referred to as a direct labour organisation (DLO) or direct service organisation (DSO) for the right to run certain services such as refuse collection, catering in schools, management of leisure facilities, etc. The procedure of placing work out to tender is called competitive tendering. Where authorities are obliged by law to put services out to tender, the process is called compulsory competitive tendering or CCT for short. CCT is now being extended to local authority financial services.

Cost centre

A cost centre is a local authority function or service area for which a specific budget is prepared, and costs identified within the authority's accounts. Generally, the expenses of a cost centre will be under the control of a single manager.

Council tax benefit

Council tax benefit is available to give people on low incomes help towards their council tax bills. Benefits staff will apportion a 'share' of the council tax bill across all liable persons in a dwelling, and award 100 per cent rebate on the 'share' of the bill apportioned to people in receipt of Income Support. In other words, people will usually not have to pay council tax for the period for which they are in receipt of Income Support.

Other people on low incomes will have their bills reduced. Benefit entitlement for people not in receipt of Income Support is calculated by comparing the income of the person to a 'needs' level (the applicable amount) set by the government. Benefit is reduced by 20 pence for every pound that the person's income exceeds the applicable amount. The amount of a person's benefit entitlement will be reduced if there are other non-liable adults living in the household on a non-commercial basis (e.g. adult relatives of the liable person).

Financial regulations

Financial regulations are a set of financial guidelines, produced by every local authority, which govern the financial affairs of the authority. Financial regulations may consist of broad statements of principle and be supplemented by a code of practice. It may sometimes be necessary for officers to request that financial regulations be waived when the circumstances of a transaction are not directly covered by them.

General fund

All district and borough councils have to maintain a general fund which is used to pay for day-to-day items of revenue expenditure such as wages and salaries, heating and lighting, office supplies, cleaning, etc. The equivalent of the general fund in county councils is called the county fund and in the City of London it is called the city fund. General fund spending is counted towards a council's expenditure for capping purposes.

Housing benefit

This is a benefit paid to people on low incomes to help them meet the costs of rents and certain other specified housing costs. Housing benefit is a Social Security benefit administered on behalf of the Secretary of State for Social Security by local authorities. The government pays local authorities a grant for administering the benefit and 95 per cent of the cost of most benefit payments.

Housing investment programme

Annual housing investment programme (HIP) submissions by local authorities are used by the government to set annual capital guidelines to help meet local housing needs. An authority's HIP allocation is the housing equivalent of the annual capital guideline.

Housing revenue account

Local authorities must keep a separate account called the housing revenue account (HRA) to administer the income and expenditure arising from the provision of housing. Since 1990/91, local authorities have not been allowed to transfer monies between their general fund and their HRA. This is known as 'ring fencing'. The system is designed to encourage authorities to set market rents for council tenants.

Housing benefit payments to council tenants are included in the HRA.

Housing subsidy

Most authorities receive HRA subsidy from the government to cover the costs of providing, managing and maintaining dwellings, allowable debt charges and paying housing benefit to council tenants. HRA subsidy is payable when the authority's notional HRA expenditure exceeds its notional HRA income (i.e. from rents and interest on receipts), as determined by the government.

Internal audit

The *Accounts and Audit Regulations 1983* require all local authorities to maintain an adequate and effective internal audit service. Internal audit is, almost universally, a function of the treasurer within local authorities. The internal audit service has wide-ranging responsibilities covering the economy, efficiency and effectiveness of local authority activities, and including the prevention and detection of fraud. There will usually be a close degree of co-operation between the internal audit service and external auditors appointed by the Audit Commission, to ensure the efficient exchange of relevant information.

Minimum rate of return

Currently, most local authority direct labour/service organisation trading accounts have to make a profit each year (the others only have to break even). The minimum rate of return is a percentage of the value of the capital employed (land, buildings, etc) used by the DLO/DSO.

Minimum revenue provision

The minimum revenue provision (MRP) is the minimum amount that a local authority must include in its revenue accounts, to repay the principal element of its borrowing for capital purposes.

NDR

NDR stands for non-domestic rates. These are paid on commercial, business and non-residential property, i.e. any property which is not a domestic dwelling. The level of NDR is determined by the Chancellor of the Exchequer, although local (billing) authorities are still responsible for its billing and collection. The level of NDR can only be increased year on year up to the level of the increase in the Retail Price Index.

The proceeds from the tax are pooled and redistributed amongst local authorities in proportion to the Registrar General's mid-1992 resident population (all ages). In areas served by more than one authority, the amount per head is split in proportion to each authority's share of council tax for standing spending.

Performance indicators

The Audit Commission is required by the *Local Government Act 1992* to publish a set of local authority service performance indicators each year for every local authority. The indicators are part of the government's Citizen's Charter and are designed to help people assess the performance of their local authorities. The services covered by the performance indicators range from refuse collection to the collection of council tax.

Precepting authority

There are two types of authority which may issue a precept (i.e. a request for money) to the appropriate billing authority. These are:

- Major precepting authorities:
  a) a county council
  b) a metropolitan county police authority

   c) the Northumbria Police Authority
   d) a metropolitan county fire and civil defence authority
   e) the London Fire and Civil Defence Authority
   f) the Receiver for the Metropolitan Police District.
- Local precepting authorities
   a) the sub-treasurer of the Inner Temple
   b) the under-treasurer of the Middle Temple
   c) a parish or community council
   d) the chairman of a parish meeting
   e) charter trustees.

Before the 1 March in the financial year preceding the one for which the monies are required, major and local precepting authorities will issue a precept to the billing authority, based on the basic amount of council tax they require to finance their revenue spending that year.

The billing authority will determine its council tax bill, by adding to the amounts which it has calculated as its own tax, the appropriate amounts calculated by each of its major precepting authorities (e.g. the county council) and, for the appropriate part of its area, the amount calculated by the local precepting authority (e.g. the parish council).

Each billing authority is required to keep a collection fund, into which are paid the amounts of council tax which it collects, and out of which are met the precepts issued by its major precepting authorities and its own spending demands (which include those of local precepting authorities).

Provision for credit liability

The provision for credit liability (PCL) refers to the amount an authority has to set aside to cover its borrowing. It is made up of the 'reserved' part of capital receipts, and the minimum revenue provision (MRP).

Receipts taken into account

RTIA (aka 'Rita') is the amount of usable capital receipts that the government assumes local authorities will have available in a given year. The basic credit approval (BCA) (i.e. the amount the authority may borrow in a year) is calculated by taking the RTIA figure away from the annual capital guideline (ACG).

Recharges

This is an accounting term which refers to the cost of the charges levied for a service provided by one department within an authority for another department.

Revenue support grant

This is the grant which the government pays to local authorities to bridge the gap between council tax and NDR income on one hand, and the total assessment of an authority's need to spend (as measured by its standard spending assessment or SSA) on the other. The payment of revenue support grant (RSG) attempts to ensure that differences in spending needs and resources between authorities are equalised, in order to permit each authority to support a standard level of spending.

The SSA is thus used to calculate the amount of RSG payable to each authority. SSAs are calculated each year for every local authority in England and Wales (except parish/community councils). The SSA is the amount of money which the government calculates it would cost the local authority to provide a standard level of service, consistent with the government's plans for the total aggregate of local authority revenue spending called total standard spending (TSS). The total amount of money which authorities receive directly from the government, which includes RSG, redistributed NDR income and a number of specific and transitional grants, is called the aggregate external finance (AEF).

RSG for each authority is calculated as the difference between the SSA and the sum of its NDR allocation plus the amount which could be raised by levying the authority's council tax for standard spending (CTSS). If all authorities spend in line with their SSA, council tax levels (excluding transitional relief and other local adjustments, e.g. for parish expenditure) would be broadly the same across the country.

Section 151 officer

Section 151 of the *Local Government Act 1972* states that, 'every local authority shall make arrangements for the proper administration of their financial affairs and shall secure that one of their officers has responsibility for the administration of those affairs'. These days, Section 151 officers come under a variety of job titles, including Treasurer, Director of Finance, Chief Financial Officer, Head of Financial Services, etc.

The Section 151 officer must be a member of one of the recognised chartered accountancy bodies (e.g. CIPFA). Sections 114–116 of the *Local Government Act 1988* set out the responsibilities of the Section 151 officer and the authority in the case of serious financial problems. The Section 151 officer must report to the authority if any members or officers of the authority are mixed up in unlawful financial activity involving the authority, or if he/she believes that the authority's expenditure is likely to exceed its resources in any financial year. Copies of any such report must be sent to all members of the authority and to the authority's external auditor.

Service level agreement

Service level agreements or SLAs are part of the process of devolving local authority budgets to give more responsibility to individual service managers. This will involve the negotiation of price and performance standards by individual sections who provide or receive services from other parts of the local authority. SLAs are usually seen as an essential step towards preparing services for CCT.

SLAs may also be referred to as TAGs or trading agreements, although some authorities use TAGs as the agreement itself, which then refers to the detail contained in the SLA.

Single regeneration budget

From 1 April 1994, most urban group programmes including Urban Programme, City

Challenge, Estates Action, Derelict Land Grants and Safer Cities, were transferred to the Single Regeneration Budget (SRB). The SRB is co-ordinated by government regional offices and will be used to support economic, social and environmental schemes, with an emphasis on partnership between the public and private sectors.

Standard spending assessment (SSA)

The SSA is used to calculate the amount of RSG payable to each authority. SSAs are calculated each year for every local authority in England (except parish councils). SSAs are also calculated for each local authority in Wales (except community councils); although the method of calculation differs for English and Welsh authorities.

The SSA can be defined as the amount of money which the government calculates it would cost the local authority to provide a standard level of service, consistent with the government's plans for the total aggregate of local authority revenue spending called total standard spending (TSS). In theory, if every authority budgeted in line with its SSA, then council tax could be set at around the same level across all areas of the country. In reality, the formulae which are used to calculate the SSA are not sensitive enough to achieve anywhere near such a perfect equalisation of local spending needs.

SSA totals for each authority in England are calculated from seven main service blocks. These are:

- education
- personal Social Services
- police
- highway maintenance
- fire and civil defence
- capital financing
- all other services.

In broad terms, each SSA element is calculated by multiplying a unit cost by the size of the underlying client group (e.g. the number of pupils for education) Allowances are made for the variation in standard costs which authorities might encounter in providing a particular service (e.g. additional employment costs in London and South-East, differing socio-economic circumstances, etc.).

The SSAs for district councils outside the metropolitan areas, are almost wholly determined by reference to the All Other Services Block. This covers 31 different services areas, including environmental health, refuse collection, council tax collection, economic development, administration of council tax and housing benefit, etc. However, the control total for the All Other Services Block is not broken down into the different service areas. Therefore, it is impossible for authorities to tell if the SSA allowance for an individual service within the All Other Services Block is a fair reflection of their needs.

Virement

This is an accounting term which refers to the switching of resources between budget heads. Financial regulations as to the level at which virement may take place without the involvement of members vary from authority to authority.

Index

Index to Acts of Parliament